From
SPITFIRES to
VAMPIRES and
BEYOND

GRUB STREET • LONDON

For my daughter Deborah and son Andrew, and my two grandchildren Simon and Jennifer, with love

To all the RAF's New Zealanders, past, present and future

From
SPITFIRES to
VAMPIRES and
BEYOND

A Kiwi Ace's RAF Journey

OWEN HARDY

Edited by
Air Marshal G.A. 'Black' Robertson

Published by
Grub Street
4 Rainham Close
London SW11 6SS

A CIP record for this title is available from the British library

ISBN-13: 978-1-911667-49-0

Design by Myriam Bell Design, UK

Printed and bound by Finidr, Czech Republic

CONTENTS

INTRODUCTION

Owen Hardy served with my father on 72 Squadron during 1942, both in the UK and later in North Africa. While Owen survived the war unscathed, 'Robbie' Robertson[1] was shot down on 20 December 1942 by Erich Rudorffer, the forty-seventh of over 200 victims claimed by one of the Luftwaffe's foremost *Experten*. It cost him an eye. Gliding apart, he flew only once more in the RAF: forty minutes with his erstwhile colleague in a Miles Master on 23 October 1943. At the time, Owen was serving with No. 61 Operational Training Unit (OTU) at Rednal, near Oswestry in Shropshire.

The two friends remained in contact after the war. I had the pleasure of meeting Owen in November 1985 at a reunion of 72 Squadron wartime colleagues, hosted on my father's behalf at RAF Wattisham. Some nine years later, on 20 August 1994, the pair were among thirty-one pilots who gathered at the RAF Museum, Hendon, for a Fighter Pilots' Symposium. After individual introductions and a question-and-answer session under moderator Christopher Shores, the morning concluded with a standing ovation from the packed audience. After lunch the veterans sat behind a line of tables so that the public could talk to them and obtain signatures in copies of books they'd bought, notably Shores' *Aces High*,[2] which had just been published.

These personal connections were lost after my father died in 1999, predeceasing his younger comrade, who passed away on 4 January 2018 aged ninety-five. But a happy coincidence, the publication of the first of two books about my father's exploits,[3] put me in contact with Owen's daughter, Debbie Elliott. Through her I learned that Owen had written about his own experiences.

Owen's memoir was never intended for publication, certainly in its original form. But thanks to the encouragement of family and friends, *Through my Eyes* became available on the internet in 2010. His story 'is not one of aerial battles but a reflection of events and emotions typical of those experienced by most fighter pilots during the war and the exciting years thereafter beginning with the new age of jet aircraft, missiles and computers'. It comprised a record of Owen's 'service in the Royal Air Force', reflecting 'the gratitude which forever will be owed to those of [his] generation who . . . gave their all for a better world'. His preface ended with a simple dedication: 'May they continue to rest peacefully.' Debbie had long harboured an ambition to interest a publisher in an updated version of her father's story but knew that the original manuscript would require a good deal of work, not least in changing the voice – Owen had studiously avoided use of the first person singular. Given our family connections, I was more than happy to take on the task. Indeed, it was an honour. Thus it was that *Through my Eyes – a personal impression of life in the Royal Air Force from 1941 to 1970* became *From Spitfires to Vampires and Beyond – A Kiwi Ace's RAF Journey*.

In editing this new version I'm indebted to Owen's daughter, first, for entrusting me with such a personal task. And second, for providing new material and photographs that reinforce the original narrative. Third, and most important of all, for ensuring that throughout this book it's her father's distinctive voice that the reader hears.

Three sections – the preface, Owen's years of disillusion and, in particular, his reflections in the final chapter – proved the most difficult to adapt; each reflects considerable editorial licence. Corrections elsewhere are generally limited to matters of fact. They also reflect the need to reduce the original text substantially while losing nothing of substance. In the interests of authenticity, as far as possible the narrative reflects Owen's original language. Given that it was written some twenty years ago, there are few, if any, concessions to modern sensitivities. A man of forthright opinions, not least about his colleagues, where Owen omitted to name specific individuals, he left clues to their identity which the curious may wish to follow up, as I have done. But out of respect for his discretion they remain nameless.

Finally, my sincere thanks go to Owen's daughter, Debbie, for allowing me the privilege of adapting her father's fascinating story and to my publisher, John Davies, for his encouragement and support.

Black Robertson
Cheltenham, January 2023

FOREWORD

This account of my life was never meant to be a book. It wasn't intended for publication. It represents a personal impression of my time in the Royal Air Force, purely for the enlightenment and enjoyment of my family. I consider it a poor reflection on my eighty years that nothing material marks my presence on this earth. Everywhere there remain monuments to great men. They stand in stone, reflecting achievements in the arts, sciences and in learning. By this measure my life has been worthless – one of destruction, not construction. In part it was this realisation that prompted me to place on record something of the men I knew and of the special age in which we lived. This in the hope that there will remain with my kin a tangible trace of my small contribution to freedom at a time of crisis in British history.

As a boy I knew no one who had fought in the First World War. It troubled me who these men were, men who withstood the terror and horror evident during my visits to the Auckland War Memorial Museum. The relics from that awful conflict seemed so primitive and ghoulish, the battles so brutal. How could men face death for so long and still go on fighting? This question worried me; but it went unanswered despite extensive reading of land, sea and air battles. The more I read, the more those men appeared as heroes. Yes, that was it. They must have come from a race of people blessed with valour.

People tend to regard veterans of the Second World War as heroes, but I hope that these writings will dispel any such ideas. Like those I fought alongside, I was no hero. We were ordinary people doing an extraordinary job in extraordinary times. True, a few airmen considered themselves heroes and acted the part, both during and after the war. Thankfully, there were few such individuals and they were seen for what they were, eventually, if not at the time. Some even enjoyed the conflict. For the majority, though, it was simply a crisis not of their making which could only be resolved by fighting. There was fear too, of course. Except for an unfortunate few, it was suppressed. Danger, even if overlooked, was rarely far from the subconscious mind. We never lingered on mortality either. The regular movements of pilots, on leave or on posting, helped conceal the prolonged absence or even loss of a friend. It didn't pay to get too close to comrades – a lesson quickly learned. Each new day was treated separately when it arrived. Inevitably, there were hectic parties, but few individuals ever got blind drunk when on operations. There were those you could trust implicitly and others you relied on only at your peril.

It was a mix of ordinary people with ordinary emotions drawn from ordinary walks of life who fought in my war. They weren't heroes in the true sense of the word, nor did they consider themselves to be. But they certainly had guts. It was a privilege to know and serve with them during the war, and to work with those who bore the burden of conflict with distinction thereafter.

Most of my time in the service was spent working with others; I saw achievements as ours, failures as mine alone. In the cast of a six-year conflict I was a bit player, not a leading man, a consideration that adds to my unease with this first-person narrative. Furthermore, in putting together a book long after the events it describes, I've had to rely mainly on memory. For any errors I can only apologise. But I make no apologies for the views expressed herein. After all, it's the story of my time with the Royal Air Force seen through my eyes.

Owen Hardy
Gulf Harbour, New Zealand
April 2004

» Chapter 1
WHERE IT BEGAN – NEW ZEALAND

'Owen! Come along will you?' It's unfortunate that the first words I remember from my mother expressed irritation – but understandably so. No more than five years old, I'd been riveted to the spot for some time, utterly fascinated by my first sight of a working model aircraft. We were visiting a small park in Parnell, now a well-to-do Auckland suburb, where two boys were regularly launching a little white machine into the sky above them; after a couple of circuits it returned apparently unharmed to the ground. It was some time before I realised the engine powering these flights was simply an elastic band, twisted and tensioned by winding the propeller. By then I'd become utterly absorbed by the magic of model aircraft and the fascination of flight.

By the time I was ready to leave school I'd progressed from kites to larger and larger models, culminating in original designs and a six-foot-span petrol-engined aircraft. It was time and effort well spent. This practical background in aerodynamics would, I felt, prove invaluable when the time came to pursue my own flying ambitions. It was England and the Royal Air Force for me, or so I thought. But Hitler intervened. The advent of the Second World War changed everything. While recruitment was now to be handled by the New Zealand Air Force, my sights, my ambitions remained firmly focussed on England.

It was an apprehensive lad of eighteen-and-a-half who took the train that night from Auckland to Levin, some 300 miles further south – a lad who'd never been more than 100 miles from home, and then only with his mother. One who'd never been in a pub, never drunk a beer and never even been out with a girl. Worldly wise I was not. Isolating myself in the corner of the carriage for the lengthy journey, my mind was a jumble, not least because I was conscious of the soul-searching my parents went through before eventually signing the air force application papers. Concerned as they were for my safety, they recognised my burning ambition to fly. It was this that tipped the balance and prompted a decision, and a level of support, for which I was eternally grateful.

The month at Levin was of little consequence, although time passed quickly because we were kept so busy. There was drill, basic navigation, fiddling with obsolescent RAF Vickers and Lewis machine guns, boring lectures on air force law – and peeling potatoes. This latter represented punishment for such heinous crimes as failing to polish uniform buttons. If accommodation was spartan and sources of amusement limited, regular meals proved partial compensation – meals where quantity made up for a notable lack of quality. It seemed we'd only just arrived when it was time to move on. Personal assessments complete, exams passed, we were off to begin flying training. For me it was Whenuapai and I couldn't wait. It was the base I'd requested, near home.

No. 13 Course arrived at Whenuapai one Sunday in the autumn of 1941, somewhat disconcerted by the absence of any red carpet or reception committee to welcome New Zealand's latest heroes. The only sign of life was a junior NCO (non-commissioned officer), who directed us to our accommodation and pointed us towards the mess, a building that, flying apart, would be our central focus in the weeks ahead.

With little else to do that day we decided to take a stroll and explore the airfield. In the absence of any flying activity, the centre of attraction became a hangar, or rather a small gap between two large sliding doors. All it needed was a hefty shove and we were inside. The hangar was chock full of yellow-painted Tiger Moths. So these were the aircraft on which we'd learn to fly – but they seemed so incredibly small! The excitement was palpable – so much so that sleep came late that night. Too many thoughts were buzzing through my head, too much adrenalin still coursing through my veins.

The first few days of the course were taken up with induction lectures and administrative matters, including a medical examination that caused considerable alarm. My heart rate was much higher than normal – adrenalin perhaps? The doctor sucked his teeth while I had visions of training being delayed or, much worse, possibly being terminated. What to do? 'Come back tomorrow for another check young man,' he said. The twenty-four hours that followed were utterly miserable. But thankfully the second check showed that my pulse was back to normal. I was declared fit for a course scheduled to last six weeks. Flying for half of each day and ground school for the rest allowed two overlapping courses to be run concurrently. Each flying instructor had four pupils, two on the senior course, and two from the later arrivals. My instructor was Pilot Officer Tony Guild, a quiet, reserved young man who preferred to teach by example rather than by the spoken word. Long after the event, I learned that Tony had been killed in the Pacific; another aircraft chewed into him from behind when landing. In war especially, survival often depends more on luck than on skill, as I would go on to find from personal experience. But I'm getting ahead of myself.

My eagerly awaited first flight scared the hell out of me, causing me to question my ability ever to come to terms with the business of flying. Four days later Tony went on leave. My relief instructor could not have been a more contrasting character. A needle's width out on any instrument brought a stream of shouted abuse – enough to destroy the most confident pupil let alone an innocent eighteen-year-old. This endless verbal battering resulted in a 'head in the cockpit' approach to flying – a mechanical chasing of the dials rather than a natural, 'seat of the pants' feel for the aircraft.

Battling on with growing frustration, I seemed to be slipping behind the rest of the course. It was difficult not to become depressed by the constant ear-bashing and lack of flying. Then came a huge surprise. On landing after a severe bout of criticism it was announced that the time had come to go solo! Another surprise followed almost immediately. When my tormentor discovered that my total flying hours were half that normally set for solo clearance, the event was postponed. Any disappointment felt was more than offset by the knowledge that perhaps I might, after all, make a successful pilot.

The extra hours proved no hardship and, in retrospect, I benefitted from them. Certainly my eventual first solo, on 26 April 1941, went well enough, although relief at arriving in one piece allowed my concentration to wander – like the landing run. As I came to a halt the real world suddenly materialised in the shape of a loud engine roar. Another Tiger Moth flashed by, just a few feet above, with instructor and pupil staring down at the idiot who'd balked their landing by weaving about the field in front of them.

From then on the days passed quickly. Because of the repetitive nature of the subsequent flying exercises, little remains by way of memories. Just a few incidents stick in my mind. The first was when returning from Mangere, the Auckland Aero Club airfield, flying low across Manukau Harbour we came across a pair of swans. My instructor decided to formate on them. As they curved away from the aircraft he joined on the outside of their turn. It was like a Disney film, the birds looking back over their wings with bewildered expressions in an unforgettable display: the effortless beauty of natural flight. Sadly this, my first exciting taste of low flying, wasn't to be repeated. Thanks to an earlier fatal student accident, it remained a forbidden thrill. As a macabre reminder of the inherent dangers, mangled pieces of Tiger Moth lay in a corner of the hangar – evidence of an unauthorised foray amongst the dunes at Muriwai Beach, ten miles or so west of the airfield.

Another incident with Tony Guild is etched firmly in my mind. It was a rotten day for flying: rain and low cloud. At 900 feet, skimming in and out of the bottom layer, I could hardly believe the words I was hearing: 'Spin it.' A lengthy hesitation on my part simply brought a repeated command, 'Spin it!' Was my instructor bent on suicide? 'Come on, trust me, spin it.' There was no escape. Off came the power, up came the nose, back came the airspeed, into the stomach with the stick and hard over with the rudder. Cloud and ground merged in a kaleidoscopic blur. We'd completed barely a single rotation when Tony shouted, 'Recover!' Stick forward, opposite rudder and power on. To my amazement, we'd lost only 300 feet. I learned something that day.

There's one final image I hold dear from the course. It was the day of the solo cross-country, about a month after flying began. The whole course took off at five-minute intervals, our destination a field near Whangārei, about an hour away. The weather was perfect: just a few small, puffy white clouds and excellent visibility. At my appointed time I lifted off and headed for Whangārei. With a map balanced precariously on my knee, I spent the next twenty minutes or so tracing my finger along the line drawn between Whenuapai and Whangārei – that was until a dot appeared on the horizon. As I tried to make out what it was, another and yet another appeared. They must be the aircraft that took off before me. With that I abandoned any pretext of map reading and simply followed the line of dots ahead.

Relaxed now, I was able to take in the sheer beauty of flying: sun, sky, clouds and countryside – a green carpet of hills, fields and forests. There was the Tasman Sea way out to the left, where it should be, and the Pacific just down on the right, so how could one get lost flying up this strip of land dividing two mighty oceans? Time to sit back and enjoy the wonder of it all. Time to ponder too a situation almost unthinkable a few months earlier, a time before Hitler's rampage through Europe. But even these thoughts couldn't dull the feelings I recall so well: excitement, expectation, happiness and a deep sense of satisfaction and contentment. Whangārei arrived all too quickly, waking me from my reverie. There was the landing ground, right where the line ended on my map: a grass field with rough lines of yellow Tiger Moths assembled at one end.

A sandwich lunch, lolling on the grass passing judgement on each pupil's arrival, and then it was time for the return flight. All too soon this welcome departure from Whangārei's inhibiting routine was over. With only a week to go until the end of the course, I was excited about the future. I felt that a move to Canada for the next spell of training would best serve my long-term aim of getting to England. Besides, it was said that much of the training over there was on Harvards, a modern single-engined, all-metal trainer, infinitely better suited to the budding fighter pilot than the old twin-engined Oxfords on offer locally. Already stimulated by seeing the first Harvard to arrive in New Zealand being test flown from Hobsonville, close to Whenuapai, I was delighted when my request to be sent to Canada was granted.

Those of us destined for overseas were supposed to get extra flying but mine amounted to only one short trip after a week's layoff. It meant that I left Whenuapai at the end of May 1941 with a grand total of forty-five hours and ten minutes' flying in my logbook. Three weeks later I was on my way to Canada.

» Chapter 2

CANADA DAYS

The TSS *Awatea* left Auckland in the middle of June 1941. Relatively new and built for the Australia–New Zealand run, she was one of the fastest for her size in the world; with a maximum speed of 26 knots she was nicknamed the 'Greyhound of the Tasman Sea'.[4] It was mid-afternoon when we sailed. Visibility was good and I watched the sun lighting the white face of the museum[5] from well beyond the Rangitoto Channel, until both it and the grey smudge that was the rest of Auckland faded from view. To my surprise there was no one else on deck, no one else to share the question in my mind. Would I ever see Auckland again? I recalled how often in the past my eyes had been drawn to the sparkling waters of Waitematā Harbour and the Rangitoto Channel, always with a sense that this was the direction in which I would one day go. Now, looking back in the opposite direction, I began to wonder. Was it destiny I was following, or simply a fantasy?

The ship was overcrowded, carrying at least twice the normal complement of passengers. I'd drawn the short straw: four in a twin-berth cabin in the middle of the ship and me bedding down on the floor. Fortunately though, from Fiji until the final week of the voyage, most of the time was spent on deck. Fiji was our first port of call and meant a walk in Suva while tropical fruits were stowed on board. Every day the sun shone out of a cloudless sky onto a beautiful blue-black sea, the colour of ink. Flying fish were regulars at the bow of the boat; it was fascinating to watch them gliding gracefully over the waves. And once we were surrounded by dolphins, their bodies glinting in the sun as they leapt through the air. At night I would lie on deck, looking up at the top of the mast as it slowly arced across a star-filled, moonless sky. The wind was warm and gentle. It seemed impossible to believe we were heading to war.

Entertainment had to be manufactured, with PT and boat drill a regular feature. Early on in the voyage I was standing about after PT watching an Australian shadow boxing. Reputed to be a semi-professional, he had a loudmouth in tow who claimed to be his trainer and was challenging people to spar a few rounds with his man. One brave Australian stepped forward and got a pasting for his trouble. But it so happened we had a New Zealand boxing champion with us: Dick Branch[6] was standing alongside me. It took several urgings, 'Come on Dick. Take him down a peg,' to get him to go forward. Eventually presenting himself, Dick was given a stream of assurances that he wouldn't be hurt. Initially he played along with the farce and danced about a bit; then, before the trainer could step in, he gave his opponent a few good cuffs around the ears. There was no more sparring or showing off after that.

The inevitable shipboard concert was memorable mainly for a performance by one of our course. Dressed in full highland rig he began with a Scottish sword dance – tricky at the best of times but well-nigh impossible on a rolling stage – and followed up with *Flight of the Bumblebee* on the violin. He received the longest and loudest applause of the evening, leaving me to ponder the surprising talents that often lie hidden within the most quiet and reserved personalities.

About a week out from Vancouver we were joined by a Canadian coastguard ship that was to be our escort. She was small and painted grey, which was about as close as she came to being a warship; the gun she carried up front certainly looked ineffective. It mattered not because the entire trip was uneventful. But we'd been fortunate. Later we learned that a previous voyage had been intercepted by a German raider. A couple of nights before arriving I caught moonlit reflections of a snowy skyline: the American Rockies. And soon I was gazing up at the bridge spanning Vancouver Harbour. With a few hours' freedom before the afternoon train, we were about to get our first experience of Canadian generosity. News of our berthing must have spread rapidly. Private cars were soon rolling up in droves, offering us tours of the city and accommodation if we could stay. Time was too short to see much, but our welcome was so touchingly genuine that it made a never-to-be-forgotten impression – a wonderful introduction to the good people of a great country.

By no means as pleasurable, though equally impressive, was the train itself. Canadian National Railway was to carry us to our destination on hardwood slatted seats. There were overhead pull-down luggage racks that might have served as beds, should anyone manage to clamber up that high. While most of us spent nearly three days getting corrugated backsides, the pain was eased regularly by the wonderful views as we wound our way through the Rockies and out onto the wheatfields of middle Canada. From snow-clad mountain peaks, perfectly reflected in huge, glass-smooth lakes, to hundreds of miles of waving corn, the sheer size and scale of everything we saw was impressive.

After the occasional stop to stretch our limbs we were informed we were getting there. But what was there? Very little, as we discovered when we alighted on the ground which served as the platform at Dauphin. *Where the hell was Dauphin?* A tiny town amidst the flat Manitoba wheatfields, it comprised a rail stop and a few buildings and sat right in the centre of Canada. The nearest civilisation was Winnipeg, a hundred miles or so further down the track. There certainly wouldn't be anything to distract us, or divert attention from the forthcoming training task. Not to worry. After all, we were here to fly, and I wanted to get on with things as soon as possible.

The airfield, home to No. 10 SFTS (Service Flying Training School), turned out to be some ten miles away. There were sixty-five students on the course, including a few Canadians; we were housed in a single large room, part of a barrack block. Steel frame upper and lower bunks were arranged along each side wall – all very spartan and military. At our first parade we were greeted by a French Canadian warrant officer who spoke an unintelligible tongue for some ten minutes. The only information we registered was: 'You're a good bunch of chaps and can be off until too tirty on turdy.' After the parade there was much discussion about what this meant. 'Too tirty' we understood, but was it Tuesday or Thursday? The majority went for Thursday, which meant three days' leave. But what to do? Consultation with a few Canadians on duty brought to light the holiday resort of Clear Lake, about thirty miles away. Within an hour a dozen or more of us at the airfield gate managed to hitch lifts in a variety of passing vehicles, many drivers going out of their way to drop us off at Clear Lake. The place was a gem, a lovely lake with a number of cafes offering log cabins for hire. It was to become our leisure centre during the forty-eight hours' leave we got every second weekend.

On our return to the airfield, courtesy of the customary Canadian generosity – it never failed – we were surprised to be charged with two days'

AWOL (absent without leave). But in the end nothing came of our error. The entire course was at fault due to a misunderstanding – perhaps why we never encountered that particular warrant officer again.

The airfield's wooden hangars were full of Harvards. Spotlessly clean, shiny and new, all painted bright yellow with black letters and trim. My instructor was to be Pilot Officer Gee, a tall clean-cut young man. When not dressed in flying overalls, he wore an immaculately tailored khaki uniform. Formal, thorough and reserved, he ensured that our association was maintained on a strict instructor/pupil basis. But before we could go flying there was much to learn about the aircraft: fuel system, trim settings, checks and manoeuvre speeds – all to be learnt by heart and repeated when questioned. Finally, there was the blindfold test. This involved sitting in a cockpit, eyes covered, touching without hesitation the correct switch, lever or instrument identified by the instructor.

My first trip in a Harvard, as in the Tiger Moth, was disturbing. Nearly seven weeks away from flying may have dimmed the senses, but it was also a big leap from about eighty horsepower to nearly 500. An alarmingly loud noise, like bits of metal rattling about in a tin can, didn't help much either. With the instructor seated behind rather than in front of the pupil (as in the Tiger Moth), the sight of the engine cowling shaking and twisting just a few feet away was also less than reassuring. The flying controls seemed lifeless, with a machine-like feel. All of which contributed to the impression of encasement within an inanimate mechanical contraption. Would I ever master this assembly of metal, this automaton? But, as so often in life, first impressions quickly faded. My first solo came on 18 July 1941 and, as I became more familiar with the Harvard, it soon became a joy to fly, its possibilities exciting.

Unlike many aircraft, where flipping a couple of switches or pushing two buttons was all that was required, starting the engine of a Harvard involved feet, hands and a good deal of concentration. The engine was fitted with an inertia starter; a flywheel spun up to high revolutions using the aircraft battery, which then engaged with the engine to turn the propeller. The sequence was carried out from the front cockpit on a rocker pedal using heel then toe action. Once the propeller was turning, hands madly pumped the petrol pump and, perhaps, the priming pump too – all to an accompaniment of loud backfiring and smoke from the large exhaust pipe. Simply getting the engine turning brought a sense of accomplishment from the very beginning, even before the thrill of taking to the air. The Harvard was fully aerobatic, although flick rolls were forbidden (a restriction ignored by some instructors). On the two occasions I experienced this it was astonishing to see the stress wrinkles running diagonally across the wing surfaces as they twisted under the heavy aerodynamic load. Things to watch out for: spins could become vicious, but recovery was a simple matter. Also a wing would drop at the stall, and clumsy use of rudder or brake on landing could result in a ground loop – an uncontrolled tight circle sometimes causing damage.

Flying was intensive, sometimes three trips a day. Instruction was excellent and progress checks were numerous (usually carried out by the more senior officers). Considerable emphasis was put on 'blind' flying, which was done under a hood from the rear cockpit and included recovery from spins and unusual positions. Interestingly, these tests were far more searching than those in the post-war RAF. Some of our cross-country flying was also done under the hood and it was on one such test that the course's resident comedian, a lad named Blackmore, played one of his little jokes. He was doubtless encouraged by flying with one of the two sergeant pilots assigned to the course, instructors who adopted a more friendly and casual attitude than the officers. They would even join us on our occasional short breaks at Clear Lake. Chasing needles on dials for any length of time under the hood, especially on hot summer days, was a tiring business. After a bit, his instructor told him to put back the hood and take a rest. In Blackmore's words, 'I got bored after a while and fished out a fag, lit up and decided to blow smoke down the Gosport tube.[7] Every time I puffed, a stream of smoke squirted out from each side of the instructor's helmet, by his ears. The harder I blew the bigger the stream of smoke. It was ever so funny to watch.' Blackmore got away with his little prank – smoking in aircraft was strictly forbidden, of course. I lost contact with him after training in England but will always remember his irrepressible and at times inappropriate sense of humour.

The weather during our stay in Canada was warm and wonderful, with night flying under star-filled skies an eagerly awaited delight. We had to do forty solo night landings. Ground control was exercised by an instructor and half a dozen pupils at the approach end of the runway. Permission to land was requested by flashing the navigation lights on and off on the downwind leg of the circuit and waiting for the Aldis lamp reply: white for OK, red for go round again. Before lowering the wheels we had to make sure that the klaxon was working. The horn sounded a warning if the undercarriage wasn't down when the throttle was closed, as for landing. It became my habit when testing the horn to slam the throttle closed. It caused the engine to backfire loudly while huge flames shot out from the exhaust pipe just below the front cockpit on the right-hand side. The glow from the flames was enhanced by reflections from the Harvard's yellow paintwork, giving the impression of fire dancing across the fuselage and wing. The louder the bang the bigger the flash and kick of adrenalin. It seemed fun at the time but rumour had it that on an earlier course the backfiring display was sufficiently realistic for a pupil to bale out, thinking he was on fire. Had he never been shown the full effect of this phenomenon?

Never to be forgotten were the warm, king-size egg sandwiches waiting in the crew room after night flying. No egg sandwich since has ever tasted quite as delicious as those at Dauphin. Nor has anything ever matched the magic of the Northern Lights, the backdrop to our night runway duties. The whole sky seemed filled with moving shafts of bright colours and patterns of every description. It was breathtakingly mystical, majestic and humbling too.

Related memories are the short walks on warm evenings to the Coke machine. A dime in the slot produced an ice-cold, thirst-quenching Coca Cola, the outside of the bottle soon sweating moisture. Again, no Coke has given quite the same satisfaction since. Another habit quickly acquired was the Canadian breakfast. There was much speculation early on about the compatibility of pancakes and maple syrup with fried egg, sausage and bacon. But after a few mornings no one refused a full plate swimming in syrup.

Time at Dauphin passed all too quickly. Half of each day was given over to flying, the other half to ground school. A number of nights were spent either flying or blind flying in the Link Trainer,[8] doing cross-countries and beam approaches. My final test in this tedious little machine produced a perfect result, criticized by some in the belief that 100 per cent was never achievable, but that was of little concern to me.

After what seemed endless flying tests, exams and interviews, the big day arrived: Wings Parade, and the unveiling of the student passing out top. Uniforms pressed, buttons polished, we all lined up in front of the Canadian national and air force flags. The small, seated audience included a few girlfriends from Clear Lake, while the officiating party was led by a middle-ranking officer accompanied by an aide. Names were called, students stepped forward and saluted, wings were pinned to breasts, a few words, a handshake, a salute and back into line they went. When my turn came I noticed the aide whisper to the officiating officer. Then, as wings were pinned to my uniform, a few words of heavily alcoholic congratulation were breathed in my ear. To my astonishment, I'd passed out as course senior student. It was a slightly confused little airman – the result of those whisky fumes perhaps – who staggered back into line. Whispered enquiries passed up and down the ranks as we marched off: 'Who'd come out top?' But Leading Aircraftman Hardy wasn't telling. He was sitting on a cloud, happy in the knowledge he was first in line for promotion to officer rank.

The immediate result of this unexpected honour was that I was made responsible for delivering the course, complete with documentation, to the dispatch centre at Halifax. With some wanting to explore the rest of Canada it was an unenviable task. But in the end the majority stayed together, spending a day in Winnipeg and a few in Toronto and Montreal before meeting our Halifax deadline. The rail journey from Dauphin was a complete reversal of our previous experience. This time it was a Canadian Pacific Pullman car with porter, bunk beds and proper meals. The first flakes of snow fell at the end of September when we were in Winnipeg. There some said goodbye to their Clear Lake girlfriends – apart from the fool who got himself married there!

While at Toronto five of us hired a car for the day and drove down to Niagara Falls – an impressive sight and the closest we got to America. Without passports or civilian clothes we couldn't officially enter a country not then at war, although the few who did manage to cross the border were treated to a whale of a time. Toronto was clean and spacious but we saw little of the sights. On the other hand, apart from visiting the top of the Royal Bank of Canada building, once the highest in the British Empire,[9] Montreal was unimpressive; we weren't particularly well received and were happy to move on.

During one of the customary stops to stretch legs on the long rail journey that followed, a group of us were engaged in conversation by two old dears. Where had we come from? Where was New Zealand? And how long had we been in Canada? Our answer to the latter question brought a memorable response: 'Haven't you learnt to speak English quickly!' On reaching Halifax my orders were to assemble the course next morning at a reception arranged by the local Women's Institute. Announcement of this commitment met with mutinous hostility but in the end sufficient members of the course turned out to guarantee respectability. In fact, those who did attend were agreeably surprised to be hosted by several attractive young ladies. The result was a pleasant morning, but there were no offers of sightseeing rides as in Vancouver. In any event, England was now calling urgently and we really couldn't afford to keep her waiting. Within days we were all aboard ships heading for the dangerous waters of the Atlantic.

» Chapter 3

ENGLAND AT LAST – SPITFIRES

The Atlantic crossing from Halifax to Liverpool on board the *Capetown Castle* was exceptionally fast. Our convoy included fourteen requisitioned troopships, all doing well over twenty knots and changing course every fifteen minutes or so. How they did this while keeping station in the pitch-black nights was quite bewildering. The weather was cold; the boat was cold too – she'd been built for the mail service from Southampton to South Africa.[10] Visibility was mostly poor, no sun; no scares either, just one or two depth charges barely sensed in the far distance.

The ship was again full to the gunnels, overflowing with French Canadian army men. Boat drill was held at regular intervals and my penalty for now being an officer, all of nineteen years old, was to be placed in command of a Carley float,[11] a lifeboat to be shared with thirty or forty surly and dishevelled French troops in the event of a catastrophe. The French language was as incomprehensible to me as was English to my charges, so communication between us was impossible. We just stood there in silence, trying to balance on a rolling deck, while I attempted to maintain an air of dignified authority in front of my ragged charges, huddled together three deep. Staring at the pitifully small float, I wondered how long I'd last attempting to control these cut-throats trained to kill, each fighting for a place. No one would have lasted long in the cold, miserable, heaving North Atlantic at that time of the year.

The cloud cover that had accompanied us since Halifax suddenly broke as we steamed up the Mersey. Shafts of light lit up the twin towers of the Liver Building in the distance and highlighted the two lines of silvery barrage balloons flying from buoys marking the channel every half mile or so. A Spitfire crossed high overhead, leaving me wondering where this lone fellow had come from and where he was going; how lucky he was. The cloud then returned with a vengeance; visibility closed in as a storm of heavy rain passed rapidly through. Once the skies cleared and the sun came out again there wasn't a barrage balloon to be seen. They'd all been swept away by the squall.

The train from Liverpool to Bournemouth was the first of many crawling journeys across England. It took almost a whole day and night to cover what seemed a relatively short distance. Bournemouth was a smart, middle-class holiday resort on the south coast, respectable and reserved in peacetime. Now, though, it was very dead. The Australian and New Zealand aircrew located there could do little other than walk the cold and windy promenade or gather in pubs, neither of which appealed. Time passed slowly and frustration set in. There was one day of interest, however, when four of us took a bus and taxi trip to see Stonehenge. It featured regularly in our school history books and had always interested me. But what surprised us most was that few of the locals seemed ever to have heard of the site.

Roll call at Bournemouth was at 0900 hours each morning on the promenade, about ten minutes from our spartan hotel billet. It was a bit of a rush to dress, shave in agonisingly cold water, face a miserly breakfast (if there was any left) and get to the parade on time. Many failed to make it but there was always someone on hand to answer for the missing person(s). My own absences usually presaged a late breakfast at Bobby's store. They became too regular, however, and resulted in three days' orderly officer duty. At least the task made a change and enabled me to witness the airmen eating better than we did. Then came a period of great excitement amongst the staff; the King was coming to inspect his loyal Commonwealth troops.

Briefings and rehearsals became top priority for a couple of days and included instructions that, in an outburst of uncontrolled enthusiasm, we were to break ranks and run after His Majesty's car when he departed. To my mind this was taking loyalty beyond acceptable limits. On the day King George VI arrived all that could be seen was the top of his hat, bobbing along the front row of servicemen, a few of whom he spoke to for a moment. Then his car was on its way and 'three cheers for His Majesty' was interrupted by the pounding of running feet. But many, like me, stood fast. This display had nothing to do with loyalty, we felt, and would surely never have been approved by His Majesty, had he known about it. Sure enough, in newsreels covering the visit, 'the loyalty of Commonwealth airmen scrambling to get close to their King' was prominently displayed on the big screen.

And so passed three weeks at Bournemouth before we learned our fate. On arriving there, when we had filled in our records of service, we'd been asked which type of flying we'd prefer: bomber, fighter, coastal, training, army cooperation etc. There were three orders of preference. My answers were Spitfire, Spitfire and Spitfire, which I hoped would get the point across. And it did. No other officer from our Canada course was posted onto Spitfires. Not without further incident, it would lead to my arrival at Heston, where Neville Chamberlain had landed in 1938 proclaiming 'peace for our time'. It was a peace which brought thousands like me halfway round the world. Hard to believe that it was only seven months since I climbed into a Tiger Moth for the first time.

The journey from Bournemouth to Heston was tedious, taking nearly a day. Travel in wartime England was invariably slow and, for those in the services, rarely if ever direct. This was certainly the case for the five Australian and three New Zealand officers lugging all their worldly belongings from coach to train, another train and then coach again. With plenty of standing about in between, the day had been a test of strength and patience. Hungry too, why were we now locked out of this RAF base in a cold coach on a miserable, misty November afternoon? Notwithstanding our travails, chatter was jovial; the banter carried an air of expectation and excitement. After all, we were about to fly Spitfires – and in a role of some importance too. So why were we being kept waiting? Our puzzlement was manifested as humour, much of it forced laughter over possible reasons for the delay.

Movement at last. A service policeman approached and opened the gates. He spoke to the driver who nodded. Beyond the gates a tractor appeared, moving slowly down the drive and towing a trailer. Airmen were walking behind. What was that thing on the trailer? Everyone moved to one side of the coach to get a better look: a coffin draped in a Union Jack. It must have been a hurried, makeshift affair since the tractor and trailer looked to have come straight from a farm. We could not have been more shocked by this welcome to Heston had the Reaper himself been standing by the coffin, scythe in hand and nodding to us. The silence in the coach was deafening, each turning to his own thoughts. It later transpired that the funeral was for a pilot who'd been killed when another aircraft landed on top of him. It was the sort of thing that happened in wartime.

Heston's grass airfield lay on the outskirts of London to the south-west, close to where Heathrow is now. Its location as a Spitfire training unit was hardly ideal. While easy access to the high spots of central London was welcomed by almost everyone, proximity to that huge metropolis made for a number of hazards to flying, especially in winter. It was our misfortune to be there at just such a time – a time when the capital's smoke and fog meant there was hardly a day of good visibility. And poor weather wasn't the only danger. Virtually in the airfield circuit stood the gasometer at Southall, over 300-feet high, lurking menacingly in the mist. As if that wasn't enough, the airfield sat in the middle of three clusters of barrage balloons: London to the east, Slough to the west and Brooklands south-west. That said, with Heston at the centre of this triangle, the balloons could prove helpful when there was total cloud cover. Provided they were visible above, getting home was simply a case of picking the centre spot, then spiralling down through cloud to the airfield. Considering that the majority of pilots were accustomed to flying in the clear skies of Commonwealth countries, it was something of a miracle that we all survived. If nothing else, the weather forced us to develop our map-reading and navigation skills. The Thames, in particular, was an excellent landmark and a pathway home. Every inch of the river from London to Oxford became familiar, as did a long causeway in one of the large Staines reservoirs that signposted the final few miles.

The Spitfires at 61 OTU were mainly Mk 1s. There were also a few Mk 2s but any differences between the two escape me. The undercarriage was raised using the right hand which meant changing hands, flying with the left while pumping with the right. An awkward transition just after take-off was even more difficult in formation – a juggling exercise involving throttle, control column and pump handle. First solos, and a few take-offs thereafter, were amusing to watch as Spitfires disappeared into the mist hunting up and down as the pilot moved the control column backwards and forwards in time with the pumping motion of his right hand. The radio was also cumbersome, a useless piece of one-channel HF equipment with a great lever moved back and forth to transmit and receive. Range was about ten miles at best and the voice at the other end came like a whisper from the dead – if it worked at all. It was certainly a dead loss as a homing device.

The jump from flying a Harvard, with its short nose, to flying a Spitfire with four yards between you and the propeller, and with twice the power, was mind boggling. But in the air the Spitfire was docile by comparison. The controls were light and sensitive, and there wasn't a trace of viciousness if the aircraft was mishandled. In fact, the Spitfire could be flown along straight and level completely stalled. It wouldn't even drop a wing when stalled under high G loads in a steep turn – always provided coarse rudder wasn't applied. Indeed, the Spitfire had none of those nasty characteristics which might prove fatal. Those it did kill likely killed themselves.

My first flight in a Spitfire, on 22 November 1941, was a nervous thrill. Nervous, because I was uncertain of my ability to handle this magnificent machine and get it back on the ground in one piece; a thrill, having the chance to prove myself. Sitting in the cockpit on the ground with that long nose pointing upwards there was simply no view ahead. So cautious taxying, turning the aircraft from side to side, was essential. Take-off was quite straightforward, taking care not to let the tail up too high to see forwards lest the propeller strike the ground. Retracting the undercarriage took longer than expected and I started a turn before I'd finished pumping the undercarriage up. I didn't want to lose sight of the airfield. From then on flying was simply a pleasure – until opening the hood for landing. My dislike of fastening the helmet chinstrap suddenly became an unexpected distraction. Air pressure lifted the helmet from my head, making the curved approach a contest between landing successfully and avoiding strangulation by the radio cord around my neck. Fortunately, the landing won, although the reluctance of the aircraft to touch down was surprising; it seemed to float along forever. Our Spitfires were light then, of course; they weren't carrying an operational load.

At the end of the course two of us were chosen as staff pilots to assist with training the next course: myself and David Waters, another New Zealander. His training had been delayed in Canada due to illness. Our reward for this extra six weeks at Heston was the guarantee of a posting to a front-line squadron in the south of England, which suited us both.

Life as a staff pilot at Heston was great fun. It was a marvellous experience sharing the company of so many Battle of Britain aces, being accepted by them and treated more or less as an equal. If their attitude was a total joy, it was also difficult to understand. To me they were close to superhuman – survivors of so many air battles. A complete novice with no operational experience, I had to learn everything the hard way. Yet they gladly took me into their circle at work by day and, off duty, on jaunts to London and other nearby fighter aerodromes. We were stopped by the police only once, late at night. One look at the arms and legs sticking out of the car and we were waved on our way with an exasperated comment, 'Royal Air Force pilots!' which could be heard even above the din of our tuneless singing.

Heading an impressive list of individuals then serving at Heston was 'Sailor' Malan, the top-scoring RAF fighter pilot at the time.[12] We didn't see much of him. We saw more of his brother 'George',[13] then a sergeant going through the course after mine. He would later become a good friend and we would often fly together. Then there was young 'John Willie' Hopkin,[14] a little fellow with a twitch like St Vitus' dance, a nervous but happy chap. Bob Holland, a wizard on the piano, survived the war only to die in an aircraft accident several years after.[15] Derek Forde[16] would go on to join 72 Squadron eight months after me, just before we left for North Africa. He was another happy chap whose only boast was to have photographed the *Scharnhorst*, despite the flak from Brest.

The chirpy, full of life little Frenchman, Maurice Choron,[17] was always smiling. He adored Michael Robinson,[18] the ace who'd just taken over the Tangmere Wing. Maurice was beside himself with excitement when Robinson flew into Heston to ask if he'd like to fly as his number two at Tangmere. Sadly, they were both shot down and killed two months later.[19] Then there was Paddy Barthropp.[20] He wasn't much older than me and became a good friend during my short time on his flight. Paddy was an easy going, devil-may-care fellow who rarely took anything seriously – certainly no one in authority. Something of a fatalist, he lived life to the full. That said, the look of anguish he wore as he slid into the seat of the car after having to identify a dead trainee pilot reflected a deeper, caring nature. Always willing to help less fortunate friends, a number of celebrated fighter pilots had Paddy to thank for his various kindnesses post-war. A couple of months after I left Heston, Paddy returned to operations and was shot down.[21]

Finally, there was Brian Kingcome,[22] a nodding acquaintance who was to play a major part in my operational future. He was posted as CO (commanding officer) of 72 Squadron around the time my own posting came through – to 1 Squadron at Tangmere doing night intruder work in Hurricanes. Hurricanes! After all my hard grind on the Spitfire? No Sir! As it happened, my colleague, David Waters, was also due for posting and had casually asked Brian in the bar if there was any chance of getting to 72 Squadron too. I saw this as my opportunity. Why not me also? The happy outcome was that we both went to 72 with Brian.

And so, after nearly a year's training, with thirty-five hours on the course and another twenty as a staff pilot – a grand total of 216 hours in my logbook – I was about to begin operations against the enemy. Well, not quite right away, as it turned out.

» Chapter 4

72 SQUADRON

In March 1942, when the two young sprog pilots from New Zealand joined 72 Squadron it was based at Gravesend, a small aerodrome to the east of London just south of the Thames. It was aptly named. A number of pilots had crashed trying to land on this postage stamp of an airfield – including me on my first flight there. What an ignominious introduction to the squadron! Clambering out of a Spitfire with no wings, wheels or propeller was no way to thank Brian Kingcome for his generosity in taking me on. In spite of his assurances that no retribution would follow, I was crushed by disgrace and humiliation. That my shameful exhibition of 14 March didn't make me the butt of ridicule was simply because so many others had suffered a similar fate. My flight commander, Ross Gillespie, had laid great emphasis on the smallness of the field and the need to bring the Spitfire in slowly. Forgetting that it was fully armed and heavier than any I'd flown before, I took his advice too literally. But even with my limited experience I should have been able to feel the imminent stall considerably better than I did.

Gillespie was in no hurry to get us started on operations. Within a week the squadron moved to Biggin Hill where another fortnight passed with the same excuse each day: we weren't ready. It was frustrating. Not only were we treated like student pilots by this old woman of a Canadian, we felt rejected, forced to stand around on the fringes of excited conversations as pilots returned from operations. Then one day it happened. Thirteen aircraft took off on operations but only ten returned. Gillespie, Al Hake and Tom Watson were missing, never to be heard of again.[23] Our flight had taken a heavy blow, but there were two new pilots thankful that they 'weren't ready'. Almost immediately a replacement flight commander, Australian Hugo Armstrong, arrived on posting from 129 Squadron; he had an impressive record and would soon collect a DFC.[24] Two days later, on 8 April, I began flying sweeps into France. My recollections of those first few trips are strictly limited – the slowly revolving tailwheel of Hugo's aircraft as I stuck to him like glue, and the flak coming up at us from Boulogne. The tracer seemed slow to arrive at first; then it gradually gathered speed and swished by at an unbelievable rate. It was a sight that never lost its fascination – provided it didn't come too close, of course.

While never a cause of great concern, the dangers associated with flak were never far from one's mind, especially when flying within range of machine-gun and rifle fire. The highly decorated Wing Commander 'Sheep' Gilroy[25] scared the daylights out of us in North Africa with his reckless disregard of danger. Whenever he turned up at dispersal to fly with us the sergeant pilots made themselves scarce, hoping they wouldn't have to fly with him. He had a reputation for losing his number twos. 'No need to worry about flak,' he regularly assured us. But that was before a rifle bullet passed up through his parachute and embedded itself in his backside! 20-mm cannon fire, usually tracer, was also a danger from a few hundred feet up to about a thousand. Above that, 40-mm Bofors filled the gap to nearly 10,000 feet. This too was tracer and arrived in strings of about five shells – lovely to watch as it went by and never much of a threat. 88-mm heavy flak was even less of a threat. It could reach 35,000 feet but to my knowledge no fighter boy was ever shot down by it. Only once did heavy flak come close enough for me to hear the characteristic crump, crump, crump and feel the Spitfire jump from these explosions. It was my own fault – giving the German battery a good half-hour to do their sums as I flew up and down the same patrol line at the same height.

I recall a couple of flak incidents that did cause a bit of heart pumping. The first was over the invasion fleet shortly after D-Day. A Fw 190 popped out of cloud and straight back into it, right over the mass of ships involved in the landings. I thought this worth investigating but as I did all hell let loose – even though I was supposedly safe, above the prohibited firing height. It only needed one idiot on the battleship below to start firing to set the rest of the fleet off. *Typical Navy!* Golf balls of every description coming up at me from all directions – a real firework display. My saviour was the cloud, as it was for the 190. It was a worrying moment that seemed to last for hours.

The second occasion was a few months later when two of us were stooging along just inside the French coast near Calais. Thick cloud had forced us down to about 2,000 feet when lots of golf balls appeared close by. So urgent was the need to escape that I entered cloud vertically. What to do now? All the flying instruments had toppled: direction indicator spinning like a top, artificial horizon flicking from side to side, turn-and-bank needles twitching about like drunken metronomes and very little airspeed on the clock. Fear of spinning made me handle the controls lightly. Best put on full power, ease the stick back, hope to complete a loop, pop out of cloud at the bottom and sort things out from there. Emerging below cloud again, I levelled the aircraft and reset the artificial horizon before re-entering cloud – safely this time. Eventually I emerged from the top of the cloud, sorted out where home was, and reflected on how close I'd come to killing myself.

The Spitfire is universally acknowledged as a beautiful machine, an object of grace from every angle. Its lines could never be improved and its shape remained much the same despite endless modifications to improve its performance. There was, however, one pilot on 72 Squadron who did a bit of redesign work himself, quite unintentionally, of course. One drawback on the early Spitfires was the hood, which had flat sides and wasn't very wide. This, together with the oxygen mask sticking out in front of one's face, made it very difficult to check behind to cover the area from which an attack was most likely. We spent as much time looking backwards as anywhere else. Weaving from side to side instead of flying straight and level thus became a habit. But it was annoying to keep banging the oxygen mask against the slab-sided hood each time one turned to look behind. The problem was eventually solved with a design change in 1942. Meanwhile we continued with the slab-sided hood incorporating a small 'knock-out panel' on one side. It could be forced out with an elbow to equalize the pressure inside and outside the cockpit. (During a fast descent it was thought that the greater pressure on the outside would hold the hood in place, preventing the pilot from jettisoning it should he wish to bale out.)

Well, on this particular day our hero, a stocky, powerful fellow and a good pilot, was diving down over the Channel at great speed when there was a loud bang. 'God, I've been hit,' thought our hero and yanked back hard on the stick. When he recovered after blacking out there wasn't an aircraft to be seen anywhere. His Spitfire seemed to be all right so he hurried on home to Biggin. A few hours later the aircraft caught my attention as I cycled past on my way to dispersal. It was standing head on to me in a servicing bay and looked as though it was about to clap its wings together over its body like some great bird. Curiosity justified closer investigation, which established that a good nine inches had been added to the dihedral on each wing! The wings on a Spitfire are attached to the body by three large and five smaller bolts of specially hardened steel. After the wings had been removed I was shown a large bolt, over an inch in diameter, distorted into the shape of a crankshaft. Why it didn't fail completely, and how the ground crew were able to drive it from its location bent into that shape, was an engineering miracle. No one to my knowledge has torn the wings off a Spitfire in the air but on 13 July 1942 Robbie Robertson almost succeeded.

It was about this time that the Fw 190 began to appear in numbers over France. In the absence of detailed information, rumour tended to exaggerate the capabilities of this new fighter. That said, in most respects it was a better aircraft than the Spitfire Vs we were flying. Mutterings about the advantages it brought the Luftwaffe must have reached higher authority because Sholto Douglas, Commander-in-Chief Fighter Command,[26] soon arrived at dispersal wanting to meet all the pilots. He sat down with us and said, 'Right, what do you chaps want? Feel free to speak.' The question caught everyone by surprise. After some hesitation and shuffling of feet the first request was for more ammunition. 'Six seconds of cannon fire was far too short for combat, especially fighting a running battle in France.' Next came the matter of the hood. 'Why couldn't our aircraft be fitted with bubble hoods?' We knew they were fitted to Photographic Reconnaissance Unit Spitfires. Finally, we needed more power for increased speed and rate of climb. The C-in-C assured us that our comments would be looked into and much of what we wanted would soon be provided. Sure enough, bubble hoods arrived and were fitted within a couple of weeks. But it took a further two months before the response to our other requests arrived in the shape of Spitfire IXs.

Life was never dull at Biggin, quite apart from operations. There was a memorable occasion when an American pilot on 133 Squadron (of which more later) was seen climbing from the cockpit of a Spitfire, only to be followed by a WAAF.[27] Unfortunately, the incident was seen from the air traffic control tower and reported, which led to the pilot being court martialled. With all the pilots at Biggin on the side of the American, the trial was a scream. Asked to describe what happened, he admitted flying down to Tangmere to see his girlfriend, the WAAF in question. But parting had been so difficult that he decided to fly the light of his life back to Biggin. With the parachute removed and the lady positioned on the seat, he sat on top of her. Flying the aircraft hadn't been a problem. Asked later if he'd be prepared to incur the wrath of the Air Council[28] by committing the same crime again he replied, 'Oh yes, if it was with the same WAAF. She knew the form.' Punishment was a reprimand.

Then there was the day another American tried to fly a Tiger Moth for the first time. I witnessed his efforts on the way to dispersal one morning. Taxying in a strong crosswind he was applying more and more power in an effort to keep straight. But the more throttle he applied the worse the situation became. He finished up travelling downwind at great speed, straight for a team of workers laying concrete at the end of a runway. They scattered in all directions – as did the concrete when the Moth arrived in the middle of it.

All pilots at Biggin were issued with yellow-painted bicycles, referred to as 'yellow perils'. With the airfield on top of a hill, they were great for evening runs down to the local pubs – always accomplished at high speed in the absence then of any traffic. The journey back was a different thing, of course, and much more taxing. We tended to cycle from the officers' mess to dispersal in groups of two or more. How the practice began is beyond me, but someone started a game which involved carrying out quarter attacks on bicycles. The aim was to come in at some speed from the side of your quarry and hit his front or rear wheel as near at right angles as possible. A successful attack would see the victim's wheel fold up completely as the frame thumped down with a jolt. The victim was deemed shot down and claimed as 'destroyed' amidst gales of laughter. Such were the simple pleasures enjoyed by grown men – possibly the external release of internal pressures at a risky time. We were fortunate that this practice came to a halt – the bicycle section unable to withstand its combat losses – before news of it reached the station commander.

In the spring of 1942 every effort was being made to think up new tricks to engage the Luftwaffe over northern France. Sweeps directed at their airfields accompanied by a few medium bombers would often provoke a reaction, although not always combat. Only if German fighters had a height advantage would they come near us. And such was their respect for the Spitfire they would rarely seek combat beyond the French coast unless the odds were heavily in their favour. A bright spark at HQ Fighter Command then had the idea that a dawn thrust by the Biggin, Hornchurch and North Weald Wings (nine squadrons in all) directed at the Luftwaffe airfields around St Omer might stir up some action. The plan was to take off in the dark with navigation lights on, rendezvous with the other two Wings over the Isle of Sheppey at 15,000 feet, climb to 25,000 and arrive over St Omer around sunrise. One would have to be naïve or stupid to believe that German pilots would turn out of bed at that time in the morning, let alone for a lot of English idiots milling about at that freezing height. However, anything new seemed worth trying.

No pilot was at his best at four o'clock in the morning. A few grunts were all one got for conversation at breakfast, and that had to be rushed to get to the briefing by five. Our wing commander, Jamie Rankin,[29] was to lead the whole show, flying with 72 Squadron – a comforting thought as the other eight squadrons would be stacked at higher altitudes, protecting us against attack from above. There was, however, some doubt about the weather so it was agreed we would go to dispersal, kit up and be ready to go. The signal for take-off would be either a Verey light fired from the control tower or a telephone call to dispersal. Hanging about in the dark all togged up was about as inspiring as the early morning call, the only difference being the element of expectation, half wishing we could get on with it, half hoping it would be scrubbed.

Vaguely visible little groups stood around, recognisable only by the yellow of Mae Wests and occasional glow of a cigarette. There was much muttering and staring in the direction of the control tower. Five minutes passed, then ten. We were all getting impatient, especially Jamie Rankin, who trotted to the telephone several times. At last a red flare climbed heavenwards and most of us turned and headed for our aircraft. Almost at the same time there came a gasp and a few nervous laughs. Attention again turned to the tower. Not a trace of the Verey light which only seconds before had been sailing majestically upwards. Then, as we stood gaping, the flare suddenly reappeared, fell to the ground and burnt out. There were a few curses but most were struck silent by thoughts of the horrors that might have been. Had the cloud base been a little higher, had the Verey light not been fired vertically, total chaos would have ensued. Three squadrons would have launched into cloud less than a hundred feet from the ground with the inevitable result: disorientation, collisions and crashes. Few would have survived.

Despite this close shave, the operation was carried out a week later. It was a memorable sight. Navigation lights floating about above us after leaving the Isle of Sheppey gave the appearance of lights on a huge Christmas tree waving in the wind. Needless to say, there was no reaction by the Luftwaffe as we sat in the half-light of dawn over St Omer. Looking down at the featureless dark of the earth below one could imagine smiles of bemused satisfaction flickering across the faces of the German pilots lying comfortably in their beds.

Then there was the day the King was to visit Biggin. A chance for more behind the scenes theatricals. According to the plot thought up by the propaganda machine, the King would watch his intrepid fighter pilots launch themselves into battle with 72 Squadron centre stage. Photographers were falling over themselves as he made his way down the line of pilots dressed in full flying gear (except parachutes, thank God!), shaking hands with each of us and stopping for a brief word with some. He still spoke with traces of a stammer. (It had gone when we met again two years later.) Meanwhile the other two squadrons[30] were taking to the air. By the time we joined them for a mass flypast – so that the King could be photographed waving farewell from a dais – the first aircraft had been milling about burning fuel fast at low level for a good fifteen minutes. For once we provoked a vigorous Luftwaffe response but, with two squadrons down on fuel, Jamie Rankin wisely decided not to push on into France. After stooging up and down off the coast several times, watching the German fighters do the same on the land side, we came creeping back to Biggin. So much for the media's subsequent claim that the King had spent the day waving his gallant pilots off into battle. Some battle!

If Biggin Hill was considered the premier Fighter Command station during the Second World War, Abbeville on the Somme was its Luftwaffe equivalent. The German pilots there, 'the Abbeville Boys', were worthy foes. One of our aims – it became almost an obsession in the spring of 1942 – was to stir up trouble for them as often as we could. Sometimes our incursions would meet with success, marked by great jubilation on our return. On other occasions, arriving home safely would bring silent relief; the fright, sweat and confusion quickly forgotten. The standard German tactic was to climb up sun or inland after take-off, depending on the threat direction. The earlier they learned of our arrival, the greater their potential height advantage. Our counter to this ploy was to fly at wave-top height, below the German radar horizon, until sighting the French coast. We'd then climb like hell to a point well up sun of Abbeville in the hope of arriving there before the Boys. On more than one occasion it worked a treat. However, being the baby of the squadron, it usually fell to me to fly at the back end of the flight – 'arse-end Charlie' as it was known. The only reward, if it could be called that, of occupying this vulnerable position was the thrill of flying at ultra-low level, legally.

One such experience sticks firmly in my mind. Zooming over a country estate in Sussex (later used by Sotheby's as an auction house) at chimney-top level, I noticed what appeared to be a large garden party less than a hundred feet below. I've never forgotten that summer's afternoon and the stark contrast it so vividly demonstrated: between a pilot's sweaty cockpit and all the finery of those below. Momentarily it brought to mind the gap between the risks faced by those in the armed forces and the safety of civilians in a war-torn Britain. Heedless of the excitement our sudden massed flypast must have generated, on we roared, out across the coast and over a sea that was oily smooth, flat as a millpond. Hazy sunshine and lack of any horizon made height judgement difficult. Helped by the occasional glint of light off the water's surface we flew on, only partly aware of the danger. Then, suddenly, to my amazement, two dolphins appeared to rise into the air in front of me. I had a perfect view of the pair but it wasn't until their dorsal fins cut the surface that I realised they were still in the water. Low flying could be fun but this was frightening. Arse-end Charlie had learnt a lesson. Never again was I such a smart arse, so complacent over water.

Provided nothing big was on, one day each week at Biggin the squadron was released from operations for a so-called 'training day'. In fact many pilots went off to see family or friends, flying wherever possible. My first training day trip was to visit an old college friend who was on a wireless operators' course near Oxford, at Upper Heyford. Oxford was on the Thames and the river, together with the surrounding countryside, was familiar from my time at Heston. A quick check of the map. Yes, just follow all the well-known features to Oxford, then Upper Heyford was a couple of minutes on a rough heading of such and such. Can't miss it. Would be good to see Phil again after a couple of years half a world away. A lot of water had gone under the bridge since our yacht sank in Auckland Harbour and we had the extraordinary good fortune to be rescued late that evening by the only other vessel in the area. And I'd get a great kick out of showing him over my very own Spitfire.

It was a leisurely flight to Oxford recalling this town, that village, this island and that weir and lock. How green and lush everything looked now that spring had arrived. Biggin Hill and the war seemed no longer real as I floated along placidly in my own little world. Ha! There was Oxford. Time to drop down to a thousand feet and head for Heyford. Minutes passed … no sign of a big airfield. More minutes and still no airfield. Must have missed it. Time to climb back to Oxford and start again using the map this time. Unfolding a large map in a Spitfire, orientating it properly and finding the bit you want is by no means simple; it always seems to be on a fold. Soon the map spreads out to cover all the instruments, not least the compass. A seemingly simple task quickly becomes frustrating, irritating; it's like trying to read a large national newspaper in a crowded railway carriage. All this time I was flying a lazy orbit round Oxford, head down. Suddenly everything darkened as a shadow whipped across the cockpit. What the hell was that?

A quick glance out to the right revealed a thick cable sloping back from a silver biplane; I could just make out the helmeted head in the back seat as it flashed under my wing. With a few seconds to recover from the fright and return a skipping heart to something approaching normal, I realised my error. I'd flown under a Hotspur glider towed by a Hawker Hind, up the cable and over the tug itself. Fifty feet up or down, a bit further to the right and the resulting accident would have been put down to a brash young Spitfire pilot showing off by beating up a glider and tug. In reality the cause was an idiot who thought he could find his way without using a map.

I eventually arrived at Upper Heyford to find that Phil had left a couple of days earlier, having completed his training. He went off to a bomber squadron and we didn't meet again until the end of the war. In the meantime he'd been shot down twice and spent two spells as a prisoner of war. Later he returned to New Zealand and became a successful farmer.

My second training day trip was to Oakington, near Cambridge, to see a friend flying Stirlings. Ben and I had been close throughout training. At Biggin we rarely used the runway so it was a new and slightly bewildering experience to find myself in the middle of a great expanse of asphalt; I'd used less than half the runway length. The only thing visible was the top of the control tower. I had to find my way there using the taxiways – the grass looked very rough – and couldn't afford to hang about because the Spitfire engine overheats quickly on the ground. I eventually found a parking place but there wasn't an airman in sight. The airfield was dead. The only living thing in the control tower pointed out the officers' mess in the distance; it turned out to be as dead as the airfield. It took some time to locate Ben's room, where I found him asleep. As I later discovered, so were most of the others on the aerodrome. Ben had been on a 'freshman' operation the previous night, a trip to Brest. This sort of short-range raid allowed crews to gain experience at the beginning of their operational tours. Awake now, Ben dressed and we wandered down to take a look at his aircraft.

Oakington was eerily silent. The contrast with the bustle and noise of a fighter airfield during daytime reflected the contrasting role of Bomber Command. Standing beside a massive black Stirling, waiting for darkness to hide its path of terror and destruction, was a disturbing sensation. It was a steep climb to the cockpit, twenty-two feet above the ground, enormous by Spitfire standards but surprisingly small and cumbersome given the size of the aircraft itself. Looking out at the two engines either side with their tiny three-bladed propellers it was obviously underpowered. It had difficulty in climbing to 13,000 feet – just about out of range of light flak but a sitting duck for everything else thrown at it, especially night fighters. On the way out Ben showed me a 'hush hush' box under a cover: a new navigation aid, GEE he called it. (Radio navigation meant nothing to me then.)

Time for Ben to see my Spitfire now, a toy by comparison; he didn't seem much impressed. A happy farewell, a quick circuit of the aerodrome, a beat-up of Ben's lone figure, a couple of 'upward Charlies'[31] and off to Biggin. We met again a couple of times in London, where Ben and his crew spent much of their time on great binges. It was something all bomber crews seemed to do – a bonding exercise that made for trust and created a close-knit family of friends, far more so than between fighter pilots. It was probably their way of suppressing thoughts of the inevitable. Losses in Bomber Command were appalling and to my mind the Stirling, in particular, was nothing more than a flying coffin. Three months after my Oakington visit the bodies of Ben and his crew were washed ashore on the Zuider Zee.

Tragedy could strike fighter squadrons too, mostly when least expected. Dickie Barwell[32] was the fiery little station commander at Biggin during the summer of 1942. His torso was encased in plaster following a crash which damaged his spine after the engine of his Spitfire failed on take-off. Ignoring medical advice, he flew with the squadrons as often as he could, sometimes as leader but more often as number two to Jamie Rankin or a squadron commander. At the time Luftwaffe Me 109s[33] carried out a regular late evening 'milk run' along the south coast. They'd come in high near Beachy Head, run along the coast in a gradual dive to Dover then escape to France relying on speed for defence. It was a tactic that worked, as witnessed one evening from Sir Philip Sassoon's home, appropriated as the officers' mess for the airfield at Lympne, near Hythe in Kent. The magnificent view out over Dungeness to the English Channel was suddenly interrupted by the sight of an Me 109 diving down out of cloud with a Spitfire some 500 yards behind. The sound of engines at speed was accompanied by the rattle of cannon fire as the Spitfire pilot opened up at his rapidly receding target, more in hope than expectation.

Similar lack of success against these regular visitors became sufficiently annoying and embarrassing to stir Bob Oxspring[34] into doing something about it. Bob was CO of 91 Squadron at Hawkinge, near Folkestone, which carried out weather reconnaissance sorties. It was Bob who first sighted and gave warning of the dash by the *Scharnhorst*, *Gneisenau* and *Prince Eugen* up the English Channel – a warning which went unheeded until too late. That was in February 1942. Months later Bob flew up to Biggin to express his concern about the 'milk run' 109s and work out a plan of action. That same day, it was 1 July, with Dickie Barwell as his number two, Bob took off at sunset under the control of Bill Igoe in the Biggin operations room. The plan was to lie in wait near Beachy Head for the intruder. Unknown to them a pair of Spitfires under Tangmere's control were also in the area. In the not unusual confusion which plagued the control system, the Tangmere pair were vectored onto Bob and Dickie, who recognised them as friendly. As the leader passed over the top of Bob, he looked back towards Dickie and was horrified to see his aircraft on fire. The other Tangmere Spitfire was shooting at it. Dickie was never seen again, swallowed up by the sea. It later transpired that the two Tangmere Spitfires were flown by Czechoslovakian pilots with no operational experience.[35]

Fifty-two years later at the RAF Museum[36] there was another Barwell sitting alongside me. It was Dickie's younger brother, Eric, who earlier that day had given a short talk. He became an ace, and later CO of 125 Squadron, flying the Defiant, an aircraft he didn't rate highly. Despite its initial success, Luftwaffe pilots quickly learned not to attack from behind where they were vulnerable to the four .303 machine guns mounted in its power-operated turret. Attacks from ahead and below were far more successful. So much so, in fact, that Barwell lost almost his entire squadron. The Defiant was soon withdrawn from day operations. It had little success at night either and soon fell from use completely. The younger Barwell was lucky to be alive.[37]

Dickie Barwell wasn't the only station commander to be shot down. In May 1942, as 72 Squadron was returning from a sweep over France, Bill Igoe came on the R/T. 'Hello Brian. Grandad next door has fallen in the drink.' With typical dryness Kingcome replied, 'Silly fellow.' Grandad was Group Captain 'Batchy' Atcherley,[38] station commander at Kenley, a few miles from Biggin. A member of the successful British Schneider Trophy Team in 1931, stories of his outrageous flying were legion. On this particular day, Batchy decided he'd take on the Luftwaffe all on his own, with a little bit of help from the operations controller at Kenley. His plan was to sit high above the Channel in the hope of catching any Germans chasing aircraft returning from sweeps over France. But he paid the price for not sitting high enough. The controller warned him there were hostiles about, giving their height too.

Content that he was above them, what Batchy didn't know was that we always added another eight or ten thousand feet to any 'angels'[39] we were given. Judging height by radar was an inexact science and it paid to err on the safe side. He was fortunate to be picked up from the Channel, an (even) older and a wiser man. I can still picture Brian Kingcome sitting on a bar stool, acting out the story of Batchy's solo onslaught against the Luftwaffe. It was a scream.

Tragedy of a different form struck Biggin's 133 Squadron, the third RAF 'Eagle' Squadron, formed before the United States entered the war and manned by American volunteers. It was always puzzling, trying to understand the thinking of the Fighter Command planners, never more so than at the end of July 1942. We had just re-equipped with the new, more powerful Spitfire Mk IX, the second Fighter Command unit to do so. Then, only a week later, the squadron was split up and on its way to Scotland under a new CO, Bob Oxspring. Flying north, Bob received instructions to report to 11 Group HQ as soon as he landed. The upshot was that he and a number of our sergeant pilots returned to Biggin Hill to reinforce the inexperienced squadron which had replaced us there. This was in preparation for the disastrous Dieppe raid.[40]

At the beginning of July we'd moved down to Lympne and sat with our aircraft painted like zebras[41] and hidden under cover, waiting almost a week for the raid which was eventually cancelled. The sudden lack of activity by Fighter Command during this period must surely have alerted the German High Command that something big was brewing. Little wonder that the raid a month later ended in such tragic loss of life. It was regarded by many as a military blunder, though not by Lord Mountbatten,[42] chief of Combined Operations. At that time the pilots of 72 were fuming over the decision to withdraw us from operations. Here was one of the top units in Fighter Command, equipped with its best aircraft, being replaced by a cobbled together outfit, most of whom had no combat experience and little opportunity to work together as a team. Bob was as disgusted as the rest of us, not least by the heavy responsibility mortals of lesser skill had heaped upon him.

Our move north meant handing over our Spitfire IXs, some of which went to 133 Squadron. A little over a month later, 133 and two other squadrons were tasked with escorting a large number of American B-17s in a raid on Morlaix. The mission was on the limit of the Spitfire's range so the three squadrons moved down to Bolt Head, near Salcombe in Devon, to reduce the distance to the target. On the day of the raid, only about half the B-17s turned up at the rendezvous point; they then set course for the target with the fighters some distance behind. Total cloud cover meant that the run to the target was done on dead reckoning. The Spitfires stayed with the bombers until the limit of their range, then turned back. Estimating they were nearing England, they let down through cloud only to find they were still over occupied France, Brest in fact. All hell let loose!

Unable to reach England, eleven new Spitfire IXs from 133 Squadron were lost. Four pilots were killed, six ended up in enemy hands while one baled out, evaded capture and eventually returned to England via Spain.[43] The only other pilot to make it back that day had to return from the raid early.[44] The cause of this misfortune was the weather: solid cloud and a hundred-mile-an-hour tailwind on the outbound leg. It was the first time any of us had heard of jet streams. It wasn't until 1954 that I heard a first-hand account of the events of that day, from one of the American pilots involved. He spent the rest of the war as a POW after a forced landing in Normandy – all because of a wind.

Looking back on those Biggin Hill days after all these years, it's only unusual events that stick in the memory. One day was much like another; only the weather, the target or the type of operation made a difference. The squadron worked as a team. It didn't matter where a pilot flew in the formation, he knew what was required of him. Procedures became instinctive, a matter of course – like radio silence, enforced from climbing into the aircraft until over enemy territory and broken only when enemy action demanded it. Pilots in a disciplined squadron rarely spoke, even in combat, except to give warnings. Squadrons that clogged the air with excited shouts and chatter scared the hell out of people – until they realised the situation didn't involve them.

More eerie, but just as nerve-wracking, was the sound of a radar beam sweeping over the formation. It began quietly, a slow pulsating beat; the sound level would then increase before fading away. It would start as we climbed out over Kent at about 10,000 feet, a sequence that was repeated until about halfway across the Channel. Alone in a cold, confined cockpit, perched high in a rarefied atmosphere, the effect of this monotonous intrusion could become unsettling. One pilot likened it to a voice saying, 'Look behind you. Look behind you' – the direction from which an attack was most feared.

Acting as top cover on sweeps into France at upwards of 30,000 feet, it always came as a surprise in fine weather to look down and see the Channel with the land on each side exactly as shown on a map. The view extended as far up the north-west coast of Europe as the Dutch islands and down to the coast of Normandy in the south-west. Even the curvature of the earth was discernible, while directly overhead the sky was dark blue – a contrast with the lighter horizon. Twenty to thirty minutes at such an altitude in an unpressurised, unheated cockpit left one nearly frozen. My hands suffered most. The issue flying gauntlets were too clumsy, making it difficult to find the right switch in a hurry or feel the right place on the gun button, a three-position rocker switch. The silk inner gloves were better but gave little warmth and it became my habit to bang each hand alternately on a knee to keep the circulation going.

Another annoying feature of flying at high altitude for any length of time was misting. The armour-plated glass of the front windscreen was about two inches thick and slow to react to changes in air temperature. A fast dive from height could cause it to mist over, or even freeze up, in the warmer, moist air at lower level; not conducive to good formation keeping and hopeless when following an enemy vertically down – the usual Luftwaffe evasive tactic. German fighters were faster in a dive than the Spitfire, and there wasn't much hope of cutting the distance when they pulled out from their dive – they'd be lost from sight under the Spitfire's long nose. Very frustrating.

Wrapped cosily in its small cockpit, flying the Spitfire you soon became part of the machine. This allowed you to concentrate on the critical tasks: searching the whole sky for the enemy and making split-second decisions in combat. Most of the time on operations was spent concentrating on what was happening around you. Then, suddenly, you could be jolted back to the reality that you were connected to a machine on which your life depended. The slightest change in engine note would have you anxiously scanning the instruments, only to find that all was as it should be. Good old Rolls-Royce! However, my concentration would sometimes be broken by a strange sensation, a tiny spot of light revolving like a spinning firework for a fraction of a second. It puzzled me for a couple of years but I never mentioned it for fear of seeming foolish. The riddle was solved on my first night sortie. Outside air could be fed into the cockpit by a small scoop located just below the windscreen panel on the right. It was hand operated and, when opened, tended to collect incandescent carbon from the engine exhaust. It was something of a relief to discover that my mysterious daylight distractions were caused by these particles, some red, some white hot, spinning as they cooled.

No amount of praise could do justice to the devotion of the ground crews who kept our aircraft smart and serviceable. Two men were allocated to each, an engine mechanic and an airframe fitter. Other trades, such as instrument fitters and armourers, were shared. The pilot might fly the aircraft but the ground crew owned it. The pilot might fire at the enemy but the ground crew shot it down – and sometimes danced on the wings with joy. It was the ground crew who strapped the pilot in, who polished the windscreen and patted him on the head for luck before jumping down ready for start-up. And long before the aircraft stopped taxying they knew from the absence of patches over the machine gun ports that you'd been in action; the grins on their faces told you so. The first words you heard as you threw off the harness straps were, 'What happened, Sir?' They were part of the action and proud of it.

They'd be up at dawn, or earlier if necessary, testing engines and they'd still be there long after we'd departed at night. They'd listen patiently if this or that wasn't right and immediately set about fixing things, no matter the hour; and they wouldn't stop until every problem had been rectified. They could change an engine and overhaul an aircraft in a night. Such was their enthusiasm and involvement that they would gather around a radio set and listen for any conversations while we were on operations. Their resourcefulness was astonishing. Witness the occasion when an aircraft taxying out suffered a burst tyre about fifty yards from dispersal. Almost at the sound of the bang an airman was bowling a wheel out to the aircraft; another followed carrying a spanner with at least six more in hot pursuit. Arched backs under the wing lifted the oleo off the ground. The wheel was off, the new one on and locked in what seemed less than thirty seconds. And the pilot was on his way without even stopping the engine.

During the spring and summer of 1942 the squadron would occasionally be tasked to provide a flight of six aircraft on standby for air-sea rescue work. We'd position at Hawkinge in Kent, a couple of minutes' flying from the Channel. There we'd lie down on the grass alongside our aircraft, kitted up in our Mae Wests, ready to go at a moment's notice. Instructions would be passed to us once airborne. Relaxing in the sun, it was difficult to imagine that within minutes we could be engaged in a battle for survival. Only once did it happen to me. Gentle birdsong gave way to the sound of engines, hundreds of them. Away in the distance a cloud of dots moved slowly out over the Channel with a heavy rumble. A sweep was climbing towards France, looking and sounding like a swarm of bees. We'd soon be in the air, I thought.

It was about thirty minutes before the first few Spitfires came screaming back – the sure sign of a scrap. We were scrambled shortly after and set course for Boulogne. When we arrived a little yellow dot was floating about three miles outside the harbour entrance trailing marker dye. We set up an orbit overhead at about 10,000 feet. That was until a larger force of 109s arrived, whereupon we moved a little closer to England. But let it not be said that we gave up our charge, because as soon as more Spitfires arrived we resumed our role as minders. Amusingly, this shuffling about went on for about an hour as the forces on each side increased both in number and in height. Not a shot was fired throughout this aerial dance. In the meantime two RAF rescue craft going like hell were cutting a long white swathe towards Boulogne. With about fifteen minutes to go rescue seemed certain. But alas, another launch, possibly an E-boat, came streaking out of Boulogne and looked likely to reach the dinghy first. Once we were certain of this our cover faded away and we headed for home, safe in the knowledge that we were 'all right, Jack'.

But what about the feelings of that poor chap in the dinghy? Hope and exhilaration when the RAF were overhead. Misery and depression when the Luftwaffe took command. Joy and relief when the rescue craft were sighted. Bewilderment when the German boat appeared. Anxiety, wondering which would arrive first. Then the awful realisation that he faced years in the bag.[45] The poor chap had probably been through enough stress to give most people a heart attack. He had my sympathy.

In June the squadron moved to Martlesham Heath in Suffolk for a week's air-to-air firing; the target was a ten-foot drogue towed behind a Spitfire. It was a waste of time because few of us got more than a couple of shoots thanks to poor organisation of the towing aircraft. However, a week away from operations provided a restful break. The weather was fine throughout and the extra two hours afforded by double summer time meant the evenings didn't end until nigh on eleven o'clock.

After a physically and mentally relaxing day, cycling back to the billets along lush overgrown lanes, winding our way through fields of ripening corn on those warm evenings was absolute bliss. The relief of being alive brought a sense of peace and contentment, a sense too of being someone important in the nation's hour of need, of playing a leading role at a great moment in history. But even in such peaceful moments the signs of death and destruction were never far away – bomber boys disturbing the tranquillity of those rural evenings. Sitting on a stationary bicycle one evening I watched in wonderment as these four-engined monsters struggled across the heavens, silhouetted against the pale sky. As they laboured to gain height in their slow passage eastwards, to a fighter pilot they looked like sitting ducks, waiting to be shot out of the sky. No wonder the German night fighters were knocking down so many, some pilots reputedly up to six in a single night. Watching the bombers set off it was impossible not to feel both pity and admiration for their crews – crews all too aware of the terrible odds they faced. The contrast between their chances of survival and my own, between the stress they were under and my personal anxieties, simply didn't bear thinking about. So I pedalled off to the billet and to bed.

It was horrifying to learn that none of the pilots who trained with me and went on to fly bombers survived the war – most of them killed within six months of starting operations. Those who served in Bomber Command were unquestionably brave, worthy of greater recognition than they got at the time. Representative of armed forces that delivered everything an idealistic world asked of them, were they alive today would they recognise the world they fought to save? I fear they might blame politicians for destroying their legacy. We'll never know, but looking back it's hard not to reflect on the loss of so many fine men and an apparent diminution of the national pride that meant so much to them.

At barely twenty, I was very much the baby of the squadron at Biggin. Like so many others, my flight commander, Hugo Armstrong, was a good deal older. Possibly because of his age and experience, at twenty-six he seemed to exhibit a smug sense of superiority where I was concerned. Invariably the worst positions in the formation fell to me. That said, my aircraft survived untouched on our numerous sweeps into France during the spring and summer of 1942. It was partly due to luck, good eyesight and, dare I say, a modicum of skill. One particular memory of Hugo stands out. I was whistling while shaving one morning when he asked what I had to be so cheerful about. 'It's my birthday,' I said. 'Then make the most of it, it's your last,' was his strange reply. He left 72 in July to take over 611 Squadron and was shot down and killed in early 1943.[46] I bore no grudge against a man who was never a good friend – we had several tricky moments over France – but, regrettably, there were doubts over some of his claims when with 72 Squadron.[47]

There were others whose imagination outweighed their skill against the enemy, notably an Irishman operating from an airfield close to Biggin who was regularly claiming aircraft destroyed when our pilots were getting nothing out of the same skirmishes. The newspapers moved in and made quite a hero of him. News of his demise was broken to us one morning by Brian Kingcome, who'd been through the war from the beginning and was renowned for underclaiming – he had a higher ratio of damaged and probables to destroyed than any other pilot.[48] He burst into the dispersal hut proclaiming that so-and-so had been shot down; then, as a note of warning, he added, 'You see what happens to pilots who overclaim?'[49]

Brian Kingcome had a major influence on my flying career. By arranging my posting to 72 Squadron and hence to Biggin Hill, he ensured that my operational flying began right at the heart of things and with the best of teachers. In some ways the squadron's rigid discipline inhibited individualism; only those up front got the chance to do any shooting. But because 72 flew as a team we rarely suffered losses. It was unforgiveable not to provide cover for your leader, or to break away from him if attacked. Inexperienced as I was, for months it was my lot to follow and not to lead. I had little chance to shoot, even though I was often the first to see the enemy. But I gained considerable experience in terms of defensive tactics. This may be why my aircraft was hit only once during the entire war – by a rifle bullet fired from the ground – despite attracting the Luftwaffe's attention on numerous occasions. It wasn't until we began operations in North Africa that the defensive constraints of the Biggin days were replaced by a more aggressive approach.

To get back to Brian Kingcome, he was a quiet individual with a wry sense of humour. Nothing ruffled him. A lover of parties and high living, he never ate in the mess and was invariably in the company of beautiful girls with expensive tastes. One of his wealthy companions gave a silk scarf to every pilot on the squadron. Operational flying involved a lot of head twisting, searching the skies behind, and a soft scarf avoided painful neck scuffing from the rough material of our battledress. It certainly wasn't worn for effect as the public seemed to imagine. Mine was brilliant yellow with red hammer and sickles and bundles of wheat sheaves all over it. Should I wear it, and face the consequences if shot down and captured, or not wear it and face interrogation by the CO? It finished in my trunk after a few trips, the excuse being that it was sucked out when opening the hood for landing.

Among the things I remember about Brian was the scar across his face from a motor accident. He always wore soft rubber-soled shoes, never the regulation pattern. And he had a habit of hitching up his trousers at regular intervals, sailor fashion, with a slight jump; and when he was surprised his eyebrows would leap upwards forming high arches. Brian's dog, Gus, was a young Bull Terrier, as stupid as they come. It was a laugh a minute to watch him square up to Ben, the ground crew's pet rooster. Combat always took place on the grass in front of the dispersal hut where initially Gus was driven off with a puzzled expression. But after several months he got the hang of things, leading Ben to take refuge under the hut. The rooster would only reappear and queue up with the airmen when the NAAFI van arrived – always provided Gus wasn't around.

Apart from Hugo Armstrong's claims, pickings for the rest of the squadron were rather slim, including Brian. He was muttering to himself one day and my ears picked up. 'If I don't get a Hun soon … ' but the rest of his self-admonishment was lost. Clearly, he was beginning to worry about his performance in front of his own pilots. He had no need. A great leader, he'd already proved himself during the Battle of Britain and was highly respected by everyone. He was deservedly promoted to take over the Kenley Wing towards the end of July 1942. However, it was a loss to the squadron and we were all sorry to see him leave.

There were two other New Zealanders on the squadron: Flight Sergeant McCutchan, who arrived ahead of me, and David Waters, who joined with me from Heston. Time didn't allow me to get to know McCutchan, he was killed early on.[50] I'll never forget the sight of his Spitfire slowly rolling onto its back, trailing white puffs of glycol, with a 109 a few hundred yards behind. It was the first time I'd felt so angry and helpless, sitting there watching his Spitfire, hoping for a parachute as it entered a vertical dive and eventually disappeared into the darkness below. A tragic sight. It was the first and last time the squadron was 'jumped' and caught by surprise during my tour. It took a lot of willpower not to break off from the squadron and go for another German who cheekily flew up alongside us just a few hundred yards away. I could almost sense him gloating. All he wanted was for one of us to break formation and follow him down as he dived away, knowing he could outrun us and that his colleagues were waiting for any hot-headed Spitfire pilot so tempted. Despite my anger, sense prevailed.

Regrettably, Dave Waters was also killed, shortly after McCutchan.[51] The circumstances were a mystery. Dave was a good pilot. On one occasion, returning from a sweep short of fuel, he landed in a small field on the Isle of Wight. When ground crew arrived with petrol they had to lift the wing of his

Spitfire back over a gatepost to increase the take-off room. It's a measure of his ability that he managed to get the aircraft back into the air safely. On the day he was killed we were returning from a sweep to St Omer. We weren't in visual contact but I could hear his leader's voice on the R/T. They were flying at sea level investigating an object on the water (it turned out to be a raft) when the leader said he thought a Spitfire had crashed. A minute or so later he said, 'Yes, it looks as though an aircraft has gone in.' This had me worried and when my brief calls to Dave weren't answered there seemed little hope for him. My suspicions about the accident remain to this day. The pilot Dave was following was well known for recklessness and stupid accidents. A ham-fisted flyer, he wasn't nicknamed 'Dangerous' for nothing. I wondered, had he been flying in a split-arse way that left Dave no room for manoeuvre? Had Dave been forced to concentrate more on his leader than on his own safety? The official explanation given at the time was that 'he hit the sea'.[52] Just another wartime statistic with no answers as to how or why.

A close comrade had been lost. Others would follow in time, Ronnie Kitchen[53] and Jack Ratten.[54] Both these characters were considerably older. Indeed 'Kitch' treated me like a son, often mocking me as 'boy' with haughty but humorous distaste. Flying together regularly brought a strong bond of friendship and respect between us. On quiet evenings at a local pub, with few others present, he'd occasionally knock out a tune on what passed for a piano. It was amateur stuff, a limited repertoire where mistakes added to the evening's fun. But hearing those old songs again always brings back precious images of our moments together. Kitch was a Manxman and never failed to return from training days at home on the Isle of Man with lots of goodies simply not available in war-torn England. He left Biggin in August 1942 but a little over a year later, learning of my location, he came up to RAF Rednal to see me. The trouble he took to visit, to speak of old times and comrades, is a mark of the respect generated between those briefly thrown together in wartime. I took it as a compliment. That was the last I saw of him. Word had it that he was killed on operations over Italy. But I would long remember his quiet smile and superior air when faced with one of my frivolous observations. 'Disgusting boy,' he'd say with a chuckle.

Jack Ratten was an Australian mining engineer from Tasmania who joined the squadron a few weeks ahead of me. With a bristling moustache under an almost bulbous nose, his face usually wore an amused, quizzical expression. It's there on every photograph taken of him at the time. Old he may have been but he was very much a boy at heart. Scourge of the station bicycle section, the airmen there must have cursed the day the antipodeans arrived. Jack was in the other flight and we flew together only once – in a Tiger Moth to an evening party at Kenley with Brian Kingcome again. I flew the aircraft over and, after an amusing argument, Jack took us back. Perhaps it was the tight circuit and heavy sideslip into land which put him off me? Or perhaps he thought me drunk, for that was my feeling about him. Anyway, the situation was quickly resolved amid much laughter. It may have been that my unselfish concession was influenced by Batchy Atcherley's comment on our arrival. He'd seen it and, on greeting us, asked who'd been doing the flying. I took the grin and grunt of approval from this legendary figure as a compliment.

No one was in the Biggin mess when we returned. It was late and the bar was shut. The only mischief we could get up to was to run at speed down the long hallway and skate across the polished floor. Great fun – until the door opened and in walked Dickie Barwell, the station commander, to be all but knocked over. 'Been to a party?' he asked. 'Having fun?' The sheepish look on Jack's face could not have been more innocent or amusing. 'Yes, Sir,' he replied, whereupon the group captain bade us goodnight.

Just before 72 moved north, Jack left Biggin to join an Australian unit, 453 Squadron, first as a flight commander and later as CO. On my return from North Africa we met again at Hornchurch where he'd become the first Australian to command an RAF fighter wing. My vain hope was that he might be able to pull enough strings to get me onto one of his squadrons. But all I managed was an invitation to the party to celebrate Hornchurch's 800th, or was it 900th Hun? That Hornchurch party in the summer of 1943, a night of hectic revelry, was my last contact with Jack Ratten. I later learned that he spent the final days of his life in charge of the Australian Personnel Dispatch Unit at Brighton before succumbing to TB in February 1945. And so another good friend and personality who helped colour my flying career fell from the sky; thankfully, not this time at the hands of the enemy.

One of Jack's great pals was another 'oldie', 'Timber' Woods, the other flight commander. Tall, with white, baby-like skin, his cheeks coloured and his bottom lip trembled whenever he was embarrassed – as he was the day he led a shipping reconnaissance sortie in the Seine Bay. We came across a number of fishing boats and, much against my feelings, we shot them up. After landing we were met at dispersal by Dickie Barwell, who asked what had happened. When Timber told him we'd found some fishing boats Dickie said, 'You didn't beat them up, did you?' Timber's face turned beetroot-red and his bottom lip shook with guilt at incurring the station commander's displeasure. Dickie must have sensed our embarrassment because he said nothing more. But it was obvious that, like a number of us, he wasn't happy.

There was a Canadian in Timber's flight, an ex-bush pilot who was always trying to impress Brian Kingcome – never blatantly, it must be said, so we simply accepted him. Returning from a couple of days' leave I learned he'd gone missing on a sweep late that morning. Feeling responsible and concerned for one of his pilots, Timber asked for volunteers to carry out a search. So there we were, six of us at sea level in a fruitless search for a dinghy. We were spread out in line abreast, flying up and down with me only a few hundred yards from the Belgian coast. Had any 109s been around we would all have finished up in the sea. Looking back now, the things we did, the risks we took as a matter of course, scares the hell out of me. But blasting defenceless little fishing boats out of the water when they weren't even the enemy, and risking all in the hope of saving a fellow pilot were typical of the many sides of Timber's nature. He too left the squadron when we moved north. A year or so later his life came to an end over Yugoslavia.[55]

At the beginning of July 1942 my world was shattered by a posting to 41 Squadron at Debden. In an effort to avoid this unwelcome move I appealed to Brian Kingcome. Sympathetic he might have been, but he had to send someone. And intervening would have put him on the spot with one of the other pilots; clearly, for his sake, things were best left as they were. So it was a very miserable departure from Biggin on 12 July. Worse, though, was still to come. I was to join one of three squadrons of Spitfires assembling under a New Zealander, Neville Ramsbottom-Isherwood, in preparation for a move to Russia.[56] It was a daunting prospect, not least because of recent horrendous shipping losses on the Murmansk route.[57] Additionally, the squadron pilots had little or no operational experience – none had more than me, including the CO. After two miserable days moping about at Debden we were all sent on leave for a week, only to be recalled a couple of days later. The train back was crowded. London faded into the darkness, leaving me wondering. Would I ever see the city again?

Finding the CO standing in the same carriage, I made my way over to him to be greeted with the news that the whole operation had been cancelled. All pilots were to return to their previous units. His delight at this turn of events was almost as great as mine. Why the change of plan? Was it the heavy losses on the Murmansk run? It mattered not – back to sunny Biggin for me, and as fast as possible before things changed again. My return didn't last long. At the beginning of August, under its new CO, Bob Oxspring, 72 Squadron was on its way north, eventually to Ayr in Scotland – nowhere near as bad as Russia but still depressing. Bob was a twenty-three-year-old veteran of the Battle of Britain and the son of a Royal Flying Corps fighter ace. Like his father, he'd been decorated twice[58] and survived a number of close shaves. Oxspring senior miraculously lived through a mid-air collision on the Western Front, finishing up out of control and crashing into a haystack. He broke both legs but it saved his life. Otherwise there would have been no Bob and no worthy successor to Brian Kingcome.

With so many heavyweights moving on before we departed Biggin – Timber and Hugo to command squadrons, and Ronnie and Jack to take flights – I experienced what can only be described as a lost feeling. These were the comrades who had mattered to me. Other pilots moved on too but a nucleus of experience remained and it was upon this that Bob began to rebuild the squadron (72 would go on become the most successful fighter unit during the early North Africa campaign). August, September and October to an extent were boring. Months of feeling quite useless, with elements of the squadron detached for short periods to various airfields in Scotland and the north of England. By October, when we were at Ouston near Newcastle, it was clear that we were earmarked for overseas; tropical kit and inoculations arrived in rapid succession. By now there were seven Battle of Britain veterans on the squadron, another starting his second tour of operations, and at least four others who'd logged more than fifty trips into France.

There could not have been a more experienced unit; we were ready for action.

» Chapter 5
NORTH AFRICA

In the middle of October the squadron was split into groups and nine of us departed for Wilmslow, near Liverpool. There we were relieved of any heavy kit and instructed to take with us only flying gear and the little personal kit we could pack into a Spitfire: a change of underwear, a shirt and shaving equipment. Speculation was rife. Would we be flying off a carrier, perhaps, as for the reinforcement of Malta? Then late one evening as we stood in heavy drizzle by some backwater canal, a ship arrived. We quickly embarked, thankful to be away from the cold, wet and miserable gloom of the wartime blackout. Accommodation and feeding arrangements on board the *Staffordshire*[59] were completely makeshift. Loose planks had been laid as a floor halfway down the hold amidships, from where wooden stairs provided access to the deck hatch; a double tier of bunks had been erected on either side of the hold. Cooking was done in a field kitchen, standing on deck near the hatch. It turned out that this was to be our home for the next seventeen days.

The following morning we left Liverpool for the Clyde. As we sailed down the Mersey my mind went back to the sights and scenes of exactly a year ago. It was difficult to believe what had happened in the meantime – difficult to comprehend the many important changes in my life. But what of the future? It was obvious that England would be at the centre of the action that would ultimately decide the outcome of the war. Yet here we were, sailing away. Not a happy thought after coming halfway across the world to be part of these historic events. I felt sure the future of the world lay in Europe, with England in particular, and I wanted to be there with a role to play. Alas, I remember thinking, my ambitions might be thwarted.

The convoy which assembled in the Clyde and sailed shortly after our arrival was huge, perhaps forty or fifty ships. With no formalities to observe on board, we just wandered where we wished. We soon discovered that the cargo was crated Spitfires but with no destination markings. No one appeared to know where we were going. If the captain knew, he wasn't telling. Speculation ranged from the Far East – dread the thought – to every country along the Mediterranean, with France high on the list. But if we were to use the Spitfires in the hold, where were they going to be assembled and where did we fit into the equation? It would take time to build and test the aircraft, so what would we be doing in the meantime? No one had any sensible answers as we plodded out into the Atlantic.

At times the convoy was moving no faster than about four knots, a fast-walking pace, as it coped with heavy rolling seas. To airmen used to talking engine speeds of hundreds of revolutions, it was strange to hear the captain calling from the bridge down to the engine room for alterations of a quarter and sometimes a half revolution a minute to maintain station. Lying in our bunks at night, conversation quickly got round to the likelihood of submarine attack and the consequences of being torpedoed. Some bright spark cheered everyone up by saying that the blast from the explosion would vent out through the hold, taking us with it like a shot from a gun. Pointless, he said, to speculate about rescue.

Derek Forde, the Heston instructor who'd just joined the squadron as B Flight commander, wasn't taking any chances. He had his escape all planned. He'd collared the upper bunk nearest the deck and slept every night with his top half dressed and his trousers draped over the side of the bunk for easy access. We all thought these precautions very amusing but quite ridiculous – that was until they were put to the test a week or so later. A tremendous bang in the dead of night saw Derek up, dressed and on deck in his lifejacket while the rest of us were still milling about in the darkness below. Someone stuck his head through the hatch and reassured us all was well, so the alert amongst us crept back to the warmth of the bunks on which those with slower reactions were still sitting. Morning revealed all. In a heavy swell a derrick boom had fallen from its crutch, crashing down onto the steel deck almost directly above us. The incident was our only alarm during the voyage, although there was one other amusing event.

There were about six lines of ships in the convoy, ours being last in the line one from the outside. With nothing else to look at, the surrounding vessels and their places in the convoy soon became familiar to us. We were therefore concerned to discover one morning that the last ship in the line inside ours was missing. Hours later a vessel appeared on the horizon dead ahead, swept round behind the convoy and took up station in the empty slot. Commenting on the incident much later to a 111 Squadron pilot and telling him of our surprise at the time, he replied, 'Not half as surprised and worried as we were finding the convoy gone and not another ship in sight!' He went on to say that their ship had passed through the whole convoy during the night without anyone becoming aware. Finding themselves alone at dawn, they weren't sure whether they were ahead of the convoy or behind it. So they pressed on until they ran into the destroyer screen and were turned back.

We never saw any of the destroyers, although there was a carrier within the convoy. She had Swordfish ('Stringbags' to the navy) aboard and occasionally, when the carrier wasn't pitching too much, she'd launch one. It was pitiful to watch. Even at the convoy's slow speed the Stringbags rose almost vertically from her deck. It was hard to believe that the navy was willing to send good men in aircraft like that to attack the most modern battleships on the high seas, often protected by the best of German fighters. It seemed to me that, like the army and its cavalry, the Royal Navy hadn't kept up with the times, let alone thought ahead, between the two wars. It took a world war, lessons from battles fought between the American and Japanese navies, and massive advances in technology for the navy to change its approach and eventually allow their airmen and submariners to contribute fully to the exercise of sea power. To give the navy due credit, however, our huge convoy suffered no attacks; although we did hear a few distant explosions at times, much as when we crossed the Atlantic a year earlier.

After a couple of weeks the cold, overcast weather changed for the better and the convoy took up a steady easterly heading. Leaks from the ship's navigation officer suggested we were bound for the Straits of Gibraltar. Two days out the convoy split with half turning south. (In retrospect, these ships were probably destined to join the convoys from America heading for the landings at Oran and Casablanca.)[60] Passing through the Straits, together with the ship carrying 111 Squadron, we left the tail of the convoy and headed for the Rock.

That evening we were transferred to another ship anchored in the harbour. With no information about our future we mooched around for a couple more days hearing regular underwater explosions – aimed at deterring enemy frogmen apparently. In the middle of our second night we were hurriedly gathered together, shoved into an army landing craft and beached in the pitch black on a quiet inlet. After nearly three weeks at sea everyone was much relieved to be back on terra firma at last. The A Flight commander, Flight Lieutenant Ian Krohn, amused us all by dropping to his knees, picking up handfuls of pebbles then letting them trickle through his fingers repeating in a soft, emotive voice, 'The good earth, the good earth.' Ridiculous as it seemed, secrecy appeared to be paramount. We were bundled into the back of a three-ton truck, flaps closed, and driven off at speed. After being flung about for half an hour as the vehicle twisted and turned we arrived at our destination, a Nissen hut. When daylight came we found ourselves at the top of the Rock looking out at the Mediterranean. There we were incarcerated for five days – until the Allied landings on the North African coast.

Getting to civilisation, in the shape of the town, and back to the top of the Rock was a problem. With no transport it was a long walk through massive tunnels still being worked on. The grind back uphill left many a drunk on his hands and knees. We set out always hoping for a lift but were rarely lucky, such was our isolation. At night Gibraltar was a mass of lights, as were the Spanish towns across the border and along the coast – strange after years of England's blackout. The town itself had few attractions. Numerous bars blasted out Spanish music to the accompaniment of stamping feet and clicking castanets, interrupted occasionally by shouts, cheers and the sound of breaking glass. Not being a great drinker, I found the place a real bore. All we learned during five more wasted days was that all the other squadrons had flown out. Interest and pride were restored, however, when we discovered that we would leapfrog the other units and take up position as the front-line squadron. By this time the rest of our pilots had caught up with us, having travelled on various ships, some even on destroyers.

When we finally arrived at the small airfield squeezed between the Rock and the Spanish border we found both sides of the single runway stacked with Spitfires. They were the tropicalised version sporting a bulge under the nose to accommodate the large Vokes air filter and fitted with ninety-gallon belly tanks. They looked hideous. Evidently the airmen at Gibraltar had been working for weeks, assembling the aircraft, testing engines, checking fuel flow from the belly tanks and firing the guns out into the sea. None had been test flown but rumour had it that of the hundreds already flown to North Africa only one had dropped into the sea. We were allocated our aircraft, gathered up maps, Mae Wests and parachutes and given a few minutes to stow our personal kit. Then it was off to Algiers. According to my logbook three hours at medium altitude through indifferent weather resulted in a 'sore bum'. The carbon dioxide bottle used to inflate the dinghy on which we sat protruded as a solid lump; it was the original 'pain in the arse'.

The two days and nights at Algiers were tough. Patrolling the coast looking for submarines supposedly lying up during the day in isolated bays was a waste of time and petrol. We slept on concrete, cold and hungry, and were bombed the second night, the impact close enough to feel the blast. Then, east to Bône, an hour and three-quarters along the coast from Algiers. The weather was atrocious: heavy clouds and drenching rain forcing us down to sea level. It was a relief to arrive – but what a miserable scene. Looking out over the airfield, propped against the doorway of the tiny battle-scarred building once the airport terminal there was mud, rain and pools of water everywhere. Cold, hungry and wondering what the hell we were doing in this remote place, I questioned whether we'd ever see action again.

The answer came suddenly out of the clouds overhead, a dozen Me 109s, guns rattling. They strafed the road running beside the airfield then were gone as quickly as they'd arrived. Strange as it may seem, the outlook improved immediately and things began to feel much better. Even the rain stopped. A couple of hours later a Ju 88 went down in flames some three miles from the airfield and next day twin Spandau machine guns arrived. They were seized upon by one particularly extrovert pilot who discovered to his horror a grisly mess jammed between the two breech block casings. Hell! This war was becoming serious all of a sudden. People were getting killed.

We spent the first night at Bône sleeping between clean white sheets in a hotel requisitioned as accommodation for officers – our first bit of comfort in weeks and, as it turned out, the last for months. At dawn two of us clambered into our Spitfires.[61] Somewhere near Tunis two 109 pilots did the same. We were destined to meet not far from Bône airfield. It was our first contact with the Luftwaffe in North Africa and the beginning of a string of successes for the squadron: my first 'confirmed', on 19 November 1942.

Next day we moved to an airfield on the edge of Souk-el-Arba, an Arab village in the Tunis valley[62] some seventy miles south-west of the city. Two of us, led by Group Captain Ronnie Lees,[63] flew there direct while the rest of the unit carried out a sweep of the area south of Tunis. It was my job to cover the squadron's arrival. Sure enough, two 109s appeared overhead shortly afterwards, too high to engage. But our presence had been noted and we wouldn't have long to wait for the Luftwaffe's response.

Our arrival at, and first impressions of, Souk-el-Arba came as a bit of a shock. The runway lay in the centre of a long valley with a range of hills either side running down its length. The ground was baked rock-hard with inch-wide cracks, giving a crazy paving effect, and a sparse covering of stubble belied the view that this was fertile soil. The road to Tunis ran up one side of the field with a track along the other. A few gum trees on either side afforded the only shade for miles. Souk-el-Arba itself lay at the junction of the road and track, just a small collection of white mud huts; there were no shops.

With a pile of four-gallon petrol cans dumped in a ditch under the trees beside the track, our aircraft were lined up there for ease of refuelling – a terrible decision militarily. So there we stood. Fourteen pilots with little more than we stood up in, lost in thought, staring vacantly at a huge picture of isolation. No point in asking where we were to sleep, what there was to eat or drink, or who would work on the aircraft. So we set to work trying to refuel the aircraft, which were soon covered with more high octane than went into the tanks. Fortunately, after a couple of hours of sweating and cursing, a few servicing commandos arrived. These were soldiers who'd been given brief instructions on how to refuel and rearm a Spitfire. Checking the oil evidently came low on their list of priorities, as we later discovered. However, they were to do a great job for us during the next three weeks until our ground crew and, thankfully, deep-sea kit began to arrive. Towards the end of the first day the French army erected a bell tent and issued us with a blanket each. Food eventually arrived in the form of K-rations[64] while we cooked on petrol tins cut in half, filled with earth saturated in petrol then set alight.

Our days began at dawn and finished after dusk, except when there was bombing. On the second day, 109s and 190s strafed the field in three separate attacks. It's not pleasant lying on the ground with bullets flying about. Fortunately, none of the pilots was hit but we lost eight or nine aircraft and all the petrol. During the first sudden attack some of the commandos took refuge in the ditch alongside the petrol. They didn't survive the subsequent fire. One poor chap who'd been killed by a bullet lay on the ground about five yards from the flames and was rapidly consumed by them. Another who'd been manning a machine gun lay with his stomach sliced open. Fortunately this was the only time I'd ever gaze upon the gory consequences of war. My one hope in turning away from the scene was that it would never happen to me. Those killed in this and subsequent attacks were wrapped in blankets and buried, only for the Arabs to dig up the dead and steal the blankets. These light-fingered people always got a hostile reception when they approached us and we quickly learnt to have someone guard our few belongings when airborne.

At night the temperature dropped to near freezing; lying on the hard ground with only one blanket for cover made sleep difficult to come by. It became impossible when the Ju 88s started nightly nuisance raids. On the third night the fourteen of us lay in the tent listening for a good hour to a fellow making bombing runs along each side of the airfield. The last was on our side. I could feel the tension in the tent as we lay waiting. This was going to be close. Two deafening explosions, then total silence. No one had been hurt but next day revealed two bomb craters in line with the tent, the closest, only twenty-five yards away, had peppered the top of the tent with holes. Slowly it became obvious. Our white tent had shown up in the moonlight and become the aiming point. There had been early, half-hearted debates about the need to dig slit trenches. Most were mildly in favour but enthusiasm vanished on seeing the difficulty involved. From that point on slit trenches appeared as though by magic, but they became a real hazard at night when going for a final pee.

On our second day at Souk-el-Arba we caught a large column of German transport on the move and stopped the lot. There was no enjoyment in this for me, only pity for the panic-stricken troops scampering for cover. We knew the feeling. Later we learned that a German general had been killed in a strafe attack that very day. We attributed his demise to Bob Oxspring. He was the first to attack and concentrated on the still moving staff cars at the head of the column. Subsequently forced to crash-land – he'd been hit by returning ground fire – his number two saw him climb out of the cockpit.

It turned out that he'd landed between the lines. He was wondering which way to go when bullets began pinging into his Spitfire. His feet didn't touch the ground until he reached the relative safety of a heap of stones. From there he worked his way to a slit trench, following shouted directions from a welcome north country voice. With the army's help he eventually arrived back at the squadron, much to everyone's delight – losing the CO would have been a disaster. But he was a shaken man. The staff car he was in had been strafed by the same 109s who'd just attacked us. It was only because he'd seen the danger early that they'd stopped the car and got clear. Bob's experience of two close shaves in a matter of hours was just about par for the rest of us most days.

And so the battle went on, with replacement aircraft being flown in and more strafing and bombing attacks by the Luftwaffe. They were good at their job, as we discovered when watching them dispose of another unit's aircraft right over the airfield. Our main opponents turned out to be 109s from the Luftwaffe's Ace of Spades Wing.[65] Good as they were, their latest 109Gs were no match for us. The skill shown by the Ju 88 crews at night also had to be admired. The only visible signs of their low-level strafe attacks were tracer bullets and the glow from their engine exhausts. One minute you could be fast asleep, the next wide awake, sensing all was not well. Then, as the rumble of unsynchronised engines got louder, came the decision point: stay put, or grab the blanket and make for a slit trench? When tiredness cried out for sleep and cold made moving agony, we became quite skilled in making this judgement. It was a skill we refined after our deep-sea kit and camp beds arrived. By then we were in four-man tents. Occasionally I'd stand in the entrance, attempting to judge the time of the attack with a touch of macabre humour. Watching ghost-like aircraft bathed in bright moonlight glide across mist-covered ground before disappearing brought echoes of a cheap horror film.

With the arrival of the ground crew came the doctor,[66] an Irishman full of advice of little interest or value. He was horrified by our answers to the calls of nature. We just walked off a few hundred yards and did the necessary, leaving great black dung beetles to clean things away in minutes. This wasn't good enough for the doctor, who did the rounds haranguing everyone about hygiene, the need for a latrine and for people to dig it. He was right, of course, but got a frosty reception regarding manpower. Thus rebuffed, with a service field manual in hand and armed with a spade, he set off into the distance to begin construction. We watched with mild interest as he sweated away for hours, slowly sinking lower until only his head could be seen. Finally, he hopped out and stood back to admire his handiwork, at which point our interest in his activities suddenly ceased. The 109s and 190s had arrived again, guns hammering.

When all the fuss died down there was no sign of the doctor. He eventually emerged white-faced from the latrine where he'd taken shelter, albeit after the attackers swept a few feet over his head. All credit to him for surviving such a nerve-shattering experience. But as a medic he was quite useless. His solution to every ill was an Aspro, taken with water. Shortly after the campaign ended it came to light that he received a bottle of whisky each week for medical purposes. I was given a tot only once – when we arrived from Algiers with Spitfire IXs in the middle of a thunderstorm. The rain was so heavy that I remained in the cockpit, cold and wet, for at least an hour. When it eventually ceased, onto the wing jumped the doc with a tot in one hand and half a bottle of whisky in the other, purely for medicinal purposes, of course. So what of all the other bottles that arrived? With an Irishman's hands on the controls, why ask? One bottle can be accounted for, however, but that comes later.

The lack of alcohol never bothered me, though the absence of good water and tea did. The water looked and tasted bad enough, even worse – terrible in fact – once the compulsory purification tablet was added. Tea came in a small tin, was mixed with powdered milk and sugar then dumped into half a petrol can of hot water; it never boiled no matter how much petrol we put on the fire. At night these fires advertised our presence to the Ju 88s, so the tea often finished up on the fire in an effort to put it out. For those who craved something stronger, a nearby monastery provided a ready supply. With no transport, how it was collected (in petrol cans) remained a mystery. No surprise, then, that it smelt and tasted like 100 octane and proved lethal. Several of those who imbibed were laid up for days. Although vin ordinaire remained on the menu, albeit in reduced quantity, the taste of petrol never fully wore off despite repeated use of the same cans.

The arrival in dribs and drabs of the ground crew was a welcome relief. No longer did we have to scratch together our own meals after a tiring day. Christmas Day found me sitting on a petrol can under leaden skies, surrounded by mud and staring down at two slices of bully beef in a mess tin. It was impossible not to think of home, of the wonderful spreads enjoyed at earlier festive seasons. Another benefit was that we now had proper aircraft servicing, allaying our previous apprehensions about airworthiness. The servicing commandos had done a great job under extremely testing conditions, although there had been slip-ups. In my case, guns that didn't fire and an oil scare.

I first noticed the oil problem heading home, still well inside enemy territory; pressure began to fall at a worrying rate. By the time the gauge showed half the normal reading, both brain and heartbeat had shifted into high gear. It would be embarrassing to be jumped by the Luftwaffe now since I could only use full power as a last resort. My immediate concern was which of the two variables would go critical first, oil pressure or blood pressure? *Think!* The sensible thing to do was decrease power, and hence loading on the engine, and lose altitude in a slight dive to maintain speed. I found that reducing engine revolutions by increasing propeller pitch actually increased the oil pressure. The penny dropped. A chance remark remembered from years earlier. The propeller's constant speed unit used the same oil as the engine, and from the same tank. So just keep changing pitch to force oil from the propeller to the tank and hence to the engine. It then became an exercise in maintaining a delicate balance, keeping both oil pressure and engine power as high as possible. Once safely home, we found the oil header tank quite empty. It obviously hadn't been replenished between flights, an oversight that could easily have cost an aircraft. Instead, it cost me a lot of sweat.

Another body of men who didn't receive a word of recognition for the magnificent job they did under terrible, hazardous conditions that winter was the Pioneer Corps. These were men considered too old or not sufficiently fit for front-line fighting. Their job was to construct airfields. Runways, taxy tracks and hard-standings were laid with Sommerfeld Tracking – rolls of wire netting about twenty feet wide with iron rods running side-to-side about every foot along its length. This matting was pegged to the ground with heavy angle-iron stakes. Once done, all seemed ready for the wet season, but in Tunisia when it rains it's a deluge. Within a few days the airfield and its surrounds were under lakes of water; mud clung to everything that moved. Taxying required two or three men sitting on the tail to stop the aircraft tipping onto its nose; eventually airmen had to guide us along taxiways which had sunk into the mud. Take-offs and landings were frightening. Aircraft tried to nose over every time they encountered a pool of water; spray flew everywhere. Worse was to come. The matting continued to sink into the mud and tyres began to puncture on the iron stakes left standing proud.

Back to the drawing board went the pioneers. Loads of cork bark appeared and was put down as an underlay to the matting of a new runway. This didn't resolve the tyre hazard and added a new one; we bounced along the cork runway in great leaps like a kangaroo. Finally, a third runway was built and finished on New Year's Eve. At dusk, just as the pioneers began packing up, a Beaufighter arrived and proceeded to land wheels-up on the new runway, dragging masses of wire netting along behind. All this was watched by a line of pioneers standing beside the runway who immediately set about repairs. One could only admire the tenacity of these old boys. From the moment they arrived they worked day and night in mud and rain, facing strafing runs and bombing attacks which inevitably took their toll. Sadly, we never did get the chance to thank them for all they did to help keep us in the air.

By the middle of December the mud had become atrocious. Every dozen or so steps we had to remove wads of mud and clay the size of snow shoes from our boots. It was a crime to climb into an aircraft with muddy boots so we wore gum boots and sat on the wing to change into flying boots. The trick on return was to park the aircraft in exactly the same place, within reach of where one's gum boots were neatly positioned. The alternative was ground crew acting as temporary batmen to deliver one's boots, which meant considerable loss of face.

In these conditions it was fascinating to watch a man walk into great puddles of water and begin prodding the ground with a long stick. After a number of searching jabs he would thrust the stick several feet into the ground and wriggle it around before pulling it out and moving on. Within seconds the pool would begin to empty, the water disappearing down the hole like water draining from a bath. Good entertainment for those with no other amusement, apart from George Malan's portable gramophone and a few records by the Andrews Sisters. After all these years I can still hear those tunes in my head, the voices so unnatural, hollow and eerie, echoing in an open expanse of nothingness – 'Scene is a June night, flooded with moonlight. Fragrant roses in bloom.'[67]

After a couple of weeks endlessly playing with the same needle the sounds from this tiny machine were quite unintelligible, but it went on being played just the same. George was in a state of sentimental bliss, having got himself married before leaving England. However, his new responsibilities failed to stop him doing his best to emulate his famous brother, over-eagerness always trumping caution. His aggression had already seen him shot down shortly after he arrived.[68] On several occasions concern for his safety found me covering for him when it was his place to cover for me. I certainly wasn't keen to take responsibility for losing the brother of the RAF's top fighter pilot! It was this consideration, together with his habit of tearing off quite blinkered in the middle of a scrap – the moment he saw black crosses he went straight for them regardless – which rather dampened my enthusiasm to have him as my number two. And this despite the close friendship we'd formed on the ground.

Thus the squadron struggled on, surviving by its wits and skill in the air and by perseverance on the ground. By Christmas all hope of the army reaching Tunis had been ended by the resistance of the German divisions landed through Tunis and Bizerte, and by the mud which impeded movement on the ground. If conditions on the airfield were bad, they were terrible for the front-line troops under regular attack from the Luftwaffe. Unlike us, the Germans operated their aircraft off proper runways and from roads too. Inevitably, the strain under which we were living took its toll. We lost two pilots through nerves, one a screaming wreck, running wild at night. The other moved on before he broke. It was pitiful to see the sweat running down his face as he waited to fly. He couldn't stay still for a moment. His behaviour became an irritation to others but he wouldn't give up and, thankfully, was sent away before it was too late. In such cases it was the habit of authority to label them as LMF (lack of moral fibre), to reduce them to the lowest rank and to employ them on the most menial of tasks. It was a disgraceful indictment of their character. It took courage and determination for such men to suppress their inner terrors and carry on when all hope had gone.

Apart from the odd tussle with the Luftwaffe, each day was much the same as every other after Christmas. Then in mid-January we moved to one of a new clutch of airfields further up the valley towards Tunis, each named after London's main railway stations.[69] The soil was now sandy; it wasn't susceptible to flooding and there was no mud. Moreover, officers had the luxury of accommodation in a small building, previously a railway station, although there was no habitation for miles. Some comfort at last. Better still, decent food thanks to the installation of proper catering support. It's surprising what a good cook can do with K-rations.

At the end of January we were ordered back to Gibraltar to collect new aircraft. It was annoying having to leave the action behind, though this was compensated for in part by the knowledge that we would be re-equipping with the latest type of Spitfire, the Mk IXA– the type we were given at Biggin, only to lose them almost immediately. It was the equal of, and in many ways better than, anything the Luftwaffe had at the time; only two units in Tunisia were thus privileged. On the way back we stopped for several days at Constantine in Algeria, then part of metropolitan France. There was nothing to do while we waited for an airlift to Gibraltar so mornings were spent sitting in the sun in pavement coffee bars. One of our pilots, Rodney Scrase,[70] spoke fluent French and one morning found himself engaged with a number of young men and women at a neighbouring table, all chattering and laughing. The upshot was that we were invited to a birthday party.

Thus it was that four or five of us arrived by taxi at an unpretentious looking house on the outskirts of the town. There we were greeted by a little old man who, with a great smile, threw wide his arms and shouted, 'La RAF!' He turned out to be the birthday girl's father but soon disappeared. Five minutes later he reappeared holding a bottle covered in dust and cobwebs, thrust glasses into our hands, filled them with a clear bubbling liquid and proposed a toast to the RAF. Overcoming our suspicions, we took a sip – to find it was champagne he'd put down during the First World War. The taste was beyond perfection and prompted a silent vow: in future champagne was the drink for me. Eighteen months later, when the war took me to France, it was a real shock to find that champagne there simply didn't compare.

It was ten days before we eventually reached Gibraltar, there to spend a further week doing nothing. My morale dropped to zero. The only things I recall during this frustrating waste of time are the anti-social antics of the squadron drunks and visits to the cinema, where we shouted and cheered when newsreels showed a few shots of the air war in Tunisia. (Strange, because no newsmen or war correspondents ever came to the airfields.)

When we finally left Gibraltar the weather wasn't good so we hopped across to the North African coast and followed it along to Algiers. Weather held us up there for another five days. When we at last set off for the Tunis valley flying conditions were terrible; rain and low cloud forced us to weave through valleys well below the mountain tops on either sides. Arriving in a downpour, visibility was nil. Nevertheless, six aircraft managed to get into our airfield, albeit the last nosed over due to water on the runway. Torrential rain, like a waterfall, then closed the airfield and I was forced to take my number two to another airfield, Paddington. We parked just off the runway and sat in our aircraft for at least an hour while the rain belted down. In normal conditions we wouldn't have dared stay with the aircraft under our leaky hoods but in that weather there was no risk of being strafed by the Luftwaffe.

The only sign of life was a visit by the CO of the local squadron during a short easing of the rain. He enquired if there was anything he could do, was thanked courteously and informed we would take off for home, Euston, as soon as the weather cleared. The news on arriving there wasn't good. Seven of us had diverted to other airfields, a new pilot had spun in on the approach and been killed, while an experienced pilot had got lost and forced-landed. In all, we'd lost four new Mk IXs during delivery (including one earlier which crashed when landing at Algiers). Not a happy or professional episode in the history of 72 Squadron.

The Mk IX was a fine aircraft. No longer could the 109s and 190s outclimb or outrun us, although it was still difficult to stay with them in a vertical dive. We now had twelve seconds' cannon fire instead of six and a more powerful engine. The second stage of the new two-speed supercharger came in at about 21,000 feet, forcing more of the thinner air into the engine. This changeover came as a heavy clunk – a sudden fright if one's concentration was elsewhere. And because none of the aircraft changed at exactly the same height we resorted to manual changes on the leader's command. It was also kinder on the nerves. Unfortunately, greater power together with the four-bladed propeller added to the Spitfire's poor directional stability whenever there was a change in airspeed or power setting. One's left hand was flying around between the throttle and the two tail trimming wheels[71] while the right, with thumb on the firing button, was key to staying behind an enemy taking violent evasive action.

One disadvantage of having Mk IXs, if it could be termed that, was that the Luftwaffe was now putting its main effort into attacking our forward troops in the early morning and late evening. A compatriot on another squadron, who didn't arrive in Tunisia until the last couple of months' fighting, chalked up seven confirmed kills, including two Ju 87s, flying dusk sorties relatively low over the front line. Operating at height, as we were, meant we never had such luck. The only time we saw Ju 87s was when they bombed us at Souk-el-Arba very early on.

One problem with our Spitfire IXs was that they didn't have air filters to prevent dust entering the engine. It was quickly solved by our young engineering officer, 'Spanner' Farish. A university graduate who joined the squadron when the ground crew arrived, he quickly proved his worth. Despite bad eyesight, which meant he always wore tiny steel rim 'grandmother' glasses, his one ambition was to fly a Spitfire. This he eventually did much later – a trip from Salerno to Anzio, which was under attack – a quite amazing feat.[72] But in Tunisia he only got as far as incurring our astonishment and Bob Oxspring's wrath when he took to taxying our Spitfires from his servicing area to our dispersal. Leading night raiding parties to remove exhaust stubs from unserviceable Hurricanes from a sister squadron on the airfield was another of his specialities. Our own exhausts were cracking, probably due to the more powerful engine, and spares simply weren't available.

Spanner's solution to the dust problem was to cut up part of the filter from a Spitfire V, and mount it inside an aluminium frame with a simple hook arrangement to hold it in place in front of the engine intake. Left there it would radically reduce engine power in the air. So a long cloth streamer was attached and after take-off we turned back quickly over the dispersal area, pulled a lever and the contraption dropped away for the ground crew to recover. After landing these same ground crew hooked it back in place at the end of the runway. The Farish filters worked so well they were officially approved and were soon being produced in their hundreds. We also got a kick out of beating up dispersal at low level and dropping the filter at the feet of our own particular ground crew. It's a measure of the man that Spanner never ate with the officers or shared our accommodation, preferring to share his airmen's hardships day and night.

Early in 1943 American Flying Fortresses began to operate over Tunisia. We were wary because we'd suffered several unfortunate encounters with their Lightning fighter colleagues earlier in the campaign. They had no idea about aircraft identification and regarded as enemy every aircraft which didn't look the same as theirs. Initially we spent more time defending ourselves against the Americans than the Luftwaffe. On one occasion four of us jumped a gaggle of 109s and 190s attacking our forward troops. We were heavily outnumbered but my calls for help to Bob Oxspring, circling above, went unanswered. His element was fully occupied evading attacks by American Lightnings! That was the time George Malan·got himself shot down, on our side of the lines fortunately. In his blinkered rush to get at the enemy he'd slotted himself between two 190s. The Fortresses made an equally unimpressive start. An unfathomable navigation error led them to bomb Souk-el-Arba – thankfully it was after we'd all moved to new airfields. Together with the Lightnings they did get things sorted out in the end, although it never paid to go too close to either of them.

From March on, when communications with Constantine and Algiers improved, we would receive brief warnings of Fortress raids. We'd kit up and wait with an eye towards the west. When a white cloud of condensation trails appeared, moving slowly in our direction, we'd take off, clamber up to 30,000 feet, join up with the Fortresses and follow wherever they went. These raids would always provoke some reaction by the Luftwaffe, even if was only to scuttle away from their airfields. When attacks did come, it was usually only one or two brave souls.

Always remembered is one amusing incident. The Fortresses were withdrawing after bombing ships in Bizerte harbour, leaving behind them a black cloud of smoke up to about 30,000 feet that could be seen from the Tunis valley airfields. With a single flight of four Lightnings weaving around the bombers, and a pair of us keeping a wary eye on them, suddenly a 109 appeared ahead, about 1,000 feet above the Fortresses in a steep dive. He went straight through the formation firing more in hope than anything else. Pulling out of his dive too quickly he then went into a high-speed stall, the aircraft flick rolling viciously about half a dozen times. By the time he'd recovered – it was a scream to watch – he was a good 1,500 feet directly below the Lightnings. They hadn't seen him so I let them know.

A few seconds later the number three rolls over, calls his leader, repeats my message and says he's going down – on his own since there was absolutely no reaction from the other three. Seeing this the 109 pilot rolled over into the usual vertical dive. With the Lightning behind the 109 but well out of range the airwaves were filled with enthusiastic American shouts, 'Come on, Superman, give her all you've got!' as the pair disappeared from view. I've always been struck by the humour of this incident. Here, in the middle of a struggle for air superiority, a comic strip war complete with cartoon hero was being acted out before my eyes, and in all seriousness too.

A final American reflection: on virtually every occasion we met with them we'd hear 'Hank' being informed of a fellow pilot's problem. He seemed the father confessor for all Lightning pilots. 'Hank, my turbines aren't working properly. I'm turning back.' Or 'Hank, my engine's rough. I'm aborting,' and sometimes, 'Hank, my oil pressure's low'. Our hearts went out to poor old Hank who must have arrived regularly at the front line on his own. It was certainly rare to see Lightnings accompany Fortresses to the target, and once we were amused to see them patrolling the front line, waiting for the bombers to return. Fortunately, the American fighter pilots, like the Fortress crews, showed great courage in time as they progressed up the learning curve.

Rommel and the Luftwaffe had given the American ground and air forces a bit of a hammering down at Kasserine but in the last days of March they had fought back and were re-taking ground held earlier. The American squadrons there were operating Spitfires and we were sent to give them a hand with the Luftwaffe, who were having things too much their own way. It took an hour's flying to reach Thelepte, which had only been back in American hands for two days. The field was bare and there were no other aircraft in sight. There we learnt that one of our ground crew, who'd travelled down by road the day before, had been killed. During a break en route he went into a field for a pee and stood on a mine.

We were quickly refuelled and set off into a dust haze which severely limited visibility. Bob Oxspring was the only one who knew where we were and how to get back to the airfield, so we took great care not to lose sight of him. At 25,000 feet we broke out of the haze and sure enough, there against a clear horizon were the 109s. Taken completely by surprise, they disappeared as quickly as we'd arrived amongst them. How Bob found his way back to the airfield was beyond us all. On arrival we were met by a bespectacled American intelligence officer with the greeting, 'Yo'all shot one down?' who then introduced us to lunch. Our eyes were out on stalks. In the middle of this wasteland was a line of collapsible tables covered with white tablecloths and layered with every sort of food and exotic fruit imaginable. There was even ice-cold fruit juice. Amazingly, there was no sign of anyone who could have produced such a lavish display of lotus living. We descended on this feast like a horde of locusts, albeit we hardly made any impression on it. We flew back happy in body and mind after the day's events. A few days later a jeep arrived at the squadron. While at Thelepte Spanner had been hard at work on the American as well as our aircraft and had bargained a bottle of whisky for a jeep delivered to our airfield at Euston. Since he already had an issue motorcycle to get him around the airfield, he had no excuse when we confiscated his brand-new vehicle. After all, and as we later discovered, it was the squadron's whisky he'd traded – the doc's!

It's astonishing what some people will do to occupy an idle mind. At Souk-el-Arba pilots had been reluctant to dig slit trenches but at Euston the earth under our dispersal tent was excavated to a depth of two and a half feet – with bench seats along each side. What started out as a defensive shelter became a creative challenge, an object of accomplishment and personal pride to the individual concerned. To the rest of us it was a welcome means of protection. With the usual slit trench nearby, during a harmless scare by the Luftwaffe, it was puzzling to watch a pilot jump in one end of the slit trench and straight out at the other – until it was revealed that there was a snake in the trench!

It was even more surprising to see what people did for protection under the sudden threat of attack. From experience at Souk-el-Arba I'd learned to assess the Luftwaffe's intentions and, if not directly in the line of the attack, I'd stand and watch the action. I regularly found myself alone, studying the reactions of my companions. Nothing looks more ridiculous than a portly body on its knees, head down, backside proud behind a tiny concrete block. Or a line of men piled on top of each other, head down behind a thin fence of asbestos. The majority would run a short distance then throw themselves onto the ground with their hands over their heads, shutting off all visible signs of danger. Immunity came face down, never face up.

Then there was the dogged determination of Tom Hughes[73] in the face of what he thought was imminent capture. He joined the squadron mid-way through the campaign; it was his first tour on operations, having previously been an instructor. Shortly after he arrived he was forced to crash-land after his engine failed. With no idea where he was, and thinking he might be on the German side of the lines, he waited until dark before making his way back to the airfield, a hike of twenty hours. He was back in action two days later. His determination to survive by his own efforts was to serve him well much later when he was shot down, badly burnt and taken prisoner in Italy. The treatment, torture and other inhumane experiences he suffered in a German psychiatric prison were quite horrifying. Eventually, by playing dumb in front of a panel of Swiss doctors, he was repatriated to England under a prisoner exchange scheme. As he wrote to me many years later: 'I have been terrified of hypodermic needles ever since.' Seeing so many exterminated by injection, Tom carried the mental scars for the rest of his life.

Other hazards we had to deal with were the local Arabs. A track from a small village of unpainted mud huts about a mile away, worn smooth by the passage of feet over many years, cut straight across the end of the runway at Euston. To the locals it was a right of way. To be confronted by a line of Arabs and camels leisurely crossing the runway when coming in to land was disconcerting to say the least. All one could do was pull the wheels up, bang on full power and zoom over their heads as low as possible. Nothing would move or hurry them.

Even more annoying, however, was the morning we arrived at the dispersal tent to find many of our parachutes gone. The local Gendarme was summoned. With a forage cap square on his head and sporting a black moustache, his wide leather belt was pulled so tight that it divided him into two plump uniformed halves. He carried a riding whip and occasionally thumped his leather puttees with what turned out to be the ultimate stamp of his authority. Rodney Scrase was detailed off as liaison officer and interpreter and away went the two of them in the direction of the Arab village. By the afternoon we had our parachutes back, albeit opened and now useless. How had this miracle come about? A disturbed Rodney explained that the little Gendarme simply walked into the village, grabbed the first Arab he saw and beat the hell out of him with the whip. This went on from Arab to Arab until the parachutes were handed over. Thus did the French rule their protectorate territories.

Twice, when not required for flying, I grabbed Spanner's motorcycle and with a fellow pilot roared off into the hills following only goat tracks. The first time we wandered off like this we landed up in a tiny remote village inhabited solely by French peasants. With no roads, there was just a central, circular cobbled area covered with weeds surrounded by small mud and stone homes. It was quite pretty with its olive trees, colourful creepers and flowers, but the silent, sullen and hostile looks from family groups sitting in front of their homes made it clear we weren't welcome. So we moved on without greeting or being greeted.

The second ride took us to the top of a mountain range along the east side of the Tunis valley. We could go no further. Immediately in front of us was an almost vertical drop of hundreds of feet. The view out over the valley was striking. Even more astonishing were the perfect remains of a Roman amphitheatre, situated on the edge of the cliff. Overgrown with weeds it may have been but there was no mistaking its classic design and wondrous state of preservation. What sort of people were inspired to build such a place? Who sat there and where did they come from? Our presence there, and our reason for being in Tunisia, suddenly seemed insignificant alongside 2,000 years of history – construction that contrasted markedly with our own destructive efforts. We left in silent thought. Wherever we went in the Tunis valley there was decaying evidence of the accomplishments of the great Roman Empire. A humiliating thought when the only things we were building were hopes of survival.

With little movement on the front line since December, towards the end of April 1943 we learnt the big push for Tunis would start with a heavy artillery bombardment around midnight. Word was that something might be seen of it from our airfield, even though the front was forty-five miles away. We all stood out in the pitch-black night, waiting for the appointed hour and glancing in the direction of Tunis. There seemed to be a delay, or perhaps we'd been given the wrong time? But the view when it did come was staggering. Our silence reflected the awe we felt at the spectacle. The jagged outline of the distant mountains was silhouetted against the pale glow of the rising moon. Reddish light would rapidly appear, add brief illumination then fade against the background glow – a display repeated over and over again across the horizon. We retired long before the bombardment was due to end, thankful that we didn't have to fight this war as a 'poor bloody infantryman'.

The tank battles which followed were an eye-opener to we airmen looking down from above. Our armoured divisions were taking a beating but there was nothing we could do to help. There must have been sixty or more tanks involved in one battle, many not moving and most burning furiously. It came as a surprise that these metal monsters became incendiary pyres when hit. They were in open ground, easy targets for the dug-in Tiger tanks and 88-mm guns invisible from the air. It was painful to watch.

By the end of the month it was obvious that the Tunisia campaign was nearing its end. Bob Oxspring was coming to the end of his tether too. He'd shot down a 109 and watched the pilot bale out. The parachute had opened but without the German, who began a free fall from 20,000 feet. The horror Bob felt was imprinted on his face when he landed. He was edgy, withdrawn and would say only, 'Poor bastard'. His reign as the 72 Squadron CO finally ended with him vacating his aircraft to be sick just before taking off on a sweep – all observed by the doctor who confined him to bed. To add to the misery of stomach trouble, he was informed by Ronnie Lees that he was tour-expired. This came as a shock to us all and to Bob especially. The disappointment on his face, evident as well in his attitude during his last few days with us, was painfully obvious.

It was the end for me too. The squadron was to be taken over by the very man who for the past four months had left me in no doubt that he was no friend of mine.[74] Despite every effort to denigrate me in front of others my standing with them remained firm – it even grew, much to his annoyance. Finally, when a valued pilot who was given the option of flying with either one of us chose me, my fate was sealed. Under no circumstances would competition with him in the air or on the ground, which was how he saw things, be brooked. But until Bob Oxspring and others who might interfere were out of the way, I was sidelined.

The remaining weeks were miserable. Despite no act of disloyalty, words directed against me were occasionally poured drunkenly into the ears of the gullible. One other suffered the same fate, perhaps not as badly though, so it was inevitable that our departures would soon be engineered. Interestingly, the pilot who'd preferred to fly with me came to see me a year later. Decorated by then, he confided that he'd suffered a similar fate. Asked why, he said: 'Perhaps my score was getting too close to his.' Jealousy in small doses may be difficult to endure but once it becomes an obsession it must be a curse to carry through life.

With the collapse of the German resistance in Tunis came the capture of thousands of prisoners together with large quantities of war materiel. It has long remained my view that the Allies missed an opportunity to capture Tunis in November before the rains came. Certainly the Germans were taken by surprise by our landings along the African coast, so credit must be given them for their rapid and determined response. However, opportunities to snatch the ports of Tunis and Bizerte, which were crucial to German reinforcement plans, were missed. The Royal Navy feared the potential loss of shipping. As it happened, fighter bases were quickly established along the coast and could have provided enough air cover to assuage the navy's fears. Once again caution prevailed, the initiative was lost and the campaign went on five months longer than might otherwise have been the case.

On the other hand, it could be claimed that the Germans would not have lost nigh on 150,000 troops, plus equipment, if they hadn't been able to reinforce Tunisia – forces that would have been available subsequently to oppose the Allied landings in Sicily and Italy. It has to be said, though, that miles and miles of Germans marching back from Tunis to large, half-full prisoner compounds was a sight not to be forgotten. We much enjoyed belting up and down the line of marchers at head height and doing upward rolls to ram home our freedom and their predicament.

Following the collapse of German resistance in North Africa the squadron moved to the airfield at La Sebala previously occupied by the Luftwaffe, a short distance from Tunis. The evident contrast between the German pilots' lifestyles and our own was stark. They'd enjoyed all the comforts of city life while operating off roads, runways and dry fields. Meanwhile we were living and working in squalor – mud, tented accommodation and dry rations. Our morale was doubtless a match for theirs and in our minds we were far better in the air. The idea that they might shoot us down was ridiculous.

During ten days at La Sebala awaiting my fate I was asked by one of the ground crew if a route could be found for them to motor to the beaches some miles away. They wanted a day by the sea to relax and wash away months of accumulated dirt. It took about an hour's helmetless flying – it was hot at ground level – along tracks and up the odd blind alley to find a route and then memorise it. Then it was into three-tonners and off for the white sands and sparkling sea. Under blue skies with not a breath of wind it was a pleasure to watch those who'd worked so hard in the open and in all weathers enjoying a day's horseplay – complete relaxation for a change. Like them, I needed a proper wash, the first since Gibraltar. Someone had noticed water being pumped into a small reservoir in the middle of a field so, complete with soap and towel, I set off in the jeep to find it. And there it was, a raised, twenty-foot square concrete tank about a foot deep designed to feed irrigation trenches in the surrounding fields.

Crystal clear water cascaded down from a pipe a good way above, so cold it took time and nerve to stand near then under it. The sheer weight of water crashing down on my head tested every neck and leg muscle and its iciness alerted every nerve. It was fascinating to watch the soap bubbles spreading out over the tank, gathering speed then disappearing through the various openings. The cleansing of body and soul was invigorating. There was an overpowering sense of contentment sitting there on a wall, naked in the warming sun, feet dangling in the water, completely alone with my thoughts – quietly thankful at still being alive.

Two more days stick in the memory. On the first we motored across to the aerodrome at Bizerte where Bob Oxspring was flying a Fw 190 which was being recovered for testing by the RAF Experimental Flight. After take-off he disappeared, but with one undercarriage leg still hanging down. It had failed to retract. Next day he appeared over La Sebala in a Me 109, did a beat-up of the squadron followed by a wheels-up forced landing. A seized engine was no problem for Bob.

Then one day in Tunis I came across a New Zealander from another squadron. We'd met before and he had an interesting tale to tell. Some weeks before the campaign ended his aircraft had been hit, forcing him to ditch on the very beach where he'd been strafing German troops. During the crash-landing his head struck the gun sight knocking him out. He came to lying on the sand with a German standing over him armed with a large hypodermic needle. He thought the worst before passing out again, only to wake up in a

Tunis hospital. There was still evidence of his stay when we met: head shaven from front to back, blood-covered stitches forming a scar like a parting. Evidently the hypodermic holder, a military doctor, had stitched his scalp together there on the beach – and done an excellent job according to his English doctors. But his story didn't end there. As the Allies advanced the Germans were evacuating Tunis at night, their own forces together with Allied prisoners and the sick. My compatriot was on the list to be moved but was advised by a British medical prisoner working in the hospital to fake delirium. The ruse worked; he was still in the hospital when Tunis fell. He was left with nothing but admiration for the German doctor whose prompt actions probably saved his life. A triumph for the Hippocratic Oath amidst all that hate and slaughter.

Reflecting on my time in North Africa, there was a remarkable lack of intelligence available to us on the squadron. We had no idea of Luftwaffe unit locations, our own troop movements or the exact location of the front line. Radar and ground control simply didn't exist. And we had no idea that the Luftwaffe was flying in most German troops to Tunis and Bizerte. Information about such movements, together with a supply of long-range tanks to facilitate intercepts, would certainly have been useful. But we were left entirely to our own devices, left to fight the air war as we saw fit. There was never sight nor sound of an officer of air rank![75] But in many ways our freedom of action was a blessing, given that our circumstances were probably much the same as those faced by the Royal Flying Corps during the First World War. Mud and plenty of it, frugal living and feeding, dawn to dusk flying, no ground control, no news, no intelligence – and survival reliant entirely on skill. But despite all this we were happy and mostly content in the knowledge we were doing a good job, making a bit of history so to speak. It was an experience not to have been missed.

Sad as I was to leave 72 Squadron there was one crumb of comfort. I took pride in the fact that not one pilot for whom I was responsible during all my operations in North Africa – Europe too for that matter – was shot down or even had his aircraft hit. The only one to suffer injury was an Australian who arrived late on in Tunisia. In spite of being told to fly at a distance from me he would persist in clinging tightly to my tail. At times I could feel the air pressure from his aircraft interfering with my tailplane. To my great surprise, almost immediately after I'd fired at a 109, he called up to say he'd been hit. He was nowhere to be seen but on landing at Euston there was his aircraft. He had been taken off to hospital with damage to his face and an eye. In front of everyone my one and only 'enemy' lost no time in accusing me of irresponsibility and neglect in allowing my number two to be attacked. This was hard to accept, the more so because of the eager manner in which the criticism was handed out.

Inspection of the Spitfire concerned revealed a shattered hood, scars on the propeller and fuselage but not a single hole anywhere. As usual the Australian had been right behind me when I opened fire. He'd simply run into the hail of empty cannon and machine-gun cases pouring from my aircraft at a rate of seventy-five every second. The scowl on the face of my accuser when I explained what had happened was a delight to see. Sadly, though, a chance to reveal all to the Australian never did come my way.

» Chapter 6

MARKING TIME

My departure from 72 Squadron was a depressing and miserable affair, made worse by the knowledge that my going was the result of jealous scheming by one who'd joined the unit at the same time as me. He'd worked his way to the top partly because he was a good fighter pilot but mainly by subtly influencing the gullible. Respect and loyalty to anyone else on the squadron were anathema to him. He finally met his match when he crossed the path of the top British fighter pilot many years later, more of which anon. But on our last meeting there was no disguising a small sense of satisfaction when he faced me as 'Sir'.

The memory of my send-off from Tunisia still lingers. Standing in the back of a three-ton truck, looking down on the smiling faces of the pilots who'd fought alongside me and hearing their shouts of good luck brought a lump to my throat. My companion on the journey was a colleague, Homer S. Lewis, an American from Albuquerque.[76] Lew spoke with a cowboy drawl, wore high heeled boots and chewed tobacco which he spat with remarkable accuracy. His dry humour and turn of phrase endeared him to all. On one operation he found himself alone with four 109s for unfriendly company. He escaped only by slamming his Spitfire onto the ground at high speed, surviving the crash with head wounds which put him in hospital for a couple of months. The resulting scar was soon almost unnoticeable amongst the wrinkles covering his battered, weather-beaten face. It was a small price to pay for surviving an experience that left his Spitfire 'so full of holes it looked like a colander'.

Our destination was Constantine where, after two days' travel over dirt roads, we finished up choking with dust and looking like clay sculptures. We were required to report to a group captain at the headquarters, there to discover our fate. Grandiose and boastful, with an air of great authority, he sat safely behind his desk a couple of hundred miles from what was once the front line speaking as though he'd been there with us, flying a Spitfire in combat. After noting how much pleasure he got in approving my DFC,[77] he thankfully agreed my request to be returned to the UK. Lew, however, came out of the office white-faced, shaking and fuming with anger. He'd become another victim of defamation. The reason for his posting from the squadron was an allegation tantamount to lack of moral fibre. Nothing could have been further from the truth and poor Lew departed to some local maintenance unit to test Spitfires, vowing as he went to transfer to the American Air Force. I wonder whatever became of you Lew?

My companion for the remainder of the journey was a fellow New Zealander, Dennis Hogan,[78] and we were flown by Americans to Algiers, Surcouf, Marrakesh and finally to Prestwick in Scotland. We spent two weeks at Algiers, mostly on a deserted beach gazing longingly at the breaking surf – we had no bathing costumes. There we met yet another New Zealander, Jack Cleland,[79] who'd been on the same initial training course as me two years earlier. He had a deep, rasping voice which earned him the nickname of 'Four Balls'. While recovering from illness and waiting to regain his flying category he spent most of his time on the beach with us. Occasionally a little French boy of about five or six would appear. He made friends with Jack who in turn taught the boy a song. It was quite moving to hear this tiny voice, clear as a bell, singing in a charming French accent, 'You are my sunshine, my only sunshine, you make me happy when skies are grey.' I was struck by the contrast between this scene, pure innocence set against a background of sun, sea and sand, and the past six months of occasional horrors amidst the mud and grime. Yet, strangely, I found myself longing to return to the squadron and take up that life once again. Operational flying had become a drug, a craving evidenced in others both before and since.

The flight to Surcouf was hair-raising. The DC-3 pilot was a smart arse, a hot shot determined to show his two limey fighter pilot passengers how to fly at low level. Palm trees whipped past above the wingtips as the aircraft zig-zagged along, throwing us off the side bench seats with every violent turn. There were no straps. Mud huts flashed by a few feet below as goats panicked off in all directions. Now and then the aircraft would zoom up over some unseen object, pressing us to the floor, then drop down again subjecting us to negative G. Had we survived a tour of operations only to be killed by some lunatic showing off? The longer the flight continued the greater became our anger and concern. The *pièce de résistance* came with a tight, high-G circuit at nought feet, a steep turn onto the runway at excessive speed followed by a ground loop caused by heavy braking. Venting our rage at this gum-chewing, cocksure 'ace of the base' when he came aft would have been pointless. We just climbed out, thankful to be alive. With nothing to do now but await the next flight we took advantage of what the huge American base at Surcouf had to offer: an open-air cinema showing James Cagney in *Yankee Doodle Dandy* plus lavish food and accommodation. Front-line living was different for the Americans.

If nothing of the flight to Marrakesh, or even the place itself, registered with me, the flight to Prestwick certainly did. It was in a DC-4, a four-engined passenger aircraft flown by an ex-civilian airline crew. The transit was at night in the hope of evading any German night fighters operating in the Bay of Biscay. I wondered, had they seen any enemy activity on this route? 'Only once,' said the steward, 'when flares were dropped on top of us.' It was hardly a comforting thought, albeit we landed safely at Prestwick the following morning. We then hitched a ride to Speke, near Liverpool, with an ATA pilot ferrying a Hudson, for the first time it turned out. The landing was a bit of a hop, skip and jump but safe enough and we were soon away on the next train to London. While Hogan decided to return to New Zealand, for me it was a quick run out to Bentley Priory, HQ Fighter Command, to see what I could wangle for my next posting. It turned out to be No. 61 OTU at Rednal. The rail journey from London to the wilds of Shropshire was a drag, as was the long, lonely wait for transport at the isolated rail stop some twenty-five miles north of Shrewsbury – standard procedure for moving around Britain in wartime, though. Standing in the black emptiness late at night, the feeling of injustice which still surfaced in such situations simply added to my depression.

No. 61 OTU was the same unit as at Heston where my Spitfire flying had begun. It had subsequently moved to Rednal and was to be my home for, hopefully, not more than nine months – a so-called rest period – before the next shot of operational adrenalin. There were many well-known fighter personalities at Rednal. The station commander was Donald Finlay, who first made his way into the public eye as an athlete. Third in the 110 metres hurdles at the Los Angeles Olympics in 1932, he improved to second in Berlin four years later. As Britain's team captain, he went on to take the Olympic oath at the 1948 London summer games. Finlay was an aloof, reserved man and a strict disciplinarian, overly so at times, which led him to be shunned and disliked by many. That said, he showed a more friendly, warmer side of his nature to me years later. It was a cruel twist of fate that this man who kept himself fit and could run like the wind should end his days in a wheelchair.[80]

Pete Brothers[81] was also there, affecting the image of a sophisticated gentlemen with elegant gestures of his trademark over-long cigarette holder. Colin Gray,[82] the top New Zealand fighter pilot, and John Mackenzie,[83] another compatriot and one of the first to be decorated during the Battle of Britain, were there too. Among many others there was the young Canadian, George Beurling, of Malta fame.[84] He'd just come back from a tour of his home country where he was feted as a hero – a second Billy Bishop of First World War fame.[85] He'd been the subject of much publicity in the English press too. There were stories doing the rounds about his exceptional eyesight and shooting skills. My first impressions of Beurling were a mild surprise, astonishment almost.

He reminded me of the skinny, pimple-faced haystack kids seen in American comic strips, although on closer inspection his face bore the scars of smallpox. However, the most noticeable things were his decorations, not only because the DSO, DFC and two DFMs which adorned the breast of one so young were unique, but also because the ribbons were so big. As high as they were wide, they stood out like billboards, inviting attention on a battle dress of superb barathea; beautifully cut, it would have done justice to a Hollywood set. Both were doubtless the handiwork of an enthusiastic Canadian tailor, commissioned for his public engagements there.

George spent his short stay at Rednal either on the skeet range or prowling the local fields with a shotgun, the latter pastime resulting in appearances in front of Donald Finlay to answer endless complaints about poaching. This was entirely in keeping with George's renowned indiscipline and disregard for authority both in the air and on the ground, a maverick attitude which finally led to his honourable discharge from the RCAF in October 1944.[86]

Shortly after my arrival at Rednal, 'Jamie' Jameson,[87] who was later to become New Zealand's top night-fighter pilot, came to gain Spitfire experience before attending the very same gunnery instructors' course I was slated for. We sometimes flew together and became good friends. On one formation trip, after I flew a barrel roll around him, he described it as one of the most beautiful sights he'd ever seen – an apt description of the elegance of the Spitfire in its natural surroundings. The evenings were long at that time of year and, with little else to do, the two of us would walk the fields near the airfield with a shotgun. On one such outing we ran into George Beurling doing his usual stalking act and, after a brief greeting, we let him lead the way home. Walking at a gentle pace some twenty yards ahead of us as we chatted quietly, he was between two small shrubs no more than five yards apart when a rabbit emerged at speed from the bush on his left; it went under his legs towards the cover to his right. George was carrying his gun at his side and there was a bang as he spun round. I remarked to Jamie that George had missed that one – only to see him pick up a very dead rabbit from the edge of the bush on his right.

It was quite dark before we separated from George as we reached the airfield, there to witness a piece of astonishing behaviour. I've never forgotten the sight of George holding the gun vertically in front of his body as he loaded cartridge after cartridge, triggering them as fast as he could and laughing almost hysterically at the long red flames shooting out from the end of the barrels. We were dumbstruck as this display of gleeful emotion went on until a dozen or so cartridges had been expended. Clearly, there were many facets to George's unusual character. But that night confirmed that he had the reactions and deflection shooting skills of a great fighter pilot. Thereafter it became impossible to dismiss as fanciful the many stories woven around his exploits in the air. After the war he failed to settle in civilian life and volunteered for the Israeli air force, only to be killed in 1948 when the aircraft he was ferrying from Rome blew up after take-off.

In August 1943, during a brief interlude away from Rednal, I found myself at Sutton Bridge, a small wooden-hutted airfield near The Wash in south-east Lincolnshire. There was a certain irony in training as a pilot gunnery instructor at the Central Gunnery School. Having begun operational flying more than a year earlier without ever firing the Spitfire's guns, after numerous combats over France and Tunisia, I was now to be schooled in the art of air firing. What a way to run a war! But at the time it was the best option. Faced with a compulsory rest posting – nine months' comparative inactivity –

the course was much preferable to some soul-destroying squadron task in the north of England or Scotland or, worse still, a desk job. It was certainly helpful having friends at HQ Fighter Command – comforting too to ponder a subsequent return to operations in readiness for the great invasion which I felt was certain to follow in the spring.

There were fourteen officers on the course, from America, Canada, New Zealand, Poland and the UK, each one fairly experienced in day or night fighting. All flying came under the command of Peter 'Johnnie' Walker, famed for pre-war formation aerobatics in the Fury with No. 1 Squadron and for his exploits in France at the very beginning of the war.[88] Johnnie was a quiet, friendly person with great dignity and a subtle sense of humour. Never without his pipe, he was admired as a leader and a gentleman. However, as with many aviators of similar experience and capabilities at that time, he would later be shunned by higher authority, apparently deemed unworthy of more senior rank.[89] Our paths were to cross again throughout the war. It was a pleasure and a privilege to have known this honourable man.

The course ran for four weeks and was coordinated with Bomber Command's training of master gunners. The Wellingtons they used operated from another airfield and carried a number of trainees, supervised by an instructor, who took turns in manning the gun turrets against attacks from our Spitfires. It's questionable whether the course did much to improve our combat skills. Most of the exercises involved deflection shooting, whereas success in combat usually came when attacking from directly behind. The Spitfire wasn't a good gun platform against an enemy taking violent evasive action who'd often disappear from sight under its long nose. Deflection shooting was nigh on impossible as well as being scary. As the course progressed we found ourselves performing the most unlikely and often hazardous aerial evolutions. They included attacking from vertically below, hanging upside down with nothing on the clock right behind a Wellington offering a perfect target for the rear gunner. Or coming in high above from the opposite direction, rolling onto our backs and screaming down onto white-faced tail gunners who had every reason to scream back at us over the radio – especially when the Pole was flying. He frightened one crew so badly that they packed up early and flew home, complaining bitterly. A gentle public admonition from Johnnie Walker followed, and rightly so.

On the day at Sutton Bridge fixed most firmly in my memory, carrying my parachute and helmet back to our Nissen hut I was met by an unusual sight. There, lying somnolently on the sunlit carpet, was a Jack Russell normally bursting with energy, especially when his Canadian master, a Flight Lieutenant Bennett, was around. His inactivity was cause for concern. Was he sick, I enquired. 'Haven't you heard?' The tone of the reply signalled bad news. After more than a year of operations, bad news never came as a surprise, even when least expected. 'Bennett's just been killed. He hit a Wellington. They're all dead.'

Eventually the sequence of events began to leak through. Wellington affiliation exercises were usually arranged so that two Spitfires would rendezvous with two Wellingtons and split up to work one-to-one. If, as on this occasion, there was only one Spitfire the two Wellingtons would fly in close formation. Bennett began a quarter attack exercise, starting one side of the bombers then curving round to the astern position before breaking away to the other side, from where the next attack would begin. Part-way through the exercise, with Bennett attacking the lead Wellington, the other bomber was a little further away, hidden under the nose of his Spitfire. Word had it that this second Wellington had slipped back a little from the close formation position, which was why Bennett slammed into it when breaking away from his attack. But how did that dog know immediately what had happened to his master? His expression of misery has never been equalled in all my experience of human loss. It would not surprise me if the dog's soul departed that day alongside that of his master.

Back again at Rednal, the days began to seem like months. This was supposed to be a rest period but the waiting about and trying to put a satisfying effort into each day was more wearing on the nerves than any operational flying.[90] The one consoling thought, though not a particularly convincing one, was that I was missing very little. Winter weather would certainly limit the potential excitement for squadrons operating over France. Not so easy to dismiss the Mediterranean theatre, however, where I felt sure 72 Squadron would be enjoying itself.

The training at Rednal was carried out in three stages, pupils passing from flight to flight as they progressed. The syllabus comprised Spitfire conversion and formation flying first, then gunnery training and, finally, live firing and bombing. Thereafter pupils went to a satellite airfield for tactical and night flying. Training had certainly improved since my days at Heston. There, after converting to the Spitfire and a bit of formation flying, one mostly floated about the sky alone. For the three instructors in the gunnery flight, who included John Mackenzie, work comprised a few days' intensive flying and weeks of filling in with the odd lecture and debriefing ciné gun exercises. Dual instruction in a Miles Master allowed us to demonstrate the basics of deflection shooting and the patterns for air-to-air firing and for ciné. Once proficient, pupils moved on to the next flight for live firing. Ranges located on the Welsh coast meant transit over the mountains where, on average, about one pupil a month crashed in winter weather – such was the pressure to turn out pilots in numbers pending the coming invasion. If weather ruled out range flying and other exercises, low-level attacks using small practice bombs would sometimes be carried out on the airfield.

Among the usual run of accidents, one was unusual. Stepping out of the mess one afternoon, it came as a sudden shock to witness two Spitfires collide at about a hundred feet over the bombing target in the middle of the airfield. The fuselage of one aircraft was chopped in half by the propeller of the other; it then flicked over and hit the ground almost vertically with a heavy thump. The pupil in the other aircraft managed to nurse his damaged Spitfire around the circuit and land. He was a very lucky and shaken fellow and, for a change, not the one responsible for the accident.[91]

During my time there were only two other accidents that were out of the ordinary. While heavy landings were fairly common, it was amusing once to see a Spitfire floating down the runway some ten feet above its undercarriage. As I stood outside our dispersal, close to the touchdown point, I'd seen it come in too slowly. It stalled, thumped into the ground and bounced back into the air leaving both wheels rolling down the runway, their legs standing vertical. The three elements of this picture held station for at least a hundred yards, looking funnier and funnier, until the wheels decided to go their individual ways and the pupil gathered his wits, opened up the engine and went round again. He hadn't realised he had no undercarriage until ordered to land on the grass.

Then there was the drama of the Gladiators. Three Gloster Gladiators and a Wellington arrived at Rednal to do some shooting for a film about the three aircraft, Faith, Hope and Charity, involved in the early defence of Malta. Everyone wanted to fly these lovely biplanes. The word graceful barely does justice to the beauty of their flight. However, the Rednal instructors were warned off from flying them. It was therefore a surprise when forced into a bed at the airfield hospital by a cold, to see two instructors admitted to the same ward having baled out of a couple of Gladiators. Both were officers, one an Australian in the New Zealand Air Force, the other a Norwegian. Prompted by the sudden arrival of good weather and the absence of the regular civilian pilots, they'd been asked by the film unit to help out. Lacking radios, communication in the air was by hand signals but somewhere along the line things got mixed up, leading to a collision during a cross-over. Luckily no one was seriously hurt although the two Gladiators were written off. The film never did get made.

Lack of excitement at Rednal provided opportunities to experiment. A year earlier, on our first day at Bône, I'd watched Tony Bartley,[92] who later married the actress Deborah Kerr, coming in to land. It was a beautiful sight. He'd done a spell as a test pilot with Vickers Supermarine, makers of the Spitfire, and here demonstrated the aircraft's placid handling characteristics with a graceful side-slip round the final approach before executing a perfect touchdown. It was a manoeuvre well worth mastering, but there was never a chance. The Sommerfeld landing strips left no room for error and, more importantly, one had to keep a sharp eye out during approaches and landings for strafe attacks. Rednal, on the other hand, was ideal. There were proper runways, a relatively clear circuit and feather-light aircraft (we weren't carrying ammunition) in terms of both weight and touch.

I never missed an opportunity to side-slip a landing and eventually it became the signature of my arrival. Run in fast at about a hundred feet, slam the throttle shut, into fine pitch, pull up hard to the left at forty-five degrees, bang the undercarriage down at the top of the semi-loop, pop the flaps, roll partly right way up about thirty degrees off from the runway axis and kick on hard top rudder. Done properly, the Spitfire would then slide sideways down a naturally curved approach to the runway where, if necessary, any excess speed could be fish-tailed off.

Even the Mark IXs, with full ammunition, were docile enough to accept this treatment. So docile, in fact, that months later in Germany I was met with, 'Oh, you're the pilot who brings the Spitfire in backwards.' Then an old friend said, 'I knew it was you. I saw you land.' With no desire to show off, I simply delighted in demonstrating the Spitfire's superb flying characteristics. If it impressed others as much as Tony had impressed me, then perhaps something worthwhile had been passed on.

Entertainment was at a premium during those winter months. Snooker matches were a fairly regular post-lunch event with Colin Gray and me against an English or other Dominion pair – with Colin doing most of the scoring. He also organised a shoot on a local farmer's land which turned out to be pretty much of a dead loss. The only sign of life I saw, a single pigeon, found me astride a wire fence. There was a station cinema and the occasional ENSA[93] show to break the monotony – we could have done with them in Tunisia. I took as much leave as I could, in London at the home of a girlfriend's parents. Attractive as she was, she soon dropped out of my life; there simply wasn't enough time for me to deal with the opposition! Besides, marriage was out of the question while the war was on. Winter and Christmas came and went and soon it would be April, when my eagerly awaited move was due.

Bloody hell! Posted to the gunnery school at Sutton Bridge as an instructor. Over my dead body! So a quick call through to HQ Fighter Command to enlist Bob Oxspring's help. He was on leave but his pal in the office had heard him speak of me and my wish to return to operations and thought things 'could be arranged'. Then Don Finlay called me to his office and asked what my feelings were on the appointment. It was no time to hide my disappointment and hostility to the idea of such a move. To my surprise this strict disciplinarian sympathised with my predicament and offered to see what he could do.

Two irons in the fire so far, but let's try for the big one. I scorched down to London and New Zealand Air Force Headquarters with a request to see the top man, 'Grid' Caldwell.[94] No point in messing with the minions. I hardly expected an immediate response but a door was opened by a secretary and there stood the man himself, an ace from the First World War. He got straight to the point. 'What do you want?' Hardly a good start, but there was too much at stake to be put off. Out it all came: the scheme to get back to England for the anticipated invasion, the compulsory rest and patient nine-month wait, the urge to return to operational flying and the disappointment of yet another instructing job. 'You've done your bit, why not leave it at that?' I made it clear. 'Sir, I didn't come all this way to take a back seat in the final act. But thank you for taking the time to see me.' And out I marched, escorted to the door.

Back to Rednal. Time to consider further possible lines of attack. Then, the following day, there it was: a posting to No. 485 (New Zealand) Squadron! Who'd worked the oracle? Caldwell possibly? While the squadron would not have been high on my list – it had a bad reputation for vendettas and personal intrigues – best not to complain. Just hope that these disruptive cliques had disappeared and been replaced by a more comradely, competitively healthy environment.

» Chapter 7

485 (NEW ZEALAND) SQUADRON

When I joined 485 Squadron in April 1944 it was based at Hornchurch in Essex, on the western edge of Greater London just north of the Thames. Equipped with the Spitfire IXB, we were preparing to move to an airstrip on the tip of Selsey Bill in West Sussex. As part of the RAF's Second Tactical Air Force and in readiness for the D-Day invasion, we were originally assigned to No. 83 Group, which was to operate mainly with British Army divisions. Meanwhile No. 84 Group would support a mix of other army units but mainly comprising the Canadian Division. However, somewhere along the line politics, and possibly personalities, came into play. The Canadian squadrons went to 83 Group while we were transferred to 84 Group. It was obvious that the British divisions, with 83 Group in support, would be part of the main thrust across France and into Germany alongside the Americans. The switch annoyed me at the time because, as expected, the Canadian squadrons got the lion's share of the action, 485 not even the scraps.

In keeping with Tactical Air Force practice, the squadron was equipped to be mobile and live under canvas, as we did at Selsey. Our Spitfire IXBs were much the same as the 72 Squadron IXAs, except that to complement a pair of cannons they were fitted with two 0.5-inch machine guns instead of four .303s. Also the engine performed a little better at lower altitude. The CO was a Scot,[95] a reasonable enough chap, moderately experienced but hardly one to set things alight. But why a Scot? There were enough experienced New Zealanders around to take command. Perhaps it was a deliberate move to avoid the favouritism so prevalent in earlier times? In any event, relationships among the pilots appeared congenial enough. Those few with chips on their shoulders left fairly soon after I arrived. There was a small contingent of new pilots eager for the fray and quite a few on their second tour who'd previously been with squadrons of mixed nationalities; they brought skill, experience and above all harmony to 485.

With no flying during the week at Hornchurch, my first trip was the move to Selsey, no more than a large field. The three squadrons there were under the command of Fred Rosier,[96] who was to become the last Commander-in-Chief Fighter Command and oversee its sad demise. In 1969 it was absorbed into Strike Command. For a rapidly contracting air force it was convenience disguised as progress. Fred would become a kind, sincere and approachable friend during my final years in the RAF.

Our tents were in the grounds of a small country residence, Church Norton, not far from the airstrip. With screeching peacocks keeping us awake at nights, we were fortunate there was little operational flying in April. It also gave us a chance to sunbathe and swim now and then. The limited flying we did over France was a total disappointment – so different from two years earlier. Not a German aircraft anywhere. Those they had were back defending the Fatherland. Even the flak had become scarce, unless we were at low altitude where, regrettably, most of our work would turn out to be done. The thought of being shot at, with little to shoot back at, never did appeal.

Our hope was that action would pick up once the invasion started, and there were signs that it would be soon. Roads in the south of England were packed with tanks, guns and military vehicles of every description. Great floating concrete contraptions, later identified as Mulberry harbours, began appearing in increasing numbers each night off the East Beach at Selsey. All of May was given over to softening up the Germans in France. We were either throwing 500-lb bombs about with gay abandon – Spitfire dive-bombing was notoriously inaccurate – or escorting medium bombers attacking targets as far inland as Paris. And in all this time not a sign of the Luftwaffe.

Our poor ground crews worked frantically to keep up with the changing directions from Group. Aircraft would be loaded with bombs, then, following new instructions, off would come the bombs and on would go the long-range tanks. This game of bombs on, bombs off, tanks on, tanks off once had an amusing outcome. One of our pilots was involved in a torrid affair with a local woman and would arrive back each morning exhausted.

We'd been briefed for an operation requiring tanks and were waiting in the dispersal tent kitted-up, ready for the off. Then down came the order: tanks off, bombs on, with urgency dictating a quick briefing at dispersal – there was no time to move to the operations room as was the norm. Throughout all this our Lothario lay comatose and unnoticed, but he did make the take-off. After a few minutes he came up on the R/T saying his tank wasn't feeding and he was returning to base. 'You have a bomb underneath, you bloody fool!' came the voice of a well-known squadron character. Needless to say, Casanova changed his plans and stayed with us.

Towards the end of May our aircraft were fitted with the new gyro gunsight. All one had to do was keep the moving dot with its ring of ranging diamonds on the enemy and bingo, *alles kaputt!* Fine if he was flying a steady course, impossible if he was manoeuvring hard. Fortunately a modified version of the old ring and bead sight was retained as a back-up. With June's arrival came indications of momentous events – and soon. The evening of the 5th found a few of us strolling through Church Norton's grounds. It was nearly ten o'clock, the setting sun was casting its last few beams of light through the trees when the telephone orderly suddenly appeared. His job was to take messages at the tent lines, do the round of early calls and clean up generally – hence he became known as Gunk.[97] 'Briefing at eleven o'clock, Sir.' There was no doubt now. It was on at last. All those years of patient waiting at an end.

The marquee was full. There wasn't a great deal of chatter but the atmosphere was alive with expectation. Shortly after eleven the plan was unveiled: the what, where and when of the Normandy landings. Almost immediately the darkness overhead began to vibrate with the rumble of engines, hundreds of them. It went on for most of the remaining night. Paratroopers and Bomber Command were on their way.

Two trips over the beachheads on D-Day produced astonishment at the clutter of ships crowding the Seine Bay – annoyance too, at failing to get to a Ju 88 before it was shot down by an ex-pupil of mine from Rednal. He got there first, dropping down from above, whilst I was disadvantaged by having to climb. The bomber went straight in on the beachhead from 15,000 feet taking the crew with it. I lost a 190 in cloud next day (when I caught that naval barrage) and another on day three when my long-range tank failed to jettison. Otherwise I might have caught a hit-and-run merchant after his sally onto the beachhead. It seemed the gods had deserted me.

The rest of the month was given over to beachhead patrols. But no matter how far inland we stretched 'the beachhead', the Luftwaffe was nowhere to be seen. Operating below our cover were the rocket-firing Typhoons. Ground attack was a hazardous business disliked by all pilots. At least those of us privileged to fly Spitfires were employed in a variety of roles, which gave some relief from pure ground attack. Not so the Typhoon crews, who worked continuously in close support of the army and almost always faced a barrage of light flak. It was rare for a target worth striking not to be defended. Most Typhoon pilots began flying late in the war, doubtless fired with youthful visions of becoming aces. Alas, there was no glory in store for them. If they survived two months on operations they were lucky. It humbled us. We could only admire the courage and determination with which they, like their colleagues in Bomber Command, faced the stressful demands of every single sortie – day after day.

Shortly after D-Day we were warned about the possibility of attack by pilotless aircraft. There was little information so we had no real idea of what to expect. We didn't have long to wait. A couple of days later we learned that London had been hit by some of these weapons. They could end up anywhere within miles of the intended target, but London was so large it could hardly be missed. We soon got our first glimpse of the V-1. Alerted by a loud, deep-throated throbbing sound approaching quickly, we saw it first through gaps in the cloud at about 1,200 feet. Three things were immediately imprinted on my mind: the peculiar noise, the crucifix shape and its speed – possibly exaggerated by its tiny size. Its intended target must have been Portsmouth, some fifteen miles to the north-east.[98]

At much the same time Portsmouth was subjected to a rare night-bombing raid, albeit in small numbers. With total cloud cover we could see nothing of the action. But we could hear the sounds of battle: a few Luftwaffe engines, our own anti-aircraft fire and the crump, crump, crump of bursting shells. Lying in bed with just canvas above us, the only danger was falling shrapnel. Bits of it could be heard whizzing through the air then hitting the ground. It was disconcerting and led one of our number to don his tin hat while he lay reading. Clever fellow.

July saw us escorting the beginning of daylight raids by the heavies of Bomber Command. The first of these was at dusk against the German defences around Caen, which had been holding up the British Army, much to Montgomery's annoyance. Some 450 aircraft delivered their bombs from between 15,000 and 20,000 feet.[99] Watching the red, green and yellow marker flares, seeing the circular pressure waves as the bombs exploded in the semi-darkness, was to witness an awesome display of air power. Halfway through the raid the markers became quite useless as they disappeared into an enormous cloud of dust which rose to nearly 10,000 feet. It prompted a note in my logbook, 'Boy, what bombing and what a sight.'

During July and August, amongst other tasks I flew as escort on twelve daylight raids by Bomber Command and seven by medium bombers from the Second Tactical Air Force. This diversion of Bomber Command effort from attacks on strategic targets in Germany was the cause of great annoyance to 'Bomber' Harris.[100] For us they provided an interesting change, something of a novelty. More than 500 four-engined aircraft flying down a corridor stretching from the French coast to Paris made an impressive sight. As did their unflinching progress through a carpet of heavy flak. On one of these runs our wing commander, Ray Harries,[101] unwittingly led the three Selsey squadrons into some heavy and fairly accurate flak. Never did a man retreat more quickly from the black barrage. Ray may have accumulated as many gongs on his chest as anyone but he wasn't for taking risks.

Paris itself wasn't a target on these raids, just the heavy industries on its outskirts feeding the German war machine; meanwhile medium bombers targeted marshalling yards and the transport network. With V-1 attacks increasing during July, we were tasked with patrolling specific areas in France in order to protect single heavy bombers as they carried out precision bombing of launch sites. This was yet another diversion from their strategic role. It wasn't bombing, however, that defeated the V-1 threat. In large part it was the introduction of proximity-fused anti-aircraft shells.[102] At the beginning of July the odd V-1 was still turning up in our area. We'd moved from Selsey to Funtington, near Havant, for a short period – one of our occasional local moves to practise squadron mobility. While there we watched a Mosquito shoot down a V-1. It landed on the airfield and wrote off three Spitfires, fortunately none of ours and no one was hurt. The only squadron casualty thus far occurred in tragic circumstances. Ground crew were running up a Spitfire at dispersal when it tipped onto its nose, splintering the wooden propeller; a piece flew off and killed an airman standing by the wingtip.

Two other unusual incidents occurred at Selsey. Returning one day from France we found an American Thunderbolt standing in dispersal. There was no sign of the pilot. It was the first time I'd seen one of these fighters at close quarters. Compared with a Spitfire it was huge – an ugly, tubby beast with a massive radial engine. The only advantage it had over Luftwaffe fighters was said to be due to its great weight; it went downhill faster! In keeping with the trend of most things American, especially their cars, its four-bladed metal propeller was massive, and the main point of interest. The outer two or three feet of each blade was bent backwards almost at right angles. The pilot had apparently 'got too close to the Channel' – testament to the strength and construction of this flying tank.

The second incident happened when everyone was lined up on the runway ready for take-off. The R/T crackled into life: 'Look at that!' Overhead a stream of heavies were on their way to the beachhead – all but one. Bits were falling out of the sky, engines leading the way with a couple on fire and trailing smoke. The whole aircraft had disintegrated. Perhaps the load had exploded? Unlikely, there was no black smoke. Just bits – heavy lumps streaking down from about 15,000 feet, the rest more slowly. It later transpired that a Spitfire, probably an escort, had climbed up into the bomber. Was it due to a blind spot, bad luck, lack of skill and experience? Maybe a combination of some or all of these? We'd never know. One simply had to have eyes everywhere to survive. Not always possible.

Back at Selsey, word circulated that the King would be visiting the nearby aerodrome at Tangmere to hold an investiture and lunch with senior officers. Anyone who had not received their 'gong' and wished to attend could apply. With little chance of getting to Buckingham Palace – I certainly had no desire to spend time away from the squadron – best put my name forward, I thought, and lose only a single day if selected. And I was, along with two others who'd been in Tunisia with me and were now on one of the other squadrons. They would be welcome company. The ceremony would be 'in the field', so battledress was required. However, mine was more garbage than garment. There was no time to have it dry cleaned or acquire a new one, which would cost money, of course. Could anyone lend me something? Great! I acquired one just about the right size and almost new. No need to bother with the campaign 'spaghetti'[103] – I'd never even collected the ribbons let alone worn them – just pin on the one that mattered.[104] And there I was, ready for the big occasion.

I arrived at Tangmere only to find my two chums looking like patients from an emergency ward; cuts, bruises, facial plasters and one with his arm in a sling. They'd just escaped from hospital after their car ended up in a ditch the previous night, returning from a binge. Officials couldn't hide them fast enough, couldn't have them standing before the King looking like wounded heroes. What would the press make of it? Casualties this time of protocol and officialdom, they were spirited away grumbling. Forty or more of us were fed quickly through the investiture procedure as if on a production line. Asked where I received my award I replied, 'In Tunisia, Sir.' Then, rather in the tone of an admonishment, 'Why aren't you wearing the campaign ribbon?' How does one reply to that? Tell the truth – involved and humiliating – or a fib, which would need to be short and convincing? Staying silent would be rude but words wouldn't come. My obvious signs of embarrassment prompted HM to resolve the impasse: 'You will get them now, won't you?' Of course I would, 'Yes, Sir.' Phew! With that the ordeal was over.

Apart from noting the presence of a night-fighter pilot who'd earned a good deal of publicity,[105] my only other memory of that day was of the Queen Mother, standing patiently and alone to the right of and slightly behind the King. She wore a beautiful powder blue hat and matching outfit and there was a radiance about her utter absorption in what must surely have been just another routine duty. Many years later it came to light that the King, who'd taken a personal interest in the design of campaign ribbons and medals, had become disturbed by their slow distribution. No wonder he'd shown an interest in my vacant breast. Moreover, when he learned that large numbers of decoration holders were being killed before receiving their awards he instituted more investitures. After my own, the small part we played in the greatest invasion ever undertaken continued into early August. We still hadn't moved to France, although on a couple of occasions we landed there to operate from hastily laid airstrips. By mid-August, preparations were at last in hand; we'd soon be leaving England. There had been surprisingly few heart-thumping incidents in my flying career but the biggest scare, the largest and longest adrenalin rush, was just about to happen.

We began the move by relocating to Tangmere briefly, just long enough for the ground staff and equipment to cross by sea to France and make ready to receive us there. The airfield dated back to the First World War. Its quaint little officers' mess had somehow survived the bombing during the Battle of Britain, in which Tangmere played a major part. It lay in a beautiful part of Sussex between the Downs and the sea, only a few miles from the coast. Its location, as with a number of other airfields along the Channel coast, made it a sanctuary for aircrew returning from action over France and Germany, either damaged or short of fuel.

The airfield has long since disappeared but for us in that August of 1944 it was a place of wondrous luxury. A permanent mess again after four months of tented living on makeshift airstrips. Sheets on real beds, hot baths, waitresses and WAAFs to ogle – and a cinema too. These were real joys to be indulged to the full. After all, we'd soon be back to 'hard living conditions' in the fields of France and wherever thereafter. This relative luxury apart, there was no respite from the fighting. Weather permitting we flew twice and sometimes three times a day. And on this particular day, as on many others before and after D-Day, the target was enemy transport. We were to shoot up anything that moved or aided movement. 'Isolating the battlefield' it was called. Aerial combat, dive bombing and escorts were a doddle – but strafing. That was definitely a chancy and unhealthy pastime.

The early morning call, the hurried breakfast in an empty dining room, the silent, uncomfortable ride to dispersal in the back of a 15-cwt truck; then groping for damp kit in the dark before lurching into the air in the half light of dawn – all combined to dim any sense of enthusiasm. Worse was to follow: rapidly deteriorating weather. We pushed on over France at about 10,000 feet, deeper into enemy territory, weaving around great columns of heavy cloud. Against an increasingly dark and sombre backdrop it was impossible not to admire the beauty, the elegance and grace of the other Spitfires manoeuvring around me. Then the CO on the R/T: 'Jettison tanks and operate as flights.' I was happier now that tactics and decisions, the fate of the three trusty pilots following me, were in my hands. One, Allan Stead,[106] had been through part of the siege of Malta and could be relied upon to follow my every move. Surprisingly, the descent wasn't a problem and the others were able easily to stay with me as we twisted and turned to avoid cloud. Then, quite suddenly, the murky darkness below was transformed into a dim outline of fields, hedges and trees as we cautiously felt for the ground during the final thousand feet or so.

There was no sign of flak as we broke cover and a quick dash to ground level ended any such possibility. I'd no idea of our position, somewhere near Amiens at a guess, but trying to map read at this height would be madness. Three things only were important now: fly as low as possible, avoid hazards and keep an eye on the compass and fuel gauge. The early hour, poor light and dark cloud overhead made for a miserable scene. There was no rain, although the road surfaces passing below us indicated a heavy fall recently. Occasionally, a shaft of light would slant down, sparkling as it reflected off wet surfaces. I had a strange feeling of total unreality. In these conditions there was little chance of finding any worthwhile targets. The whole operation seemed to have become a useless gamble in a very high-risk game. No option but to play on, though.

Eventually, the time had come to turn back. More minutes and empty miles went by, then behold. A stationary train almost straight ahead. Was it a trap? The Germans were rumoured to put out juicy targets and surround them with lots of light flak guns. No time to worry about that, we were already committed to an attack. Careful aim wasn't necessary, the target was too big to miss. I saw flashes from exploding de Wilde shells[107] dance around the engine then turned quickly to watch the others carry out their attacks. Little smoke and no steam suggested that someone had been here before us. There was no point on wasting more ammunition so we flew on, a little more hopeful than before.

The coastal flak belt was particularly thick in this part of France – the gunners were good too after years of practice against the RAF – so we turned inland again. Thinking I'd make this the last run before setting course for home and a fast climb over the flak belt, suddenly there was a gleam of light just to the right. Christ! Look at that! One – no two – huge, covered vehicles stopped on the road a bit further back. A hurried skidding turn, right on the deck, and the glowing white cross of the gunsight came to rest on the leading vehicle, barely 200 yards away. Hardly time to fire a decent burst. But what was that? A man. He was in white overalls, standing by the cab and looking in my direction. Then he was gone in a flash, faster than he'd appeared, and only moments before my shells were splashing over his wagon.

Jesus Christ! I've had it! A massive bubble of white-hot flame boiled up at a tremendous rate in front of my Spitfire and there were great chunks of God knows what spinning end over end out of the rapidly expanding fireball. As the vehicle exploded I felt the blast in the cockpit and the aircraft leapt in the air. Time almost stopped as my mind filled with memories past. Visions of the folks at home, treasured family moments, and remorse at the sorrow they would suffer at my loss. Then annoyance with myself at what had happened. What a stupid way to go. A life lost in dismal weather over some inconspicuous bit of foreign dirt, and without due ceremony. Surely my life was worth a better finale than this? While my mind was occupied with sentiment and emotion, my brain was working overtime. Instinctively I heaved back on the control column. Shit! No hope of avoiding the fiery mass. The propeller was bound to be shattered by the debris. Engine problems would follow. Must be ready to cut the switches. Hell! The fabric tail surfaces might catch fire; best throw the aircraft on the ground at the first sign of any loss of control, regardless of speed. As I hit the ball of flame my eyes automatically clamped shut.

Complete silence. Bewilderment, surprise – and then reality as the engine gulped air and burst into life again. My eyes sprung open in disbelief to find the aircraft climbing almost vertically. A string of tracer appeared in front of me, travelling in the same direction and streaking away, giving the impression I wasn't moving. It was coming up from dead astern near the right wing and far too close for comfort. Evasion was instinctive. Half roll and haul the Spitfire round hard, down to the left. I had to get to ground level as fast as possible to escape – and force land quickly if the controls started to fail. Down on the deck there was no sign of flak and the aircraft seemed to be handling normally. The engine was running smoothly too, although I began watching the engine instruments like a hawk, especially the temperature gauge. The two radiators were vulnerable and punctured easily, in which case the engine would pack up within minutes. But so far so good. There was no point in trying to contact the others. At the height we were flying they probably wouldn't hear me anyway.

Time now to think about a climb to get above the coastal flak. In all of this, fear of the consequences had stopped me from moving the engine controls. I didn't intend to now either. But because it was still running at an economical cruise setting it would be a long, slow drag back up to altitude. A mental debate began between the merits of increasing power and possibly creating engine problems or leaving well alone, which would make me vulnerable to flak that much longer. I chose the latter. Thus began an anxious, lengthy and winding clamber to the safety of altitude. Thereafter the return to Tangmere was uneventful, the feeling of relief on landing overwhelming. It was so good to be alive and home. The Reaper had been beaten once more, although this time I'd heard the swish of his scythe all too clearly.

Twice in my youth, I'd heard that individuals who'd survived a sudden, near-death moment had experienced a flashback, a re-run of aspects of their life. At the time I'd rejected the idea. But now there's doubt in my mind. Looking back, I'm astonished at the amount, variety and clarity of the information my brain processed at such staggering speed. It could not have been much more than a second from the time of the explosion to hitting the fireball. I'm also surprised at the calmness with which I accepted my end. There was no panic or fear, although later I felt some irritation at having resigned myself so readily to the hereafter.

That afternoon I asked the engineering officer if my Spitfire could be repaired. 'No chance. It's a write-off, the back of the aircraft is broken just behind the cockpit,' came his reply. She was now standing in front of the technical hangar and on my way back to dispersal I decided to take a look at her. Surprisingly, the leading edges of the propeller had only a few small nicks, although a large amount of the Bakelite surface had gone from each blade, exposing the wire gauze over the wood laminations below. Presumably it had melted with the heat? There were also a few small dents along the leading edges of the wings, the top surfaces of which were undamaged. The undersides, however, were covered in gashes with strips hanging down and bent backwards. Both radiators were untouched, although their intakes had collected many small pieces of what looked like aluminium alloy, plywood and fabric. All a bit puzzling when I recalled those large lumps whirling out of the fireball. Apart from a few minor scratches there was no outward sign of damage to the fuselage or tail surfaces. So much for my concern over the possible loss of control.

When Allan Stead landed I asked why he hadn't stayed with me after my attack. 'I thought you'd had it,' was his reply, followed immediately by, 'we just couldn't get the other truck to burn.' That dented my egotism. He'd been less concerned about my fate than about chalking up a success. But that was typical of Allan. He was a 'press on regardless' pilot and our friendship lasted until he was killed many months later. We never did learn what the two vehicles we caught were carrying, or why they were on the road at that hour. Presumably their load was needed urgently and they felt reasonably safe from air attack in such poor weather. They obviously hadn't reckoned on meeting a bunch of idiot aviators from New Zealand.

Meanwhile, the time was fast approaching for the squadron to move closer to the battleground.

» Chapter 8
THE EUROPEAN OFFENSIVE

At the end of August 485 Squadron moved to Normandy, initially to Carpiquet, an aerodrome just outside Caen, where the British and Canadian armies had been held up by determined German resistance for over a month. When Bomber Command attempted to break the deadlock – the major raid we'd escorted on 7 July – they certainly softened up the German defences. But the cratering of the ground had been so extensive and destructive that Allied troops and armour had the utmost difficulty in moving forward. The raid thus became a lesson in the misuse of air power. As was to be expected, Caen aerodrome had been heavily damaged while the town itself was mostly rubble. Astonishingly, the cathedral stood virtually undamaged in the midst of the ruins.

During the first twelve days of September we moved to no less than seven different airfields, some back in Kent, while the Canadian Army fought its way up the French coast. One evening, from an airstrip not far from Le Havre, we could see flame throwers at work in the distance. The sickly sweet smell in the air brought back memories of my early days at Souk-el-Arba. Burning human flesh. We could only ponder the need to use flame throwers. During a short stay at another airfield Terry Kearins asked if he could borrow the 15-cwt truck to visit local friends. Shot down a year earlier and badly burnt, he'd baled out and hidden in a drain for a day or more until he could no longer bear the pain of his injuries. As he approached a farmhouse a man working nearby vigorously gestured for the 'Pilote Anglais' to go away. At this point Terry collapsed. On regaining consciousness he found himself in a barn where he remained for several weeks under the care of the farmer's family and a local doctor. Terry was eventually passed on to the French underground and after a few close calls was returned to England on a French fishing boat. He was now going to renew a strong bond of friendship with the family who had saved him from capture.[108]

They all returned to the airstrip where the family accepted an invitation to join us over lunch. The four of them – the farmer, his wife, the daughter and one other – would have been shot had the Germans caught them. It made the help they gave Terry an act of supreme bravery. This thought clearly influenced my preconceptions because it was a surprise to find they were weather-beaten, poorly dressed peasants. Humble, gracious and pleased to be with us, they seemed in awe of us too. This was somewhat embarrassing, for it was an honour to meet these courageous people, a sentiment which Terry conveyed to them together with my sincere thanks for all they had done for him. This meeting with this family bore out what we'd been told if shot down over France: avoid the landed gentry and the well off, rely only on ordinary working people, farming folk in particular.

Once the Canadian Army had broken through the defences at Caen they advanced quickly up through northern France, cutting off the German-held ports of Boulogne and Dunkirk. With strong resistance on the southern outskirts of Boulogne, 485 and the wing's other two squadrons were tasked with strafing the area. I'd never forgotten my first experience of flak there and visions of the trouble we'd stir up at low level certainly jangled the nerves. We'd no specific target so went in spraying bullets about at nothing in particular and everything in general. There were no obvious signs of flak and after a lengthy burst of fire I pulled away, breathing more easily, only to experience nervous palpitations as heavy intermittent thumps shook my Spitfire. Mercifully it was one of the machine guns running away, which they sometimes did when hot. After recovering from this quick scare, I led another run over the same area – a decision which a few weeks earlier would have been madness. All this time Ray Harries was sitting above, comfortably out of harm's way, watching proceedings and urging us on: 'Give them hell!' As expected, nothing was achieved although, unexpectedly, no one was lost. Three days later we had to repeat the attack with bombs as well as guns.

By this time, the middle of September, we were operating from Merville, near Lille. For the rest of the month, and during October too, we were employed mostly on bombing attacks. A few of these were at low level using eleven-second delay bombs against railway tunnels and 'special' targets such as observation posts used by the Germans holding out at Dunkirk. The army would mark these targets with smoke or tracer shells. The front-line troops were always grateful for our efforts and congratulatory messages were often our reward, notably after a strafing attack on 7 October. German troops were assembling in a forest prior to a counterattack but it was abandoned after we strafed the area – with Ray Harries again shouting encouragement from his usual safe position. It was on this trip that Norby King became the first and only of my number twos to be shot down.[109] Fortunately he made a forced landing behind our own lines.

Merville had a building which made a reasonable officers' mess, although we still had to live in tents surrounded by mud reminiscent of the trenches in the First World War. The size of the mess provided the opportunity to hold a party, which the three squadrons hadn't done before. On the day in question the adjutant, a portly little fellow with thick-rimmed heavy-lensed glasses, complained about the pointlessness of holding a party without women. If I let him have some transport for the afternoon he would visit Lille and try to interest some shop girls in invitations to our party. There seemed to be no harm in this so I agreed. About an hour into a rather quiet evening, despite a band conjured up from somewhere, the door burst open and a bevy of females tumbled in and made straight for the bar. Heavy with mascara, wild-eyed and clad in fishnet stockings, these were no shop girls; they were women of the streets. 'Well,' said the adjutant, 'they were all I could find.'

A couple of hours later word reached me that a woman had just performed a striptease on the dance floor. Once Johnnie Walker, who'd taken command of the wing before the move to France, heard of this he draped the naked woman with his coat and gently but firmly escorted her away from her admirers. Within two days he was ordered back to London to account for an unseemly incident not of his making. During his absence female giggles could be heard in the Belgian tent lines.[110] Fortunately he was unaware. And in view of my own unwitting part in this chaotic revelry, for the next week or two I adopted a low profile and air of innocence.

It was during October that the opportunity arose to drive up to the front line, held by the Czechs at Dunkirk. The previous evening a patrol had captured a prisoner and a few of us were to witness his interrogation. There were four Czech officers and about five of us, all seated in an otherwise bare and dingy room when the German was marched in. A small, young, skinny, dishevelled individual, he was unimpressive and bewildered – far from the archetypal blond, blue-eyed physically perfect Aryan. Only too willing to answer questions bellowed out by the interrogating Czech, I couldn't help feeling sorry for this quaking unfortunate, but at least he would live. And knowing nothing of importance, he was soon dismissed. After a quick look through binoculars at the German lines we departed, thankful that we weren't required to live and fight under front-line conditions.

November found us back in Wales for three weeks' firing at ground targets – as if we needed the practice. The bright lights of nearby Swansea, the odd dance and squadron party provided a welcome change before it was back to the battle, this time an airstrip near Bruges in Belgium. At the end of the month we saw our first German jet aircraft and a V-2 rocket launched from Holland but were powerless against these two new weapons. In stark contrast, we carried out a leaflet raid against Dunkirk offering the Germans safe conduct if they surrendered! With this act of bravado we had now conducted just about every type of operation within the capability of a Spitfire.

By December, with our arrival at Maldegem near Ghent in Belgium, we could now operate over Germany. The winter weather had arrived, forcing the army to dig in and await the spring. With little activity on the front line we reverted mostly to fighter sweeps into Germany. Halfway through December the Germans mounted a major attack into Belgium through the Ardennes; protected from air attack by bad weather, they advanced some sixty miles in heavy snow. They were stopped when the weather lifted, enabling aircraft to wreak havoc on their advance troops and, in particular, their supply lines.

It was on one such flight, as cover for medium bombers, that we ran into a new type of German jet, the Arado 234. Ray Harries was leading the wing, with me up front of 485, when the two jets were spotted coming towards us and about to slide across under me. The Arado bore some resemblance to the British Hotspur glider and my first thought on seeing the 234s was, what the hell are Hotspurs doing up here at 20,000 feet? I dropped down behind the Germans with Ray, who was firing madly in the direction of two dots fast fading into the distance. Most German aircraft smoked a bit when their engines were opened up fully, jets especially. Astonishingly it was this smoke which Ray used to claim one jet damaged. On three other occasions during the last days of December I sat behind German jets without firing a shot as they sped into the distance. They just left us standing, even when we dived down from thousands of feet above.

A revealing incident occurred at Maldegem when the thunderous roar of engines drew us from our small dispersal hangar to see what was going on. A big American Liberator raid was on its way back to England. A straggler, much lower than the rest, then began to circle the field with one propeller feathered. The pilot was obviously thinking about landing. The prospect stirred our interest since the Liberator was a big four-engined bomber and our runway was quite short, with half its length made up with steel strip. On the aircraft's second circuit parachutes began appearing below. This really was becoming interesting. Eventually it lined up with the runway some way out and started its approach. But it arrived too fast and had to be forced down halfway along the runway. With about 500 yards to go the main wheels were locked solid. Clouds of blue smoke poured from the tyres which soon burst with loud bangs. With the wheels still locked the aircraft shot down the runway tearing up metal until it ran off and eventually stopped at the edge of the muddy field. We piled into the 15-cwt and arrived at the Liberator to find the pilot standing pale and embarrassed. What had happened? 'Well, we knew we weren't going to make England so I decided to land here. I told the crew that if anyone didn't want to ride her in with me, now was the time to go. So I found myself alone!'

Ice and snow began to interfere with operations towards the end of December but at least we were now in requisitioned houses. And we had the mess, where Ray Harries brightened up Christmas Eve and Christmas Day with his expertise on the piano. We spent New Year's Eve quietly because at 0915 next morning I was due to lead the squadron on a sweep. When Gunk, the batman, woke me with the news that the operation had been cancelled because of ice on the runway, I simply rolled over and went back to sleep. But what the hell was that? Cannon fire! It was 0920 as pilots tumbled out into the street in various states of undress to watch a dozen 109s beating up our airstrip. We were completely helpless as the Luftwaffe turned up in force for the first time since my arrival on 485. We couldn't see the airstrip but could well imagine what was happening to our Spitfires. My rage at this turn of events was obvious to everyone. With not one gun deployed in defence of our aircraft the Germans were having a ball, although the way they handled their aircraft was a sure indication of their inexperience.

After the attack there was much to think about. What would have happened had our sweep not been cancelled? The possibilities were too numerous to ponder, ranging from heavy losses of our own pilots and aircraft if caught on the ground to similar losses for the Germans had we intercepted them in the air. As it was, all we could do was get down to the airstrip as soon as possible to assess the damage. All but five of our Spitfires were smouldering heaps; a sad sight not seen since the early days at Souk-el-Arba. Happily, my own aircraft, which was parked on its own in front of a small hangar, had survived; the only damage was a ricochet that had lodged in a tyre without bursting it. We soon learned that many Allied airfields in France and Belgium had suffered similar attacks, the hope being (or so we thought) that the majority of our aircraft would be on the ground because of New Year hangovers.[111] Where this wasn't the case a number of Germans were shot down. While there were heavy aircraft losses on both sides, ours were replaced within two days. On the other hand, the loss of German pilots proved critical. Apart from the odd jet, the Luftwaffe was never an active force in the air again. It was their last fling, and the final act in the Ardennes offensive.

January 1945 was an on-off month with periods of up to seven days without flying. The snow and ice had really arrived, bringing with it low cloud and foggy conditions. The initial few days saw our first casualties for over a year. Allan Stead, who had been my deputy before taking over the other flight, was killed on the very day we received yet another accolade from the army for helping them out. Having been with me when my aircraft was severely damaged months earlier, Allan had been on a similar strafing sortie. There was no indication of what happened at the time, although I later heard that he'd also been blown up. All we knew then was that he'd crashed, as had the new and inexperienced young pilot with him.[112] These unfortunate losses served to highlight the many hazards associated with ground strafing – and we were about to get another timely reminder.

In the middle of January we moved to Gilze-Rijen, a permanent base in a somewhat isolated part of Holland; the nearest town of any significance was Tilberg. Four days after we arrived the army called for a bit of bombing and strafing. The squadron was to attack a small pocket of German resistance between the rivers Meuse and Waal. Only about ten minutes' flying away, it was going to be a piece of cake. With no sign of opposition over the target, after dropping our bombs we began the strafing runs. Halfway down my run there was a high pitched 'ping' and rattle like a ball bearing in a tin can. My dear old Spitfire had been wounded, seemingly not seriously but just in case I immediately hurried off home. On landing eleven of the twelve pilots reported their aircraft had been hit by small-arms fire.

After twenty minutes' searching my ground crew could find no damage. Off they went with a flea in their ears for questioning my word. After some delay it was the flight sergeant who returned; same story, same response. Ten minutes later he reappeared with a mixture of relief and delight on his face. He'd solved the mystery; could he show me? A few small pimples on the fuselage near the tail were his first clue. The bullet had shattered inside. The second clue was a ridge on top of the starboard wing-root fillet. The bullet must have glanced off the fillet before entering the fuselage. A line projected forward from these two clues pointed to the starboard radiator. 'See, Sir?' And there it was: a pencil-sized hole in the leading edge of the radiator scoop. No wonder they'd taken so long to find it; the hole was barely visible. Lucky me. An inch further to starboard would have meant a fast radiator leak and it would have been touch and go whether I'd have made it back. Fortunately, there was no serious damage to any of our aircraft. But had we been hit by something larger than a .303 rifle bullet the outcome would have been quite different.

During the last half of January and throughout February there continued to be large gaps between flying days thanks to poor winter weather. It was during this period that our ever-resourceful Gunk, who 'never had no edumacation, Sir,' made money by selling trees from the aerodrome to the Dutch for firewood – their own trees for heaven's sake. It was bitterly cold and we were fortunate to be housed in wooden huts on a normal peacetime aerodrome. However, the only place with heating, a wood-burning stove, was the mess hut. Here we'd gather during non-flying periods, getting scorched down our fronts and freezing down our backs – marginally better than the only other way to keep warm: in our uncomfortable canvas kit beds. At least we could swap yarns, which helped maintain our interest in life and eased conflicting emotions; feeling anxious to get on with the war yet relieved at not having to. Inevitably the conversation would get around to flying and personal experiences, which led one day to an extraordinary tale.

Ted Bennett[113] was the son of a bishop, and a Māori. A quiet, reserved and sincere individual, he'd joined the squadron a few months earlier and was on his second tour of operations. We knew little of his previous experience since he never spoke about himself. Then one dank day as we sat warming our palms against the fire I broached the subject of his past flying. It took a little prompting but an interesting and puzzling story eventually unfolded. He'd been posted to a Hurricane squadron in North Africa engaged mostly in night-intruder operations. He hadn't been there long when one of the pilots reported that he'd been followed around the sky by a whitish ball of light. A few nights later another pilot reported the same thing. Ted began to wonder about the bunch of peculiars he'd joined because soon nearly half the pilots had apparently experienced a ball of light following their aircraft. By now they'd been questioned by intelligence officers and psychiatrists who kept them under surveillance. Then came Ted's turn to see it – a round, bluish-white light, a bit bigger than a tennis ball and floating about near a wingtip. It stayed in more or less the same position for about five minutes and even followed him around turns. The phenomenon was never explained and after a while never happened again. A difficult story to believe? There were certainly sceptics. But Ted was an intelligent individual, never one to lie or seek attention. He quietly got on with the job in hand and was a credit to his country. I'll always remember the quiet chuckle he gave when he talked of possible lunacy on the squadron and the arrival of psychiatrists on the scene. That touch of humour was genuine, as was everything else about Ted. What reason, therefore, to doubt his story?

A prize capture by the Allied troops as they pushed across Europe to the German border at the end of 1944 was the Belgian port of Antwerp. It was vital to the build-up of supplies needed to sustain the coming spring assault and the Germans knew it. Their goal during the Ardennes offensive had been to retake Antwerp. The Canadians faced some of the heaviest fighting of the campaign in capturing both sides of the Scheldt estuary leading to the port. We'd flown many sorties in support of the fighting to open this seaway but now, at the beginning of 1945, the Germans had resorted to attacking Antwerp with V-1s and occasionally V-2s. Gilze-Rijen lay exactly on the track of the V-1s but they didn't worry us. We weren't their target. Twenty-three buzz bombs reportedly passed overhead on one night but not one of them broke my slumbers.

Occasionally on returning from operations with more fuel than the rest of the unit, I let the others land and floated around the aerodrome for an extra ten to fifteen minutes in the hope of intercepting a buzz bomb. I saw a couple but any attempted intercept had to be quick because there was a highly effective anti-aircraft barrage less than ten miles beyond the aerodrome. Watching the guns in action of an evening was an enlightening experience. A bomb would pass overhead, the flame of its engine exhaust marking its flight path as it sped towards the gun barrage. The sky would then light up with shell bursts at a pre-set height, higher than the bomb, as flashes traced its path. This would soon be followed by a much larger flash at bomb height. Whenever we watched, these guns never failed to achieve a kill.

Cooperating with the army, it was often impossible to tell exactly where the front-line troops were. The thickness of a pencil line on a map corresponded to a couple of hundred yards on the ground that could make a vital difference. There was, however, one sure indication of the whereabouts of the battle front. If there was transport and movement on the road during daylight, the ground was ours. Nothing meant it was German territory, although occasionally there would be no movement on our side too. The Allied armies enjoyed complete freedom of movement under our air umbrella; the Germans could move only at night. We had to fly well into enemy territory to surprise anything moving on the ground.

Near the end of January I was leading one such armed reconnaissance detail when I experienced engine trouble shortly after take-off. I handed the squadron over to the other flight commander and returned to base. When the rest of the squadron landed an hour or so later there was a concerned discussion about the identity of the vehicles they had attacked. Were they ours or German? All doubt was removed when word came through that some of our transport had been attacked by Spitfires and that 485 were the culprits. Worse. It transpired that one of the vehicles involved was the staff car of General Dempsey,[114] the man in charge of the British 2nd Army. Fortunately, he was unhurt. I suggested, tongue in cheek, that it was bad enough to attack our own transport – even worse to attack a general. And unforgivably poor shooting to miss him. It was a great relief to learn that the general had escaped what must have been a very nasty experience. Needless to say there were no congratulatory signals from the army that day.

Bad weather during February, mist and low cloud, led me to make some rash decisions. Sometimes it simply wasn't possible to get the entire squadron through to the target. I'd instruct them to return, leaving me to chance my arm alone at very low level. There was much more freedom to manoeuvre when not surrounded by all the other aircraft. Gradually the stupidity of this approach began to sink in. I'd already survived over four years of a war that was obviously near its end, so why take unnecessary risks now? Sense finally prevailed when, some distance into Germany, I swung in to attack an insignificant vehicle travelling along a road. *Damn!* When reaching down to change over to internal fuel I discovered my failure to switch to the external tank after take-off. Do it now, despite the risk of being hit by flak. The engine stopped immediately. God, the damned overload tank wasn't feeding! Quick, back to the main. Thankfully the engine caught again. I was lucky not to have caused an airlock in the fuel lines (some pilots had lost tens of thousands of feet to this problem). So here I was at low altitude, miles inside Germany carrying more unusable fuel externally than there was inside the aircraft. At very low revolutions, which the Merlin engine didn't really like, I might just make it home. And so I sweated my way back, hoping the invisible Luftwaffe remained that way, eventually landing with just a few gallons of useable fuel left. It was enough to ensure that thereafter prudence prevailed; there were no more lonely escapades.

During January the wing's three squadrons had begun to re-equip with Tempest aircraft. At the end of February it was 485's turn; we were withdrawn from operations and returned to England to begin the conversion. Off we went by truck over dusty roads, by sea over the Channel and by rail almost to the western tip of Cornwall: Predannack, near Mullion on the Lizard peninsula. There we waited the whole of March and half of April for the Tempests. Only two arrived and my total flying during the period was only one hour and thirty-five minutes. Aircraft production couldn't keep pace with losses on operations. Meanwhile, 485 stood idle and as far from the battle as it was possible to get in England. There were a few blessings, however. The weather was good for the time of year and we were able regularly to sunbathe on the beach a few minutes' walk away. There was an Uffa Fox airborne lifeboat[115] at Sennen Cove which we could use too. But most appreciated were the luxuries of living in the Polurrian Hotel, requisitioned as an officers' mess, with WAAFs to cook, serve and clean up for us.

There was even a week in London for a course on the Tempest's Napier Sabre engine. It explained a lot, in particular why there were so many engine failures when it was introduced into service with the Typhoon aircraft. Twenty-four sleeve valves ensured that virtually nothing remained stationary inside the engine. So many bits and pieces moving so quickly and waiting to go wrong. As a friend flying the early Typhoons put it: 'The first solo invariably finished up in a forced-landing because of engine failure.'

With our inactivity leading to boredom and frustration, it seemed a real possibility that we would see the war out sitting on our backsides. Finally, after two wasted months, we were back in Holland on operations again, this time with Spitfire XVIs powered by the American Packard-built Merlin. Perhaps it was psychological but these aircraft didn't seem to be quite the same as the IXs. However, within two weeks the war was over.

At the risk of sounding callous, there was a great sadness and an empty feeling inside me. There was nothing ahead now, no certainty, no future except the unknown. A way of life had suddenly ended; a way which, dare it be said, I'd enjoyed. It had become a drug, bringing excitement, creating expectation. The prospect of civilian life was horrifying. The misery of my situation was destroying every hope, all interest. Unlike others, there was no hilarity or celebration for me on the cessation of hostilities. And to make matters worse, 485 was shuffled from one wing to another, finishing up alongside some Free French squadrons at Fassberg, roughly halfway between Hamburg and Hanover, close to the Russian zone. We never saw the Russians nor had any contact with them. In fact we were ordered not to fly near to or over their zone. Our reception would be from the barrels of many a gun – guaranteed.

Fassberg was another permanent aerodrome, used at times for German experimental flying. It housed a collection of Me 262 jet aircraft which had been commandeered by Farnborough for testing; unfortunately, we were prevented from getting near them. We did, however, get to play with, but not fly, a Fw 190. Not knowing a word of German we couldn't work out what the various knobs, switches and instruments were. And without knowing the engine operating limitations any attempt to fly it would be an act of total stupidity. But we did get the engine running and were able to fast taxy the aircraft around the aerodrome, which made us appreciate the advantages of a wide undercarriage. The Fw 190 was a good-looking aircraft with a fine turn of speed, although we believed that most of the German aces preferred the Me 109.

German aircraft had a distinctly unpleasant smell, possibly from some of the synthetic materials used in their construction. I noticed this first in Tunisia, where it would persist on the hands for hours. Our little games with the 190 came to an end when Keith Macdonald,[116] who'd taken command of 485 at Predannack, was seated in the cockpit trying to find the flap-operating mechanism. He shouted down to me that he thought he'd located it. A bang followed as the large, heavy cockpit canopy shot backwards and clattered to the ground. There was no sign of Keith – the cockpit was filled with smoke. When it cleared, a white face slowly appeared above the coaming. He'd tripped the hood jettison mechanism.

These sort of activities, like that of repairing a glider found tucked away in a workshop, getting it airborne with a tow from a 15-cwt truck and crashing it on the second trip, reflects the fact that we had absolutely nothing to keep us occupied while awaiting news of our futures. We were just marking time after a visit from the New Zealand Headquarters staff in London. Most aircrew wanted to be repatriated as soon as possible, which suited the New Zealand government who wanted us off their pay books quickly too. All would depend on the availability of shipping. The idea of staying on appealed to me but neither the New Zealand Air Force nor Royal Air Force looked like formulating their future policies for some time. Moreover, the trend was to get rid of all servicemen as soon as possible. Could a decision about my future be delayed by fitting me into an Empire Test Pilots' School (ETPS) course perhaps? The HQ staff would examine the possibility …

Keen to check on progress, I arranged a trip to London at the end of July. While climbing into my Spitfire an old friend, Johnnie Walker, passed by. Where was I going? All was explained. As he went on his way he said, 'Take care now and don't take any risks with the weather.' Perhaps he had a premonition. Certainly the events that followed seared his parting words into my memory forever. The weather wasn't too bad at Fassberg, although a little mist made it impossible to judge the height of the cloud base. In those days there was no means of obtaining en route weather reports. However, I'd often flown in similar conditions so set off staying in sight of the ground following the line drawn on my map. But the further I went the lower I was forced down below cloud until, finally, I set the map aside to concentrate fully on avoiding the various hazards looming up out of the mist. In these parts I couldn't come to much harm though.

Germany's northern plains were quite flat, as was Holland, so there was little chance of running into cloud with a solid centre. I could always turn back into better weather if things became difficult, of course. But on I pressed, hoping for better weather. Once past Holland and out to sea I'd angle off to the south, pick up the French coast, fly along to Calais and then head for England. I got to the sea all right but it turned out to be the Scheldt estuary. Then, out of the mist, loomed a ship. I zoomed by at deck height but what was that? A cable rising vertically into the cloud above. It was flying a barrage balloon. I'd have to avoid flying across any ships now. With plenty of them appearing ahead I was forced to weave my way down the estuary doing steep turns at deck height. At this stage the cloud base began to lift and the visibility improved so that at last I could see the balloons as well as the ships to which they were tethered. Next it was the English coast which I knew like the back of my hand, if only I could see it. Easy – there it was. Phew. It was worrying at the time but exhilarating too – winning through despite the danger. But then such excitements were essential to living a youthful life to the full.

In London all had been arranged. The test pilots' course was mine, although there would be a six-month wait. My posting from 485 Squadron back to England came through on 10 August.[117]

» Chapter 9

DOUBT, DEPRESSION AND NEW ZEALAND

I became a wanderer. Nearly a month in London and a week on a farm in Wales under a leave scheme run by New Zealand House.[118] The holiday was a formal affair; a little hay making during the day then dressing for dinner. It all felt a bit snobbish, a bore really – except for the young tutor who was looking after the hosts' two children. He too saw the humorous side of the family's airs and graces. They did occasionally try to entertain me but there was a definite feeling that I was in the way. It was a relief to all concerned when they passed me on for the last few days of my stay and I was able to do some riding.

Back in London arrangements were made to post me to Leconfield as an instructor on the Central Gunnery School there. But first there was a month of doing nothing,[119] then a move to Henlow, an engineering school a bit too far north to allow regular travel to London. The intention was for me to get some flying on different types of aircraft but all we did was to fly around the aerodrome in a Dakota dropping parachutes on test. The mess was absolutely dead, a graveyard. Not a soul in sight at night and certainly no aircrew around.

With plenty of time to ponder my future, I started to have doubts. What opportunities would there be for a test pilot back in New Zealand? And what chance was there of joining the Royal Air Force? They already had more of their own pilots than they knew what to do with. The outlook began to look depressing, a situation exacerbated by the lonely, isolated living conditions at Henlow. So much for my plans. The urge to fly was still there but the means were not, either in the immediate or distant future, or so it seemed. The only course of action appeared to be to give up my ideals, which involved a great number of important unknowns, and return to New Zealand. There I could try to pick up my education where it had been left five years earlier. With encouragement in the shape of a government bursary and the support of my new wife, Barbara – we had met at Hawkinge earlier and were married on 3 December 1945 – I made a fateful decision.

The long haul home was not a happy one. There was nothing like the contentment and expectation of my trip to England in what now seemed another lifetime. After idling away a few weeks in Brighton I boarded a train to Southampton with grave doubts and a heavy heart. I was leaving behind everything of importance to me – even for the time being my wife – and exchanging it all for an unknown and probably uninspiring future. I felt like climbing off the train.

The *Stirling Castle*[120] was loaded down with Australian and New Zealand servicemen whose eagerness to get home I didn't share. There were five or six of us in a small cabin, where the interest lay in listening to others' experiences. One chap had been a prisoner for most of the war, having joined the RAF in the mid-thirties. His tales of life in a POW camp soon became common currency but it was the first I'd heard of building escape tunnels, of the ingenious aids to escape and of the turning of German guards to provide the tools needed to make them. A jovial fellow, his temperament certainly wasn't what one would expect of a man who'd been incarcerated in harsh conditions for six years. Several times he mentioned how unpopular Douglas Bader[121] had made himself with the rest of the prisoners, and how the escape committee would have nothing to do with him. Would that I could remember all his stories of life in the pre-war air force too. The one that sticks in my memory is that he knew quite a lot about the man who designed the Napier Sabre engine, information that could have come only from personal contact. An interesting fellow.

Our route home was through the Suez Canal with calls at Taranto, Alexandria, Freemantle, Melbourne and Wellington, none of which proved interesting in the circumstances. I broke the monotony of the journey by walking the crowded decks with Harvey Sweetman,[122] exchanging experiences and views on the future. He'd already done the test pilots' course and, after a spell with Hawkers testing Tempests, he decided to give up flying. He never did go back to it, which seemed something of a loss.

My arrival in Auckland was a bit of a shock. Everything seemed so small, parochial and unexciting. Life was dull and minor incidents were magnified out of all proportion. How was I going to cope with the drastic changes in everything I'd become accustomed to? There was no time to stop and wonder; the university year was about to start.

What followed was eighteen months of failure and humiliation. It became quite impossible to get my head around the subject matter. Engineering exams which had once been so easy were now beyond my reach, no matter how hard I tried. My efforts were branding me as an ignorant fool and testing my character to destruction – my faith in the future too. It was a trying time.

To earn money between terms I worked as a labourer, cleaning out boilers at the Auckland Power House. It was hot, filthy work which simply added to my despair. An interview for a commission with the New Zealand Air Force stretched my small reserves of diplomacy to the limit. During the journey home there had been much talk of the aloof attitude taken by air staff in Wellington towards aircrew from Europe. It was difficult to believe and possibly exaggerated, I thought. Although with the threat to New Zealand from the Japanese, and their war against invasion fought in the Pacific, it was perhaps only natural that their attention was focussed in that direction. The war in Europe was too far away to have had any serious impact on the people of New Zealand. Thankfully, they'd never experienced its trials and tribulations; they weren't aware of the vast scale on which it was fought or the terrible extent of the destruction and suffering.

I soon learnt to take care when talking about Europe. It was better to say nothing than attempt to draw a comparison with the situation in New Zealand. Allowing for such sensitivities proved difficult at the air force interview. Twice, at different times, I was asked the same question: had I served in the Pacific? And again later: was I sure I hadn't served in the Pacific? Did they want me to say 'Yes' in order to justify selection? Good God, if they didn't have my service record in front of them, what was the point of me being there? Clearly, there wasn't a single officer on the board who'd served in Europe or had first-hand knowledge of the theatre.

The short service commission I was subsequently offered, with the stated probability of many months unaccompanied somewhere in the Pacific, didn't appeal. The impression was that I'd be used as a temporary expedient to fill dead-end jobs. Feeling a little insulted, I refused the offer. A number of European colleagues had similar experiences; to a man, they too refused.

Things were becoming desperate. Studies weren't progressing and a switch of syllabus had taken me back to tasks done years earlier. Even supposing I did qualify in three or four years' time there was little available in New Zealand that would bring job satisfaction and a liveable income as an engineer. It would have to be overseas, in which case probably England. By now Barbara had joined me and, to make matters worse, the situation domestically was in keeping with my poor academic achievements. This was not the way a young married couple should have to live. We shuffled between the homes of relations and friends, dependent on their goodwill and hospitality which, naturally, had its limits. At one stage we lived in one room of a flat, sharing facilities with the owners and paying out half our weekly income as rent. It was a disaster. We even lived for a while in a wooden packing case (used for a car) which had been converted into a primitive holiday chalet. At least we were on our own there, as happy there as at any time in New Zealand.

Meanwhile, on the other side of the world, the stability of post-war Europe was threatened by the possibility of forceful Russian occupation. To safeguard against potential aggression Western powers began the rebuilding of their armed forces once more. This was the context for the arrival in mid-1947 of two New Zealand officers from the RAF to recruit former aircrew on four-year engagements with the prospect of a permanent commission. Here was a way out of our miserable existence – hope for the future too.

We sailed for England on 12 August 1947.

» Chapter 10

A RETURN TO FLYING – AND ENGLAND

Of all my sea journeys none was happier than this last, a voyage in company with my wife. The movements officer at the dockside remembered me from our initial training days and although we hadn't met since, he favoured us with one of the best cabins on the ship.

The *Rangitiki* was an old vessel[123] which pottered along at moderate speed, giving us plenty of time to enjoy the passage: across the Pacific, through the Panama Canal and finally to Tilbury,[124] on the Thames. We had the company of about thirty ex-aircrew returning to England together with a full complement of passengers,[125] including a number of celebrities. Head of this list was Dr Ernest Marsden,[126] who'd been an assistant to Lord Rutherford[127] of atom-splitting fame and who, like Rutherford, was a New Zealander. There were also a couple of ex-All Blacks[128] heading for a conference and two boxers seeking their futures overseas. One of them, Bos Murphy, was to become British Empire middleweight champion shortly after arriving in England. Another of our travelling companions, who we were to meet up with many years later, was to find his destiny there too. Noel Habgood's photographs were to grace a variety of magazines, including *Country Life*,[129] for many years before his untimely death in 1975. Partying, passenger concerts and deck games meant that life was never dull. And with such erudite and well-known travelling companions, conversations were interesting and enlightening.

First stop was Pitcairn Island, where the ship had to heave-to a mile or so out to sea, there being no port or anchorage there. The islanders rowed out in two longboats to take on stores and clamber aboard to sell souvenirs, mostly made from wood. It was a delight to meet these people, many of them descendants of the *Bounty* crew with their light brown skin and blue eyes. Talk was of their rugged island. They were genuinely concerned about the decreasing population; children were leaving to be educated abroad and succumbing to the attractions of the outside world. They had to sail to another island to gather wood for carving souvenirs; they fished in hundreds of fathoms of water and shot mountain goats for their meat. Anxious to buy any .22 calibre bullets we might have, to guarantee lethality these would have to be used with uncommon accuracy.

The most fascinating feature of this short contact with the islanders was their speech. Their accent, pronunciation and phrasing was the English language of an earlier time, probably much as their *Bounty* ancestors had spoken. It was delightfully simple, almost childlike and intriguing to hear. It became difficult to imagine we weren't part of that earlier century.[130] Then down the ladders on the side of the ship they went, into their longboats and, after blessing the captain of the *Rangitiki*, away they rowed singing hymns with the same enthusiasm as when they arrived. A kind, gentle and religious people but few in number.

On then to the Panama Canal. Here we watched with interest as the ship was worked through its many locks quickly and efficiently. Across the lakes we sailed, down more locks and into the Caribbean for a bunkering stop at Colon, where we were able to stretch our legs. There was nothing to see or do, though. The port seemed full of sleazy bars oozing raucous shouts, laughter and loud music. Our one bit of entertainment was watching the crew teasing sharks with a large lump of fat on a meat hook and rope line. Our arrival at Tilbury on 23 September thus signalled the end of a pleasant journey, made all the more enjoyable by happy and companionable fellow travellers.

After a few weeks near the in-laws, spent in a Folkestone hotel, I was packed off to do a bit of refresher flying on the Harvard and Spitfire at Moreton-in-Marsh, Gloucestershire. The course lasted a couple of weeks, after which I visited Fighter Command HQ to see what was to happen next. There I saw 'Red' Bartlett,[131] who'd answered my call, intended for Bob Oxspring, requesting a change of posting back in the Rednal days. He started by suggesting an appointment to a Spitfire squadron at Llanbedr on the wild and isolated Welsh coast. Perhaps it was my look of horror, or the comment that with nearly a thousand hours on the aircraft I had strong hopes of a change to jets, that put him off. To my surprise he immediately agreed and said he would send me to No. 54 Squadron at Odiham, flying Vampires. We parted the best of friends and with me in high spirits.

I arrived at Odiham in early January 1948. It was a pre-war aerodrome beautifully sited in a lovely part of Hampshire, reasonably near to London. The quaint little village of Odiham, with its single main street, lay close by. Three squadrons were based there: Nos. 54, 72 and 247, each with eight Vampire Mk 1 aircraft on strength, half the number of a full squadron. 54 Squadron had formed the first jet formation aerobatic team and their flying displays, together with the proximity of Odiham to London, made it the premier station in Fighter Command. All dignitaries wishing to see jet aircraft in action were trotted down to Odiham.

Almost the first thing I noticed on the squadron was the unusual mix of aircrew. Most of the officers had been reduced from higher wartime rank and were dripping with decorations, while of the non-commissioned pilots few if any had war experience. The CO was just leaving, having been awarded a Bar to his Air Force Cross for his aerobatic displays. He was replaced by Frank Howells,[132] a twice-decorated Battle of Britain veteran who was captured by the Japanese in Singapore. Physically, he still bore all the starvation signs so characteristic of those who survived the ordeal of Japanese prison camps. He had not, however, lost any of his Cranwell-instilled officer characteristics and all contact with him was very much on a formal plane. Sadly, he wasn't with us long. One weekend early in April he walked out to photograph a Vampire which had returned from an air pageant, peering through his camera as it taxied back to a hangar. As the aircraft went past, the wingtip struck him behind the ear, killing him instantly. He'd been standing too close to the taxy track. It was a terrible way to die after all he'd survived. Terrible too for the wife he'd recently married; she was pregnant.

To digress for a moment, a sequel to this incident occurred forty-six years later when a number of old fighter pilots gathered at the RAF Museum, Hendon, to support the launch of a book of commemoration.[133] The event was open to the public; they were given a chance to talk to, and have their copies signed by, the oldies. A woman appeared in front of me with a photograph and asked, 'Do you know this man?' It was Frank Howells; the woman was his unborn child at the time of his death. She was determined to learn everything possible about her father's past life. I wasn't able to add much but did point her in the direction of the Air Historical Branch, advice for which she later wrote to express her gratitude.

At low level the Vampires we were flying at the time gobbled up fuel rapidly. It was the practice, therefore, to be called up by air traffic control as a reminder twenty minutes after becoming airborne and every five minutes thereafter. Short sorties, poor weather and few aircraft on strength made it difficult to accumulate flying hours. The only way to build time in the air was to climb to 25,000 feet or higher, set the engine to idle and glide around the sky gradually losing height. Doing this it was possible to eke out about three-quarters of an hour, albeit at the expense of air traffic throwing a fit of the screaming abdabs.

The Vampire was a nice aeroplane to fly but it could have done with much more power. Acceleration on take-off was poor, less than that in a modern airliner once the brakes are released. The tricycle landing gear and cockpit forward in the nose made taxying and landing a pleasure, but if the nosewheel happened to be slightly out of balance the vibration in the cockpit could nearly shake your teeth loose during take-off and landing. Cockpit heating and pressurisation brought the pleasure back to high altitude flying, although sharp manoeuvres at height and speed needed care – as we unwittingly discovered.

Twelve aircraft, with Frank Howells leading, were up at 37,000 feet on an interception exercise against a large number of B-29s. The intercept angle wasn't good so Frank banged on full throttle in a gentle dive to cut off the bomber stream; we all followed suit, trying to keep up. Then things began to happen. In my case, attempting a gentle turn brought a series of sledgehammer blows to the tail which stopped when I eased the rate of turn. Others were subjected to similar but more violent hammering and, in some cases, loss of control and height. One chap even finished up on his back. We never did intercept the B-29s and on landing the rest of the pilots were gathered together jabbering away in puzzled excitement. Such was the fuss that next day we were invaded by people from de Havilland Aircraft, builders of the Vampire, and staff from Fighter Command. They wanted to know about each pilot's experience. All we had done was to hit compressibility[134] which, for the Vampire, was not a very high Mach number – 0.72 if my memory serves me well (just under three-quarters the speed of sound).

The Vampire Mk 1s weren't with us long. They were replaced by Mk 3s about the time of Frank's death and the arrival of Bob Oxspring, of all people, to take over 54 Squadron. The Mk 3 had a bit more internal fuel than its predecessor and could also carry a hundred-gallon tank under each wing. Acceleration with a full load of fuel and ammunition was still poor but wing tanks more than doubled the endurance of the Mk 1. The Vampire carried four 20-mm cannons and was a reasonably good gun platform although misuse of the rudder could cause temporary directional instability, something that soon damped out. Without a propeller to act as a brake when the throttle was closed the Vampire's airbrakes were a godsend, especially in formation. There was positive warning of a stall but recovery from a spin was tricky, as one of my pilots was later to discover to his cost.[135]

Early in my time at Odiham came the saga of the first Atlantic crossing by jet fighters. It began, I suspect, with the American decision to fly in squadrons of F-80 jet fighters to reinforce Europe. But were the British going to allow the Americans to make history with such a crossing? Whatever the politics of the situation, the final outcome was that both countries would do a crossing at the same time. That way neither side would lose face.[136]

In Britain the task fell to 54 Squadron, who would also be required to wave the RAF flag in America with a number of formation aerobatic displays. Six Vampires were to undertake the flight with three pilots drawn from each of the three Odiham squadrons to make up the team under the 54 Squadron banner with Bob Oxspring in command. Those 54 Squadron pilots not selected to tour which, being a new boy, included me, were transferred across to the other squadrons. This resulted in me taking charge of 247 until the touring pilots returned. Bob's first task was to work up the restructured 54 Squadron into competent formation aerobatic units starting from scratch. For the next month aircraft were falling out of practice aerobatic manoeuvres in the skies around Odiham. Eventually, though, all came right and the best sorted themselves out from the good.

The route to be flown was from Odiham to Stornoway in Scotland, Keflavik in Iceland, Narsarsuaq[137] in Greenland, Goose Bay in Canada and on down to finish at Idlewild[138] in America. Each of these legs stretched the range of the Vampire and, therefore, they were to be accompanied by a Mosquito flown by 'Micky' Martin[139] of Dambuster fame. He was to fly ahead on each leg and radio back to Bob the en route and terminal weather states. It was then up to Bob to decide whether to push on past the point of no return or turn back. Micky would often fly down to Odiham and return home for the weekend. On one such visit he somehow managed to run out of runway and finished up in the middle of a wheatfield without damage, except to his ego. A Mosquito sitting serene and alone in the peaceful surrounds of a large green field somehow tickled my fancy. It looked incongruously amusing – a reminder that even the best can, and do, fall from grace sooner or later.

There was an American pilot attached to 247 Squadron under exchange scheme arrangements. A young, highly decorated officer by the name of Billy Whisner, he was further to enhance his reputation as a fighter pilot during the Korean War and as a winner of the Bendix Trophy, an annual coast-to-coast air race across America.[140] He and his wife became good friends to Barbara and me and it was distressing many years later to learn that he had died at his Shreveport, Louisiana, home from a yellow jacket sting. What a sad way to die after surviving such a brilliant career. Meanwhile, the Lockheed Aircraft Company gave a reception at the Savoy Hotel for the American F-80 visitors – all of whom were keen to meet Billy – to which some of us from Odiham were invited. It was a grand feast since rationing was still in force in Britain. There was even a Hollywood star, Martha Raye,[141] to host the occasion. All of us slept off a heavy stomach and a cocktail haze on the midnight bus ride back to Odiham. Our visitors were with us for a few days, long enough to get to know them and their aircraft, which included an accompanying B-29. This break from routine was a welcome interlude, partial compensation for missing the tour to America.

Another celebrity I caught up with at Odiham was 'Ginger' Lacey, one of the top-scoring RAF pilots during the Battle of Britain,[142] during which he also shot down one of the aircraft that bombed Buckingham Palace. He had a chequered career. As with so many of the top fighter boys, Ginger made little progress up the promotion ladder.[143] He was to spend all of his service after Odiham in rather dead-end ground appointments. Don Kingaby was another from the Battle of Britain who, for reasons known only to the hierarchy, made little progress in peacetime.[144] Rightly or wrongly, I put this down to an element of jealousy on the part of those with little charisma and even fewer battle awards.

By the time our American visitors departed, the silly season for air displays had begun. In the absence of pilots away with 54 Squadron, most of the Vampire demonstration flying fell to me, a calling – a privilege in fact – which in individual and formation aerobatic terms was to last for five years. It was the summer of 1948 and life had become varied and interesting, particularly in the air. During July, for example, besides giving demonstrations for the School of Artillery at Larkhill and a display at Gatwick aerodrome,[145] I also led the formation escorting the Shah of Persia into Heathrow. He repaid us with a VIP visit to Odiham not long afterwards.

By the end of the month I'd handed over my responsibilities for 247 Squadron to a newly promoted squadron leader, a man with no previous experience on fighters. His transport background was immediately evident in his heavy-handed use of the Vampire's controls. Yet within two weeks of arriving, and with few hours on the aircraft, he made a case for taking on the squadron's aerobatic demonstration role. My understandable reasoning against this was seen as selfish reluctance to accept competition, and concern over a possible loss of prestige. Fortunately, others with more authority were able to curb this individual's overconfidence for a month or so, by which time 54 was back at Odiham and my interest in 247 Squadron had lapsed. The man concerned, who shall remain nameless, did eventually get his way. However, his aerobatics over the airfield were so hair-raising that he was never allowed to repeat the exercise. He managed to survive for a year before, sadly, he crashed into a house while carrying out a low-level interception during a major air defence exercise.

It was good to be back with Bob Oxspring and 54 again and to be on hand when he was awarded the Air Force Cross for making the Atlantic crossing and American tour a success. By this time we had moved into a married quarter on the aerodrome; the first house we had to ourselves in two-and-a-half years of marriage. Until then we'd lived in the village in one room over a restaurant, where we had our meals. Life for us on the aerodrome had never been happier. It was a wonderful summer made all the more enjoyable by the beauty of the surrounding Hampshire countryside. Trees heavy with leaf stood magnificent amid lush green meadows with hedgerows surrounding fields of yellowing corn. The weekly walk to the cinema was a delight: peace and contentment as we ambled along overgrown shortcuts and down narrow lanes empty of traffic. Petrol was still tightly rationed and cars were for export only, not available to the general public. Life could not have been better. I was flying an exciting new jet aircraft, at the centre of the RAF's activities, entertaining test pilots and hearing about all the latest aviation developments. On top of this, we were meeting heads of state and other officials at formal and informal mess functions. It was a marvellously satisfying lifestyle, one that engendered a feeling of importance, albeit probably exaggerated since it was of our own making.

At weekends after flying had stopped there was always something going on out at the aerodrome. Usually it would be a gathering of the motor racing fraternity, fiddling with their pre-war machines in the hope of circuit racing starting again. Then when autumn arrived an evening stroll over the aerodrome would usually produce a full bag of fresh mushrooms, rarely available in shops at the time. The main attraction in September was the British aircraft industry's annual flying exhibition at Farnborough, a few miles from Odiham – an occasion for a picnic outing by a busload of officers and their wives. Requests for aerobatic displays at numerous Battle of Britain celebrations were another welcome feature of the month.

The fondest memory I have of that summer is of taxying alone around the aerodrome to the main runway prior to take-off. The perimeter track twisted and turned and dropped into little valleys here and there. Taxying could be done at speed but numerous throttle changes were required to negotiate the turns and undulations of the track; progress was thus accompanied by an ear-piercing wail. The centrifugal compressor sucking in air for the Goblin engine produced a whine that varied in loudness and in pitch, up to a scream, with changes in engine speed. There was an eerie fascination having control over and listening to this banshee instrument strapped to my backside.

It was a noise which attracted the attention of the watching public at air displays and greatly added interest to the Vampire demonstrations. However, the thrill for me when taxying at Odiham was always capped when lined up on the runway with brakes on and engine idling. Looking up during those few seconds before take-off at a blue sky with white puffy clouds dotted about, a blanket of peacefulness seemed to fall upon my world as the little skylarks hovering overhead came into view. It was as though they were showing me that they were the real masters of flight and the keepers of peace and harmony in the heavens. It was a sin to have to open up this screaming, smelly engine and tear the silent air apart. But the skylarks were always there next time singing their songs. Those moments of seemingly little consequence will die in my memory with me; they perhaps epitomised man's transgression into nature's beautiful world.

Thus the first year at Odiham slipped by with only a few hours' flying each month but with various social events and other attractions to occupy our interest. One of these was the Olympic Games, held in London.[146] On my one day of attendance it was sad to see Don Finlay of Rednal days fall in his heat of the hurdles. Typical of his determination, he picked himself up and trotted on to finish last to much applause for his sporting courage. Twelve years and a war had taken its toll of skill and stamina since his outstanding feat at the Berlin games.

Then in November came another move, this time back to my old wartime squadron, No. 72, as a flight commander. The CO was 'Buck' Courtney,[147] an easy-going fellow with a quiet personality who enjoyed the odd drink. He was courting a WAAF working in the control tower and spent most of his day there leaving me to run the flying, which suited me. They married eventually, but within two months of my arrival he was posted and replaced by Don Kingaby. Don was to become a close friend until his death in 1990 in America. He first came to prominence as a sergeant pilot during the Battle of Britain, serving on 92 Squadron alongside other notables like Brian Kingcome and Bob Holland. He was the only pilot to be awarded three Distinguished Flying Medals (and later a Distinguished Service Order and an Air Force Cross). Don never rose above squadron leader in the peacetime RAF (although he retained his wartime rank of wing commander on retirement). Why? My wife once asked this of Johnnie Johnson[148] who, after a moment's hesitation said, 'I don't know. Born the wrong side of the blanket I guess.'

Late in 1949, while on detachment to a bomber aerodrome, Don paid a visit to 'Piet' Hugo and trotted me along too. Piet was a highly decorated South African who'd risen to the rank of group captain and been at Bône in 1942 during my short stay there. By this time he'd been reduced to squadron leader rank and was living a lone, spartan existence in a room devoid of personal ornaments: a depressed and disillusioned man. He was determined to resign his commission and did so not long after.[149] Pilots from the old Dominions

Top left: Auckland, 1938, with the last of my designs. It all started like this.

Top right: At 10 SFTS, Dauphin, Manitoba, with a Harvard in 1941.

Middle: Levin, March 1941. We had no idea what we were letting ourselves in for. Of fifty-four on our initial training course who went on to train in Canada, twenty-three failed to survive the war. I'm fourth left, second row.

Bottom: Biggin Hill, April 1942. With fellow 72 Squadron New Zealander Dave Waters (right), killed in a flying accident, May 1942.

Top: Biggin Hill, April 1942. Left to right: AVM Leigh-Mallory, Gp Capt Barwell, Sqn Ldr Kingcome, HM King George VI, Flt Lt Armstrong, Plt Off Ratten, Plt Off Daniel, Plt Off Booth, self, Sgt Robertson and Plt Off Waters.

Middle: A mass flypast to salute the King as the Biggin Hill Wing, with 72 Squadron led by Wg Cdr Jamie Rankin, sets off on a sweep. It proved unproductive.

Bottom: Biggin Hill, May 1942. Left to right: Plt Off Daniel, self, Plt Off Kitchen, Plt Off Ratten, Plt Off Frahm, Flt Lt Woods, King Haakon of Norway and Gp Capt Barwell. Of the other aircrew, only Daniel would survive the war. (Crown Copyright)

Right: Biggin Hill, April 1942. Flt Lt Hugo Armstrong, seated on the 72 Squadron china mascot, chats to Plt Off Ronnie Kitchen. Between them, facing the camera, Plt Off Francis de Naeyer; behind, Fg Off Brady Parker, smoking. All four were later killed. (Crown Copyright)

Below: No. 485 Squadron at Selsey. Front row: sixth from left, Flt Lt King. Back row from left: fifth, Fg Off Stead; eighth, Sqn Ldr Ldr Niven; ninth, self; from right: third, Flt Lt Macdonald; fifth, Fg Off Kearins. (Crown Copyright)

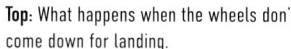

Top: What happens when the wheels don't come down for landing.

Left: A photograph illustrating 485 Squadron's proud New Zealand heritage, albeit the aircraft has suffered some damage.

Below left: Maldegem, Belgium. All that remained of one Spitfire after the Luftwaffe attack on 1 January 1945 which cost 485 Squadron a dozen aircraft.

Bottom: My own aircraft miraculously survived the New Year's Day attack unscathed.

Top: No. 485 Squadron in front of one of the only two Tempests to arrive at Predannack. Middle row from left: third, Flt Lt King; fourth, self; fifth, Flt Lt Macdonald. (Crown Copyright)

Middle: Relaxing in tented accommodation in Germany shortly after VE Day, 8 May 1945 – it had been a long war.

Right: Taken at Predannack, March 1945, where we spent a frustrating two months waiting for 485 Squadron's Tempests.

Top left: With a captured Fw 190 at Fassberg, June 1945.

Top right: Me 262s at Fassberg. This was the closest we ever got to these aircraft – they were just too fast for us.

Bottom left: A German Luger was a prized trophy at the end of the war, but I never did get one.

Bottom right: Our wedding day, 3 December 1945.

Top left: The lovely Mrs Hardy.

Top right: With Barbara on the *Rangitiki*, August 1947.

Bottom: January 1946, arriving back in New Zealand with parents, sister Gloria and niece Annette.

Top: Back in England, back in the cockpit – and this time its jets: the Vampire.

Middle: Flying is fun!

Left: RAF Odiham rugby XV; self, back row, far left.

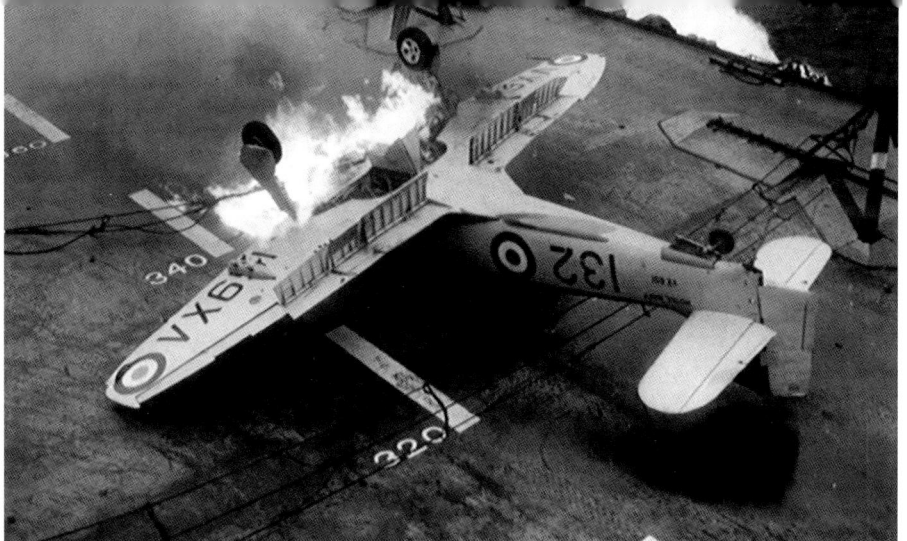

Top: A few days on board the carrier HMS *Illustrious* in 1950 were eye-opening. All too many Sea Fury landings ended up like this – or worse.

Middle: Even the photographers were enthusiastic at this Ypenburg display in July 1951.

Right: The newly produced 71 Squadron badge, with its central bald eagle embellished by three nine-pointed stars above the motto: 'First From The Eyrie'.

Top: The combined 71 and 3 Squadron aerobatic team preparing for the NATO display.

Bottom: At times we flew down to about fifty feet.

Top: The 71 Squadron aerobatic team in front of our bronze eagle trophy. From left to right: Flt Lt Smart, self and Sgt Jackson.

Middle: Brussels, 13 July 1952. Moments after entering this loop, number four (centre aircraft of the rear three) broke away with an engine problem.

Right: Another loop at Brussels – after we'd lost our number four.

Top: 71 Squadron at Wildenrath, 1952. Some of the pilots look so young! (Crown Copyright)

Middle: With an F-86 Sabre at Wildenrath, 1953, left to right: John Sutherland, Paddy Harbison, Johnnie Johnson, Mike Le Bas and self.

Left: Buckingham Palace, 1953, picking up my AFC.

Top: The 1965–66 Senior Officers' War Course. Top row: extreme right, Sir Peter Anson; fourth right, self; third left, Capt Poynter. Middle row: fifth right, Col Timbrell. Front row: fourth left, Capt Kidd. (Crown Copyright)

Middle: North Coates, 1967. The AOC's inspection parade was held inside because of bad weather. Returning my salute is Air Cdre John Manning. (Crown Copyright)

Bottom: A different parade picture (possibly featuring the Queen's Colour Squadron) which gives an idea of the sheer size of the Bloodhound missile. (Crown Copyright)

Top left: ACM Sir Fredrick Rosier, AOC-in-C Fighter Command, visits North Coates in 1967. (Crown Copyright)

Top right: AOC-in-C Strike Command, ACM Sir Denis Spotswood, meets North Coates' champion police dog, 1968. (Crown Copyright)

Middle: Marking the demise of Fighter Command in 1968: left to right, Johnnie Johnson, Peter Townsend, Bob Stanford Tuck, Sir Frederick Rosier and Al Deere.

Left: A 72 Squadron reunion at Wattisham, 1985: extreme left, Robbie Robertson; fourth left, Bob Oxspring; sixth left, Tom Hughes; extreme right, self. (Crown Copyright)

Top: Port Solent 2016. Left to right: Wg Cdr Mike Cannon, Air Adviser NZDF; Col Patrice Morand, French Air Attaché; Owen Hardy with his *Légion d'Honneur*, and Brig Evan Williams, Head NZDF London.

Bottom: Tangmere Museum 2017. Great grandson, Harvey Brinsmead, is interviewed on local radio during Owen Hardy's visit. It was marked by a salute from four 72 Squadron Tucanos on a round robin sortie celebrating the unit's centenary.

Top: Goodwood, 31 July 2017. Left to right: Matt Jones, New Zealand Red Arrows pilot Flt Lt Emmet Cox, Owen Hardy and Tim Granshaw.

Bottom: Owen Hardy's last flight, with Matt Jones in the Spitfire. (Courtesy Emmet Cox)

became a dying breed in the post-war RAF – apart from a number of New Zealanders who struggled on with varying levels of success.

Most evenings at Odiham found me tied down with correspondence studies arranged for me through service channels. I appeared to be making progress until it gradually became evident that the individual appointed to mark papers in one of my subjects appeared to know less about it than me. Coincident with this depressing discovery, the lure of a permanent commission was cast in my direction. So far, life in the Royal Air Force had been nothing short of fun and excitement. The money was reasonable; married quarters were usually available; the prospects for advancement appeared to be good; medical attention was excellent and, with a pension in the offing, personal security during and after service seemed assured. The temptation to at least try for a long-term engagement was too good to miss. So I went up to 11 Group HQ at Uxbridge for the interview. First step was a cursory chat with 'Flash' Pleasance[150] for about five minutes, then into Air Vice-Marshal Vincent's[151] office for an even shorter and chummier chat. The outcome seemed a foregone conclusion. So I had a career at last, albeit one far from the degree-based profession originally intended. On the other hand, Barbara and I were happy and enjoying a good standard of living now, rather than entertaining the uncertain hopes of earlier years.

The rest of the year followed the usual routine of aerobatic displays, exercises and parties, although it was marked by two events which certainly weren't run of the mill. The first, at the beginning of the year, saw me achieve by a considerable margin the highest air-to-air score in Fighter Command. This could be attributed mostly to good luck and partly, perhaps, to experience gained during gunnery instructing days.

The second is a much longer story. In September came a flight to Gibraltar, the first by a jet aircraft. I was to wave the RAF flag and give an aerobatic display on the anniversary of the Battle of Britain. An NCO was to fly the reserve aircraft and a small ground party plus equipment would be airlifted in a Dakota. Our route was via Mont-de-Marsan in France, just north of the Pyrenees, to refuel, then on to Gibraltar. My memory from Operation Torch of the weather in the Mediterranean at that time of the year was far from encouraging. My major concern was that if, after having to fly above cloud all the way, we broke out with only water in sight, which way should we turn to get to Gibraltar? Left or right? The first guess would have to be the right one. There was, of course, the radio. In those days the Vampire carried a four-channel set but it wasn't reliable – particularly in bad weather and at low level, where range was limited. Thoughts of jet streams and the unfortunate experience of 133 Squadron during the flight to Brest in 1942[152] brought visions of calamity. Much time was therefore spent beforehand poring over maps.

The meteorological officer had made a special effort to produce a synoptic chart for the route to Gibraltar, although he did stress that some of the 'actuals' for France and Spain were up to six hours old. Overall he thought that the en route weather and that at Mont-de-Marsan and Gibraltar would be all right. There was quite a lot of cloud over England, though we did manage a glimpse of the south coast as we passed over at about 15,000 feet. Another snatched view of the Normandy coast through a gap indicated that we were on track, but it was the last we were to see of the ground for some time as we continued our climb to 25,000 feet. The further we went the bleaker the outlook became.

Several layers of cloud had formed at altitude with solid columns of blackness rising up through them. Initially we managed to hold close to our compass course but that soon became impossible as we dodged about between these great pillars of unfriendliness. It was like wandering about in a forest of massive tree trunks. Lightning was flashing everywhere, its brilliance heightened by the relative darkness in which we were enclosed. As was only to be expected, our earphones were filled with the endless crackling of static. My fears about the flight were becoming a worrying reality. Fortunately, the gaps between the cloud layers enabled us to see and circumnavigate the lurking monsters sticking up in front, attempting to bar our passage. As long as we could continue to see ahead, the risks of pushing on were acceptable.

Our fate was soon to be placed in the lap of the gods as we scrambled up to 30,000 feet and passed the point of no return. Hope now ruled supreme. Hopefully, we hadn't wandered too far from our intended course. Hopefully, we wouldn't be too far from Mont-de-Marsan when we dropped out of cloud. Hopefully, the aerodrome wouldn't be blotted from sight by rain and cloud and, hopefully, we wouldn't overshoot our destination and run into the Pyrenees.

Letting down a little earlier than planned would reduce the chances of overshooting – but at the cost of burning a lot more fuel at low level and reducing the time available to find the aerodrome. At about 2,000 feet we broke out below cloud. With a full view of the ground, I could identify nothing from my high-level maps. A call to Mont-de-Marsan tower produced only light static. Our best move, therefore, was to alter course slightly to starboard and pick up the coast, which came into view about ten minutes later, enabling me to establish our position.

Although we were quite close to the aerodrome another call produced silence. Not until we were almost overhead did we receive a reply, in garbled English, to our request for permission to land. The confusion was to continue once safely on the ground. Since we had no information about the ability of Mont-de-Marsan to handle Vampires my instructions to the Dakota pilot were to land and offload the ground crew, who would deal with any rectification problems and oversee the refuelling. The last thing we wanted was to be filled with the wrong grade of fuel. Imagine my annoyance, therefore, after hanging about with our aircraft, at seeing the Dakota sail overhead and disappear into the distance – and this despite explaining to the controller my wish for the Dakota to land at his airfield. A swift visit to the control tower followed. Why hadn't the Dakota landed? 'Because,' said the controller, 'it was told it wasn't necessary for it to land!' We'd already lost two hours hanging about and there was still refuelling to be arranged. Fortunately, there were a few French Vampires on the aerodrome and some local knowledge of what was required. But we made sure we were on hand to check that the tanks were full.

Off we set again without food, drink or offer of hospitality, full of apprehension about what the weather had in store for us this time. Heavy clouds towered above the Pyrenees and our climb took a winding course as we skirted around them. Then, for a few moments, there was a memorable sight as a shaft of sunlight struck the sheer slopes of jagged peaks – colours and beauty that provided a stark contrast with the awesome nature of this dangerous terrain. This was certainly no place to have an engine flame-out; there was no means of relighting a Goblin engine, though to my knowledge none had ever failed. The cloud then closed off all sight of the ground as we twisted our way ever higher into the tops of towering cumulonimbus. On and up we climbed as the fuel in the tanks burnt off, but we were never able to break free of the layer of thin cloud.

'Chippy' Carpenter, flying the other aircraft, had done well to stay with me under such adverse weather conditions. Suddenly, without warning and when halfway along our route, we shot out into clear blue sky and blinding sunlight. A long way below and just off to the right was Madrid. We were bang on track. Visibility was perfect and with a little concentration it was possible to pick out a tiny dot on the horizon which was the Rock at Gibraltar. All concerns about the flight fell away with the wall of cloud now behind us and we sat back to enjoy the extensive view across Spain. Way off to the right over Portugal stood an enormous cumulonimbus, a perfect example of the classic shape. I offered up quiet thanks that we hadn't run into that monster en route.

Our arrival at Gibraltar drew a lot of interest. The few vantage points overlooking the runway from the Spanish side were lined with spectators who must have known we were coming. But our relief at arriving safely was nothing compared with that expressed by the ground crew when they turned up. Most of them had suffered severe sickness and were sporting bruises that bore witness to the roughness of their ride. The Dakota hadn't escaped damage either on the leg to Mont-de-Marsan. There was a foot-long gash along the fuselage, as though made by an old-fashioned tin-opener. It was where the aerial pylon had stood before both it and the trailing aerial had been blown away by lightning. However, to our surprise we were not the only arrivals from England that day.

Three or four Hornet aircraft, a single-seat fighter like a Mosquito but smaller, had set out to break the record for a non-stop flight from London to Gibraltar. Only one made it; the others landed at various places in Spain due to lack of fuel. They were under the command of a group captain, who took it upon himself to supervise my Vampire display and ordered that aerobatics were not to be performed below 500 feet. Back at Odiham I was accustomed to working nearer five feet for high and low speed runs and finishing other manoeuvres at between 100 and 200 feet. During one display I raised a few laughs when my jet exhaust lifted the wind 'T' out of the signals square in front of the control tower where the VIPs stood. Needless to say my 'supervisor' was fuming on the day of the display and threatened disciplinary action once back in England. But at least the Spanish crowd was happy.

The weather on the run back to Mont-de-Marsan wasn't good, although nowhere as bad as on the way out. It was a Saturday and the few people on duty at the aerodrome were in no hurry to help. The meteorological officer showed me a synoptic chart and when asked what the weather was like at Odiham gave a typically French shrug of the shoulders and said it was all right. He pointed to Odiham where, on closer inspection and in astonishment, we spotted the symbol for snow in the last three hours. Other nearby stations were showing the same information. Snow? In Hampshire in September? My queries were answered with more shrugs. Either the weather was exceptionally bad or the chart was wrong. My bet was the latter, but this was no time to be taking chances on guesses. Much as we disliked the decision we would stay the night and check the weather next day. Accommodation and the food were pretty primitive but we didn't complain since we had no French money to pay for officer privileges.

The weather looked more promising the following morning. At least there were no snow shower symbols on the chart so we made haste to get airborne and away from France. Again, not the best of weather but no worry after the conditions we'd already been through. As we spotted the French coast through a hole in the cloud I put a call through to Odiham. Up came the reply immediately, loud and clear, with news that all was well with the weather there. It was midday Sunday when we touched down and the duty crew were in a hurry to push the aircraft into the hangar the moment I shut the engine down.

The first person to hop up to the cockpit was a customs officer, also in a hurry to be off for the rest of the weekend. 'What have you brought back with you?' Nothing, I explained. 'Where is your bag?' It was in the radio compartment and while he stood on the wing an airman retrieved it for him. He began ferreting about in my small homemade bag (it could be tucked away in the odd spare places in a Vampire) and got the shock of his life. After an hour and a half at high altitude the little metal box containing my safety razor was so cold it stuck to his fingers. Try as he might, he couldn't shake it free, much to the amusement of all present. It made my day. I never took kindly to aggressive officials.

The Christmas fancy dress party at Odiham was always great fun but this time tempered by the knowledge that my stay there was coming to an end. Early in January my posting to Stradishall in Suffolk was announced. I was to run the Vampire flight at the Operational Conversion Unit there.

» Chapter 11

VAMPIRE INSTRUCTOR

Stradishall was a pre-war aerodrome between Bury St Edmunds and Haverhill in Suffolk. The station was tasked with introducing trainee pilots to jet aircraft and teaching basic fighter skills prior to their posting to front-line squadrons. Russell Mackenzie,[153] a New Zealander, was in charge of the conversion squadron, which was split into a Meteor and a Vampire flight. There were three officers with me in the Vampire flight. Another squadron on the station was responsible for gunnery training. Russell Mackenzie had joined the RAF in 1937 and spent his war on Beaufighters. We had much in common, which helped cement a firm bond of friendship. He was courting a girl in Oxfordshire and travelled to see her most weekends in his old car. His journeys were a godsend since my wife was still in married quarters at Odiham. Russ would drop me off in London on Friday nights and do a pick-up on Sunday evenings, a routine that went on for two months.

With nothing to do of an evening during the week, I took the opportunity to study for the promotion and Staff College entrance exams. This involved a strict routine of three hours' study each night with short breaks for dinner and the nine o'clock news (the current affairs paper was important). My approach was rewarded with passes in all these exams. In early spring I could therefore turn my attention to repairing the leaks in the tank of the car I'd bought. It was a 1933 MG J2, a sporty little two-seater which could be improved with a little technical attention but was otherwise in smart condition. The day of my driving test it failed to start because of a flat battery. After a mad rush to borrow a car, I arrived late at Bury St Edmunds. I persuaded the testing officer not to cancel the test but had to wait about until I could be fitted in. To cap this inauspicious start, I had to wrestle with an engine which stopped when the clutch was pushed fully home. It meant regularly having to hop out and use the crank-handle to re-start the motor – the final humiliation in my driving test saga. The examiner eventually handed over a pass ticket, no doubt grateful that he wouldn't have to suffer me again.

Two months after my arrival at Stradishall, who should turn up to take charge of administration on the station but Jamie Rankin. He'd been the wing commander flying during my time at Biggin Hill. He still held the rank of wing commander although he'd risen to air commodore between times. Jamie was a legend in the world of fighter pilots and was the best leader with whom I'd been privileged to fly. He missed the Battle of Britain; nearly all his successes were over France in 1941 and 42.[154] He played the air war like a chess board, manoeuvring the three Biggin squadrons out of danger and into position for an attack. In command of every situation, Jamie exuded a confidence that engendered an unshakable sense of security in every pilot who flew with him. He was universally respected and admired.

There was a huge gap between us when he was leading the Biggin Wing for the second time; my own tour had only just begun. He was up at the front end of the wing while I was usually right at the back; tactically there was a massive distance between us too. Now, at Stradishall, it felt strange to be on close terms with this revered individual. Our time at Biggin became the bond between us and it was good to talk and laugh about personalities and incidents from those hectic days. He left after three months to take command of Duxford, near Cambridge but, as with most of his contemporaries, he failed to make further progress.

After a month in a hotel in the pretty village of Clare, in May we moved into a married quarter on the aerodrome. Looking back over the record of my flying at a happy, friendly station, it shows an almost continuous run of aerobatic flights with demonstrations as far away as the Isle of Man. There were, however, two incidents which were far from routine.

The first was a week spent with the Royal Navy. A lieutenant commander on attachment arranged a visit to Culdrose (the navy's Stradishall equivalent); four of us were to watch pupils carrying out their first deck landings. We boarded the carrier, HMS *Illustrious*, every morning at Penzance. On day one, four Hawker Sea Furys arrived overhead, three pupils led by an instructor who landed on successfully. The first pupil then flew into the aft safety barrier and caught fire. After the debris was cleared from the deck the second pupil repeated this same performance. By this time the third must have become a nervous wreck, flying round watching, awaiting his turn. But thankfully for him, and us, he was sent back to Culdrose, low on fuel. Of the next two to arrive one made it successfully, the other became another victim of the barrier.

And that's how it went each day until Culdrose ran out of Sea Furys. The barrier claimed all those destroyed, bar one which hooked up on the arrester wire but slewed sideways into the island and another which spun into the sea on the approach. Astonishingly, this was the only fatality during four days of chaos. To add a bit of variety to the outing, a Sea Hornet and Sea Vampire also attempted fly-ons. The Sea Hornet stalled just before the round-down at the beginning of the deck, which snapped off half the fuselage just behind the wing, throwing the rest of the aircraft onto its nose. It continued on down the deck balanced almost vertically on its two engines and wheels until stopped by the headwind – which then began to blow it backwards. As the front end gathered speed we expected to see it disappear off the stern. But the pilot recovered his senses and put on the brakes, slowing things sufficiently for the deck crew to secure the aircraft. Perhaps wisely, the Vampire didn't attempt any landings, just a few 'touch-and-goes'.

Most of the time we watched proceedings from a platform halfway up the island, where the ship's photographer stood overlooking the barrier. Naturally, we took the precaution of ducking behind cover whenever a crash became obvious, since bits of metal would fly everywhere. Not so the photographer, who would lean as far over the metal wall as possible, doing his duty like a good sailor. We spent one spell on board with the batman on the stern of the ship, port side. His job was to indicate to the pilot adjustments required to his line of approach and decide whether to allow him to land or flag him away. A tricky task in a dangerous position. From there it was easy to see the hook on the Sea Furys bouncing over the arrester wires, a sequence that once started rarely stopped before the aircraft hit the barrier. After a crash bits of metal came tinkling down the deck before falling over the round-down into the sea.

Refreshments, and a break from the horrors on deck, were taken in the officers' wardroom, which was between decks near the stern. From there to our viewing platform was a short walk over a steel catwalk running along the outside of the ship. One of our party, a Captain Myers on exchange from the United States Air Force, was making his way along the catwalk alone once when he was startled by a loud bang. To his astonishment, an engine on fire shot over his shoulder and into the sea. Looking up he saw the front end of an aircraft, minus engine, balanced precariously on the edge of the deck above him. Back at Stradishall he lived on the story for weeks after.

Most of these crashed aircraft were pushed over the side of the ship. Our tame lieutenant commander said he'd seen more accidents in those four days than in the rest of his flying career. But to me the whole exercise seemed a shocking waste, and a virtual nil return in training terms. On the positive side, we did admire the skill of the deck crew and the speed with which they responded to a crash, especially the firemen who were into the flames and out with the pilot in seconds while others played extinguishers around the cockpit. This was no mean achievement when an aircraft was upside down with the pilot squeezed down onto the deck. We didn't see a single pilot suffering from superficial let alone severe burns, just one or two with sore heads.

The second diversion from the Stradishall routine is a shorter tale: a weekend at Banbury to attend Russell Mackenzie's wedding. The journey there and back was the longest run we'd done in the MG and justified the work put in every night in my garage – much to the annoyance of my wife. Her frustration peaked the evening she burst into the garage saying, 'How can I make a baby if you spend all the time under that car?' Despite all the distractions of aeroplanes and cars she did eventually succeed – to the extent of our cherished son and daughter. Andrew was born in April 1951 and Debbie in January 1953. But I'm getting ahead of myself.

Back on the subject of cars, we had an amateur racing driver by the name of Dickie Stoop[155] at Stradishall. Dickie was the son of Adrian Stoop, an England rugby international.[156] Dickie wasn't big, he was just built square, like a tank. He had two cars which, since he wasn't married, he was able to afford. One was a Formula Three, which in those days were small racing cars powered by hotted-up motorbike engines. John Cooper made his name building such cars; Stirling Moss was one of his first customers. I'd hoped that Dickie would let me drive his up and down the runway but he never did. His other car was a Frazer Nash two-seater which he raced at circuits all over England; it ran on special fuel which he obtained locally in Haverhill.

Once, memorably, Dickie took me to a meeting in his Frazer Nash along narrow, winding country lanes not built for speeding. It was an exhilarating ride, sliding along sideways under heavy braking then fierce acceleration. It didn't pay to think of what might be coming the opposite way round the next bend. On we tore at breakneck speed round corner after corner until the inevitable happened: two cyclists on the road, ten yards in front. Closing my eyes for the crash, I heard the scream of tyres, a double-declutch and then the roar of the engine as I was forced back into my seat. Opening my eyes, unaccountably the road ahead was clear and we sped on as before. I never did know where the cyclists went or how we missed them.

Finding a sad Dickie in the mess one Sunday evening I asked what was wrong. 'Damaged my car,' he said. In response to my question as to its whereabouts, he took me outside. And there stood a misshapen Frazer Nash with the big number on one side half scraped away. He'd gone off the track at Silverstone and hit some straw bales. Within a few weeks the car was back, as good as new, and Dickie was away racing again. He was in the grip of the sport which a few years later was to be the death of him. I never did learn what happened.[157]

Russell Mackenzie left Stradishall at the beginning of October 1950 to become the wing commander flying at Leuchars in Scotland. Two weeks later I too was on my way to Germany – to reform and command No. 71 (Eagle) Squadron at Gütersloh.

» Chapter 12
71 SQUADRON – GÜTERSLOH

After three weeks' leave, in which time our few worldly belongings were packed and put into store, my pregnant wife was settled with her parents and the MG laid up in a rented garage, I set off from Hendon for Germany. My first duty on arriving at Bückeburgh[158] was a visit to Command HQ at Bad Eilsen to be looked over by one Harry Broadhurst.[159] Several squadrons were being reformed in Germany and it came to light that as SASO (senior air staff officer) he had personally selected their commanding officers – hence the apparent disappointment that I hadn't previously served under him. Had he made a mistake? The wartime habit of commanders gathering their pet staff around them still prevailed in 1950 and Broadhurst had filled many key posts in Germany with favoured subordinates.

In my experience this system worked; it made for a happy and effective fighting machine. However, it was effectively countered by the introduction of the Air Secretary's Branch. By operating on paper rather than through personal influence when filling appointments and effecting promotions, the aim was to even out prospects and ensure a broader experience for all. But this new approach suffered from inherent failings. Square pegs were sometimes placed in round holes, to the detriment of both the individual and the service (as I was to see later at HQ Fighter Command). My belief was that appointments and promotions should be based purely on results, as they were in wartime. But the die was cast; times were changing.

After meetings with other members of the command staffs I was driven to the aerodrome at Gütersloh, which lay relatively isolated between Hanover and Dortmund. The next day was spent at the nearby 2 Group HQ, Sundern, meeting staff there, not least the Air Officer Commanding, the Earl of Bandon,[160] a man of great humour and one of the air force's true characters.

Gütersloh was home to three squadrons of Vampires, Nos. 3, 67 and 71, the last two in the process of re-forming. My own squadron had just received its aircraft and pilots, and ground crew were still arriving. I knew one of the pilots from Odiham, where he'd arrived straight from Cranwell. He was to prove an asset as most of the others had Meteor experience only, and many of them were 'throw aways' from squadrons who had to offer up pilots for NATO's expansion. Naturally, they didn't send their best. But fortunately there were a few arriving straight from the training machine who were promising material. One became an exceptional pilot within a matter of months. Starting from scratch with new aircraft and crews, what more could a commanding officer wish for?

One task was paramount: to build up morale and pride in the squadron. It would be an uphill struggle. Personnel had been hurriedly thrown together, separated from their families with Christmas just around the corner. But to counter any feelings of depression I had the willing cooperation of two flight commanders, each with an old sweat of a flight sergeant who knew all the tricks of getting the best from the airmen.

I began by telling the flight commanders they had sole charge of running their flights; there would be no interference from me unless advice was asked for or things were going wrong. Then it was off to show my face to the ground staff, to tell them what we were going to do and to lay down a few rules. We weren't here to form a squadron. We were going to form THE squadron, one we could all be proud of. A promise was made: we would reach that target in six months. Pride started with respect for the tools of our trade, the aircraft. They were not to be stepped on but refuelled from the ground; each aircraft was to be washed down every Saturday morning by the pilot and ground crew assigned to it. These were just some of the rules I laid down for keeping the Vampires in showcase condition and for the running of a good squadron. Much of my talk was necessarily directed at the ground crew, whose work lacked the glamour and the thrill of flying.

All too often pilots made contact with the ground crew only when getting in and out of their aircraft. Any conversation between them was generally aircraft related – hardly an approach to make junior airmen feel important and essential parts of a team which, of course, they were. It was vital that they understood this and I briefed all my pilots accordingly. Additionally, there was a board in my office with a photograph, name and trade included, of every airman on the squadron. I would look for an airman on the flight line, match him to a photograph and wander out in his direction – an apparently casual but pre-planned encounter. It was always heartening to watch his face when addressed by name and asked personal questions. A bit of trickery on my part, perhaps, but it worked. It certainly helped me get to know my men and, hopefully, for them to see me as human and not a demanding tartar. It was good to see that other pilots soon picked up the habit of spending time out on the flight line.

All this time at the back of my mind was the wish to build morale and enhance prestige with an aerobatic team. I'd seen what this had done for Odiham. And it lay behind my concern to maintain the aircraft in spotless condition. The silver paint finish on the Vampire wasn't durable and readily became dirty and scratched. (The aircraft on 3 Squadron were filthy; they looked like relics from a wreckers' yard.) However, for the time being aerobatics were put to the back of my mind. It was more important to find out what this lottery of pilots were capable of and turn them into a coordinated team in the air. Hours were spent in the crew room and the air going through the manoeuvres to be used for maintaining station as a flight and a squadron. I demanded perfect spacing and not the usual rabble of aeroplanes roughly spaced in approximately the same bit of sky. A coherent and tidily flown unit had a touch of professionalism which made an enemy think twice about attacking. And a tight and evenly packed formation impressed the ground crew when flying over the aerodrome prior to breaking up for the landings, where the aim was to get as many aircraft as possible on the runway at the same time. As a result of all this drilling in the air we were dubbed 'the training squadron' by the other units. But their jibes and smirks didn't last long.

The senior officers at Gütersloh showed no interest in the work of the squadrons, or in the problems and progress of the two re-forming units. Important items of equipment were missing and we were left to fight the supply system from our level. Thanks to endless telephone calls, and bypassing of the official channels of supply, we weren't popular with the equipment staffs at Group and Command Headquarters. My approach hardly endeared me to my superiors at Gütersloh either. But, finally, our pestering provoked a couple of visits from the top and shortages began to be resolved.

Things started to change in February with the arrival of Tom Dalton-Morgan[161] as wing commander flying. Tom was one of Harry Broadhurst's favourites. Hugely experienced, an excellent and much decorated pilot, he brought a sense of purpose to Gütersloh and supported me in everything I was trying to do. This Welsh fireball was another of the bright stars who illuminated my air force career. Then, shortly afterwards, 'Charlie' Chaplin[162] took command of the station. He was equally supportive but the complete antithesis in terms of personality. Charlie was an ex-bomber pilot of some experience, very quiet and deliberate in all that he did. In fact, he was too kind and gentle a man to survive for long in what I perceived to be the rough and tumble at the upper levels of the air force.[163]

No. 71 was the first of the three Eagle squadrons formed during the war from American volunteers. All were disbanded in 1942 and personnel transferred to the US Army Air Forces.[164] With them went the squadron's official crest, which a photograph showed to be an original and impressive design. I wrote to the office of the Chester Herald asking if we could adopt the same crest. He advised that he had written to America repeating our request and approval came shortly afterwards. The parchment bearing the crest arrived a couple of months later. I had a copy of the crest painted on a large board that was varnished and framed then hung in the hangar for all to see. Letters also went to all the major aircraft manufacturers, British and American, asking for coloured prints of their aircraft. As they poured in, with the best hung in crew rooms and the rest bartered away, it was rewarding to see the mood of the crews improving.

In February 1951 my heavily pregnant wife joined me and we were billeted in a requisitioned house about five miles from the aerodrome; a German driver ferried me to and from work each day. March saw the first of many attachments to Sylt for air-to-air firing. An island in the North Sea just out from the Danish/German border, Sylt was famed for its nudist beaches. But with nothing to do outside the working day, free time became an absolute bore for two or three weeks twice a year.

Flying was intensive with up to three firings each day against a twenty-five- or thirty-foot flag (would that I could remember) towed by a Tempest aircraft. These attachments were a testing time for the ground crew, the armourers especially, even though we were using only two of the Vampire's four cannons. The competence of the armourers was measured in stoppages per 10,000 rounds fired; for pilots the comparator was rounds on the target. Firing on the flag wasn't particularly easy or without its dangers. If a bullet cut the tow wire the iron bar and heavy weights which held the flag upright could whip back and strike the firer – as happened when one of our aircraft was damaged during the first attachment. As for our results, they weren't much better than the average for Germany squadrons. But rectifying this disappointment was marked down for future attention; a more immediate matter had arisen. Word had it that requests for RAF representation at air displays were being received at Command Headquarters. The time had arrived to look seriously at forming an aerobatic team.

Given the overriding requirement to turn the squadron into an effective fighting unit, my first priority was the building of morale, pride and comradeship in all personnel. The two aims were interdependent but finding the flying time to devote to each separately was difficult. The squadron had to meet a specific training programme each month, which required every hour of the working day. Any other flying we might want to do would have to be done in our spare time. The best time to practise aerobatics was during the evening when the air was relatively calm and the aerodrome free of traffic. Volunteer ground crew were encouraged to turn out on the understanding that they would be first in line to travel with us to any displays. Thus, from this part-time beginning, and for all subsequent practice aerobatic training, a team was built up which was to represent the RAF at air displays around Europe for the next two years.

Our first commitment was at Oslo at the end of May. At the time the squadron was on attachment to Wattisham in Suffolk and the team flew from there to Gardermoen, a Norwegian Air Force station near Oslo, with a refuelling stop at Sylt. The first person to poke his face into the cockpit at Gardermoen was another New Zealander, Bill Crawford-Compton.[165] It turned out that he was the air attaché in Oslo and was as surprised to see me as I was to see him. Since the city was some distance from Gardermoen we didn't see much of each other during the following three days. The display was at a different airfield, a small one on the outskirts of Oslo, so we had no idea how it went. That evening we were having drinks at the home of the station commander when Bill rang, asking why we weren't at the official dinner. We didn't know there was one. 'Must have the team here. Everyone wants to meet them, you're the stars of the show. Put the station commander on the phone.'

It was nearly midnight by the time we arrived and the party had died. After a few courteous introductions and handshakes we were on our way back to Gardermoen, very tired and very, very hungry. We'd eaten little lunch and had no meal that evening. Next day the Norwegian air force gave us a short tour of some of the attractions around Oslo, the main one being the Kon-Tiki Museum, devoted to Thor Heyerdahl's achievements.[166] The following day we flew back to the relative comfort of Gütersloh, where Barbara and I had now been allocated one of the only three married quarters on the station.

In June we gave two local displays, one organised by Tom as a farewell to the Earl of Bandon. It was arranged so that we beat up his car, stopped it on the autobahn and then did the display, much to the astonishment of all the other drivers who stopped to watch. July saw the squadron back at Sylt, where I managed to chalk up a scoring record for Germany to go with the one in Fighter Command two years earlier. A little bit of thinking and cunning use of the gyro gunsight paid off. It was also pleasing to see the squadron average improve, putting us near the top of the list now. At the end of July we flew to Valkenburg in Holland for a three-day display at Ypenburg in The Hague. Here we were to come up against the team who were to become our rivals in Europe – the American Skyblazers, flying F-84Es.

Typically, they were supported by a publicity crew who dealt with the press and the radio commentary during displays. The F-84 was ideally suited to close formation flying. The cruciform symmetry of the aircraft with its long wingtip tanks made for eye-catching formation patterns. They were good – after all, it was their full-time job – but according to the press reports we still stole the show. At last 71 Squadron was coming to the fore. Moreover, we'd already been selected to provide escort for General Eisenhower during his visit to Gütersloh on taking over as NATO's first SACEUR (Supreme Allied Commander Europe).[167] Jibes about a training squadron were no longer to be heard.

By September we were well into a period of major exercises which kept us moving around aerodromes in Germany and Holland; we were now fully mobile and equipped with our own transport. However, all this rushing about and sleeping in tents in cold conditions finally caught up with me in Holland when a touch of pleurisy put me into a field hospital. While sedated I picked up part of a conversation about a dead pilot but it made little sense. When my flight commanders visited later that evening I mentioned this; however, they denied any knowledge so I dismissed the matter from my mind. In fact it was the squadron's first fatality but Tom had instructed my visitors to say nothing to me. As so often seemed to be the case, he was an above average pilot, one of those least expected to kill himself. The aircraft of all three squadrons were carrying drop tanks for a long flight over England and were taking off rapidly in pairs. After a number of these the air at the end of the runway had become very turbulent, powerful enough to throw our young pilot, who was formating on his leader, back onto the ground. With a heavy aircraft he simply didn't have enough speed to retain control in such conditions. I didn't learn of this sad event until my discharge and return to Gütersloh five days later.

We gave a display at the end of October and another in November, by which time the silly season for air shows was over. By the end of the year Tom had left, having been promoted to group captain and taken command of the aerodrome at Wunstorf. It was a sad day for everyone at Gütersloh, particularly for me. Then within a couple of months Charlie Chaplin went also. The new station commander was not a popular man and I was lucky not to have to serve under him for long – rescued by the planned move of all three Gütersloh Vampire squadrons to Wildenrath. But that's jumping too far ahead. Back to a time not long after Tom had left, I was feeling rather smug about the progress we'd made during the year. No.71 Squadron had arrived on the fighter scene and established a name for itself in several ways. Best of all, there was a spirit of pride among the crews in what they'd accomplished. In fact, we were just ripe for a fall, which wasn't long in coming.

Our Vampires could be fitted with racks for carrying three-inch rockets. For training, two rockets with sixty-pound concrete heads were carried under each wing and fired individually. The location of the air-to-ground range, on the Dutch/German border, was such that carrying out four attacks stretched the Vampire's endurance. It was a Monday morning in December and 71 had the first range slots, but Monday mornings were when Charlie Chaplin held his commanders' meetings. As this one dragged on I became impatient, wondering what was happening to the weather; it was getting darker by the minute. I'd left the flying programme to the two flight commanders but the forecast wasn't wonderful and matters weren't expected to improve.

Once the meeting was over I found the aerodrome half blotted out by a thick fog rolling up the runway. I learned we had two aircraft in the air and they'd been up sometime. Over to the control tower. There was only one controller on duty when I arrived and he was in a confused state of panic. He hadn't alerted anyone, didn't know how many aircraft were in the air and was incapable of any sensible action. It transpired that four aircraft were airborne, two of mine and two from 67 Squadron which had been up only a short time; one of these two was requesting a GCA (ground-controlled approach) while the other was diverted to Wunstorf. But where were my two? Only one came up on the air when called. He'd been to the range and was halfway back, and beginning to panic. He wouldn't have enough fuel to attempt a GCA and all other aerodromes were further away from him than we were. It was a hard decision to make but I ordered him to return to the range and land the aircraft wheels-up on the small emergency strip there. He didn't make it and finished up in a field.

There was no sign of my other aircraft but the pilot had heard the panic back at Gütersloh and landed safely in Holland. But he had me worried, for which he got a blast for not letting us know what he was doing – plus a pat on the back for doing it. The pilot flying the GCA had two attempts at landing. He couldn't see the runway even though we could see him going along no more than fifteen feet above it after a perfectly executed approach. With little fuel left he could only climb up and bale out.

Nos. 67 and 71 Squadrons had lost one aircraft each but, thankfully, no pilots on what afterwards became known to us as 'Black Monday'. Boards of Inquiry followed and, yes, questions in the House! Was the air force asking too much of its pilots in Germany? We weren't popular with our senior officers at Group and Command and 71 had dropped to the bottom of the heap. It was back to the drawing board for me.

The climb back into favour started in March during yet another attachment to Sylt. Meanwhile the major move to Wildenrath was about to happen.

» Chapter 13
WILDENRATH DAYS

Wildenrath was the first of the large NATO aerodromes to be built in Germany west of the Rhine. With all three Gütersloh Vampire squadrons moving there I planned a quick check of the new base before we left for Sylt. I didn't want the other two squadrons laying claim to the best of what was available while we were isolated for a month during the transition.

Wildenrath was to be commanded by another of Broadhurst's boys, Johnnie Johnson, the top Allied fighter pilot. He wasn't there during my brief visit but David Scott-Malden,[168] in charge of administration, was. Wildenrath was to be my first contact with these two celebrities of the fighter world and to serve under both at the same time was a rare privilege. David confirmed that the squadron's interests would be safeguarded in my absence. The hangars were up and allocated, married quarters were proceeding at the rate of one a day and I could select mine now if I wanted. Borrowing David's car, I drove around the quarters with a plan of the site and chose one only partly finished that stood apart from the rest. Out on the aerodrome I inspected our hangar and found all construction was being done by gangs of Germans working three eight-hour shifts a day under the station works officer, a Pole! No wonder work never stopped. After thanks and farewells to David I lifted off the 2,000-yard runway for Gütersloh. A couple of days later I left for Sylt, encouraged by the prospects of a happy future at Wildenrath.

At Sylt I passed on to all the unit pilots the trick of using the gyro gunsight against the flag. With much time spent checking the camera-gun recording of each pilot's shoot, scores got better and better. It was satisfying to see enthusiasm grow as the competition between pilots became infectious. At the end of the attachment the squadron's average score was just over two and a half times that of any other in Germany; on one very full day's firing it was almost four times better. An intrigued station commander came to verify the results for himself. And all the armourers were trotted in to see the large board recording the day's shooting, sharing in the exhilaration running through the crew room. We'd worked our way back into favour with the hierarchy again and flew back to our new base at Wildenrath in the middle of April a happy squadron.

The two celebrities running Wildenrath were a complete contrast in personalities. Johnnie adopted a vibrant approach to everything he put his mind to. He was the leader at the centre of events good and not so good. He was the perfect host at service functions, but if mischief was afoot you could bet Johnnie was the instigator, although never guilty. He was a good friend who many times acted in my interests, support I returned with even greater loyalty. He could also be a terrible enemy, especially to any who didn't come up to his standards or who let him down. To me he was a loveable rogue and it was an honour to have shared in a small part of his life.

David Scott-Malden was a quiet, reserved and studious individual with an excellent academic record and a wry sense of humour. A single man, he was making his way towards marriage. But at the time none of us, including Johnnie, his closest associate, were aware of this. He was reputedly the youngest group captain of the war[169] but suffered a few physical setbacks in later years. The first, tuberculosis, cost him a lung. A few years later, as a passenger in a Norwegian air force Harvard that ditched, he spent a long time in the sea before being rescued; his health suffered further as a result. He was quick to appreciate a joke and I always enjoyed his company, both at Wildenrath and whenever we met again afterwards.

The end of April was marked by a piece of good fortune. The sooner my pilots got to know the area around Wildenrath at night the better. So a couple of weeks after our arrival I set in hand a programme to that end. The airfield lighting had been tested but never during flying and since the runway lights seemed a bit weak here and there I asked for them to be backed with gooseneck paraffin flares. All went well and the lights of the aerodrome stood out surprisingly bright, set as they were against the dark background of field and forest. The lights of the Ruhr were a brilliant landmark, although it was difficult to work out where the lights of one city stopped and those of the next began.

At night the air usually becomes quite still and the darkness makes for a fascinating change from the occasional monotony of day flying. There's no sense of motion, just a pleasant, lulling sensation of hanging in the remoteness of space with only the stars as companions. Snuggled comfortably in a warm cockpit it was easy for the mind to wander as time floated away. Hell! Where has Wildenrath gone? Should be down there; drop down for a closer look. Still no sign. The aerodrome had suffered a power failure and the standby plant hadn't cut in. No one had bothered to test that part of the system! Dropping to a lower altitude I picked up the pundit flashing the aerodrome identification code, WI, and then the gooseneck flares on the runway. Phew. On landing I saw the control staff sensibly putting out more goosenecks for the benefit of others – we had many in the air that night. Had it not been for those initial few goosenecks we could have lost a number of them. There's always an element of luck in flying, perhaps more so when operating in new and unfamiliar situations. A few heads on the station might have rolled, possibly including mine, had the gods not guided me to requesting those goosenecks that night.

Group had decided that an aerobatic competition would be held to determine which squadron would represent the RAF in Europe during the summer of 1952. It was held at Gütersloh at the beginning of May with a team from each station taking part. We were perhaps fortunate to win – one of the other teams was surprisingly good. The contest was on a weekend and since my wife was still living at Gütersloh I took a break for a couple of days while the rest of the team returned to Wildenrath. The telephone rang later that afternoon: bad news. On landing at Wildenrath all the team's aircraft had shot off the end of the runway into the mud. Good news: none of them was damaged. How could such skilful pilots make such a simple mistake?

The long concrete runway at Wildenrath stood out as a great white scar on the countryside so it had been camouflaged with a creosote paint. Visually it worked quite well but it was raining when the team landed. The combination of creosote and rain made the runway surface worse than sheet ice; the tyres simply wouldn't grip. Much money and effort had gone into painting all this concrete; now more had to be spent on sandblasting it off. This, however, proved to be another bit of luck.

On our arrival at Wildenrath we learnt that 3 Squadron had a large bronze eagle tucked away in their store room. Years earlier they'd 'acquired' it from

Wunstorf, where it had stood as one of a pair on the gate posts at the entrance to the aerodrome. While I dared not ask how this giant monument, which took four men to lift, got into my pilots' crew room, I was happy to issue files and emery cloth together with instructions to scratch the bird clean. Weeks passed without much success, then on catching sight of the giant sandblasting machine out on the runway an idea struck. Armed with a couple of cartons of cigarettes and with the bird now in our Land Rover I sped off to the men blasting the runway. With the help of a little sign language the Germans soon understood the nature of our proposition. With the pressure of the grit blast reduced, a short trial produced marvellous results. But the Germans wanted something better. The huge machine was shut down, all the grit emptied out and fine sand loaded into the hopper. A minute or so later our eagle glowed brighter than gold in the sun. It was whipped back to the crew room while brushes and seaplane varnish were acquired from stores – seaplane varnish in the middle of Germany! The end result was perfect. More cigarettes and different German labourers produced a concrete plinth in front of our hangar where the eagle was finally mounted. It stood there, good as new, long after my departure.

Flying in a UK exercise from Duxford in late May and early June I was able to catch up with Jamie Rankin and all his news. It was the last time we were to meet. Later in a quiet month came a couple of trips to practise for a display in France that would prove anything but quiet. We flew down to Lyons on 5 July in weather good enough to admire the Alps in their snow-capped splendour. The meeting to organise the following day's display was a disaster, a foreboding of what was to come. After about an hour of heated argument, all in French and way over my head, the Skyblazer's leader came across to me to say they were off and did we want to join them? With our requirements in the hands of a helpful air attaché, we left the scene of hostilities.

Visually, the Skyblazers were probably the best display team on our side of the Atlantic. The four pilots were far from the self-opinionated American boasters I'd sometimes come across. The leader had two brothers flying either side of him and a tall lanky chap who flew directly behind.[170] He was so close beneath his leader that the top half of the fin and rudder on his aircraft were streaked with black from the exhaust of his leader's engine. Proof of how close he flew, it was never cleaned off.[171]

Our display was programmed for the afternoon so we didn't turn up until late morning. It was a lovely warm day and we sat down in the sun, idly watching a small airliner load passengers. After take-off, to our surprise the pilot did a tight turn followed by a low pass along the front of the assembled crowd. Horrified, we then saw a tiny biplane coming from the opposite direction. It was very low, almost stalled, with its nose high, flicking from side to side yet under perfect control, an attitude that meant the pilot couldn't see the airliner coming towards him. We froze – a collision seemed certain. But at the last moment the airliner lifted over the biplane, missing it by only a few feet. The biplane's Belgian pilot was in the right. He'd been given permission to practise his manoeuvre, but was so alarmed by the incident that he refused to fly in the afternoon. It was the second of two bewildering introductions to an air show that hadn't yet started.

Our display went well enough in the afternoon despite the heavy turbulence. I hardly had time to catch my breath on landing before being dragged to the broadcast system to respond to words of congratulation: unexpected and, dare I say, a little embarrassing. About an hour later the Skyblazers gave their usual faultless display. Next on stage was a Nord 2501, a large twin-engined transport aircraft.[172] Once airborne the pilot commenced a low run down the runway on one engine as the Skyblazers were landing from the opposite direction. The team's leader told me later that the Nord was so low that he seriously thought of running off the runway to get out of its way.

Shortly after it passed over him the radio burst into life with shouts of panic. At the end of the runway the Nord, still on one engine, pulled up, the climb getting steeper and steeper until almost vertical. I jumped up from my chair and shouted to the air attaché: 'He's had it!' We stood transfixed as this large aircraft leisurely completed a stall turn, four turns of a spin then finally hit the ground sending up a tall plume of smoke. The accident seemed to occur in slow motion; it was difficult to accept that it was actually happening. I was jolted back to my immediate surroundings by the sounds of women becoming hysterical; some were fainting while others were already stretched out on the ground. It was my first experience of herd behaviour – an astonishing scene.

After a short break came an official decision: the show would go on. What followed was tame by comparison, until the final act: the *pièce de résistance*, a mass drop by French paratroopers. Down they came, great hobnailed boots crashing into the crowd and onto cars in the carparks. One man landed just a few yards from us, demolishing a wattle fence marking the crowd enclosure. What a shambles! The troops had been dropped at least 500 yards the wrong side of the drop zone. As for the Nord pilot, it was rumoured he'd spent time drinking in the VIP tent and invited the celebrated French woman aviator, Maryse Bastié,[173] to accompany his five crew members on their demonstration. All were killed, a tragedy that threw a cloak of gloom over the dinner that evening. We were all glad to leave behind some horrid memories of Lyons when we took to the air the following day.

Around the middle of June Group Headquarters asked whether it would be possible to increase the number of aircraft in the aerobatic team. We didn't know it at the time but a big NATO air display, the first of its kind, was scheduled for the following month. This would be a challenge. The size of the team had been dictated by two factors: the number of squadron pilots with the necessary skills and the need for high manoeuvrability. I aimed to keep the display as close to the public as possible consistent with safety and within the boundaries of the aerodrome where feasible. At times we were only fifty yards from the crowd and fifty feet from the ground. There was only one other pilot on 71 Squadron who might make the grade in time so the search was extended to the other two squadrons.

It came to light that 3 Squadron had been looking at building a team of their own, but not seriously. Well, let's get serious and see what happens – time's short. After a week or so's concentrated practice they tested themselves over the aerodrome. With a little help the prospects of a couple of them making the team looked excellent. One aircraft was taking up an unsightly attitude in rolls because the pilot was using excessive rudder and countering its effect with aileron. Ten minutes in the control tower talking him through the manoeuvre solved the problem. By the end of June I was ready to start working up a 71 Squadron [sic] team of six.

The previous maximum number of Vampires in an aerobatic team had been five. Not only were we breaking fresh ground, we had only five days to prepare. In order to spend maximum time in front of the crowd I decided to start our display as a six then separate into two formations for synchronized formation aerobatics, something that hadn't been tried before. A few days before the NATO display we were visited by our C-in-C, Air Marshal 'Pussy' Foster. Pussy was a dear old English gentleman and a very young member of 54 Squadron during the First World War.[174] He was a kindly man and didn't take much persuading to agree to us painting the aircraft of the two formations in different distinguishing colours, one blue and the other red. It helped that all the command's aircraft would soon be camouflaged, so our flashy colours would be short-lived. We were all set for Brussels.

The Vampire was a good but not ideal display aircraft. Its twin-boom configuration meant that formations lacked the pleasing symmetry of other types like the F-84. Being relatively light, it bounced about in even moderate turbulence. But its main disadvantage was lack of power. I needed sufficient speed for every manoeuvre, especially those in the vertical plane such as loops, yet manoeuvring tended to kill speed during a display. I couldn't offset this problem by using a high power setting. The others needed a considerable reserve to keep station and change formation quickly. All this dictated a maximum speed start to the display with loops entered fast from a long dive. For loops, rolls and wingovers I used elevator trim alone, letting the aircraft fly itself, to give the others a smooth ride. A commentary on what to expect next also helped ease their task.

My habit of using elevator trim threw up a peculiarity of the Vampire. Most aircraft would twist when looped on trim alone. Aileron inputs were invariably necessary to ensure we entered and exited the manoeuvre on the same heading. My conclusion, right or wrong, was that this twisting was due to the gyroscopic effect of the engine compressor and turbine rotating at around 8,000 or 9,000 revolutions a minute. Such were the peculiarities of aerobatics in a Vampire.

We flew to the civil aerodrome at Melsbroek, Brussels, on 11 July 1952 and took part in a full display rehearsal the following day. That same afternoon test pilot David Morgan[175], flying a prototype Supermarine Swift, broke the London to Brussels speed record, setting a time of eighteen minutes twenty-one seconds, an average speed of 667 mph. But he arrived a white-faced and shaken man after experiencing control and compressibility problems – a foretaste of some of the issues that were to lead to the Swift's early demise.[176]

A warm and sunny end to the day found us attending the traditional Ommegang medieval carnival held in Brussels' magnificent Grand Place.

The large cobblestone square was packed with groups of tumblers, jugglers and dancers, all dressed in period costume. Towering above were huge dolls, twirling and dancing to the music of drums, whistles and stringed instruments, all in keeping with the ancient scene. It was a spectacular, jolly and highly entertaining show – one not to be missed and now locked away forever as the happiest of memories.

The weather was fine on the day of the display, which was attended by the king of Belgium, political and service representatives of NATO countries and an estimated 150,000 spectators. David Morgan did speed runs around the aerodrome and Neville Duke[177] did the same in the Hunter, creating the first sonic boom many of us had heard. We started our performance as a six late in the afternoon before splitting into two formations for the synchronized routine. Things were going well but imagine my horror at the top of our second loop when, looking at the other team at the bottom of theirs, I saw the aircraft on each side of the leader, Des Blake, overshoot and sheer away from him. What the hell had happened? He called immediately to say his engine had failed. Swinging straight into our old routine, I carried on as though nothing was amiss and even took a chance by adding an extra manoeuvre we hadn't practised for some time – flying between the other two aircraft from head on. It was an eye-catching risk that worked in our favour because we crossed in front of the VIP dais, just a few feet off the ground. Little did the appreciative crowd know that this was solely by the grace of God and by guesswork.

When Johnnie Johnson arrived at our aircraft to find out what had happened he was faced with a silent and disillusioned group. Later we discovered that Blake's engine problem had been caused by a barostat failure, leaving him with just idling revolutions and very little thrust. Landing the aircraft safely in these conditions was a tribute to his quick reactions and piloting skill. However, the depressing fact remained that all our efforts had come to a somewhat embarrassing end that day. I suspect that Johnnie conveyed our disappointment to the air officer commanding, who left the VIP enclosure to console and congratulate us for turning our misfortune into a partial success. At least we hadn't fallen from grace with the hierarchy.

The reception that evening was a cocktail affair after which Johnnie and many others, including David Morgan and Neville Duke, were in full partying mode, so we all piled into his staff car and set off for an evening's fun. Of the little I remember, Johnnie's frightening driving and car parking stand out. With no obvious spaces he just bumped his way backwards and forwards until the staff car was snugly in place. The floor show passed me by but not the drinks, which were prohibitively expensive. When we left for our hotel at three in the morning we all had to club together to settle the bill, with just enough left for a taxi.

At the end of July our team of six flew to Soesterberg in Holland for a two-day air display at The Hague. This time everything went as planned. Regrettably, it was the last time we flew as a six and prompted these comments in *Aeroplane* magazine:

'But the next item – formation aerobatics by six RAF Vampires of No. 71 Squadron – soon had the crowd on their toes. Three of the Vampires had red fuselages and tailplanes, the others blue; and after racing across the field [in fact we looped] they split into two flights for a flying display in the finest Hendon tradition. Never going far beyond the small grass airfield they looped, rolled and banked in perfect harmony. When blue flight was at the top of a loop, red flight was at the bottom. As blue flight banked vertically past the enclosure in ever tighter circles, red flight was diametrically opposite, as if on the other end of an invisible rotor. The final full throttle shoot up from opposite sides of the field, rocket climb and breakaway made one realise that the Royal Air Force can still produce aerobatic teams to match any others in the world.'

In August we faced the tedium of another three weeks at Sylt, this time punctuated by four days in England. Our aircraft required a small modification at No. 5 MU (Maintenance Unit), Kemble, in Gloucestershire. A refuelling stop at Tangmere en route brought back memories of incidents and friends from long ago. Reflecting on the many changes in my own life since then, I began to feel the war had never taken place. It's a feeling that continued to grow until now it appears almost entirely imagined, as if it happened to another person in another time.

Meanwhile, back at Sylt we learned we were to do another display shortly after our return to Wildenrath. With no aerobatics for over a month we urgently needed a practice so we squeezed in a trip late afternoon on the penultimate day of our attachment. But aerobatics at height were no substitute for practise at low level over an airfield. Halfway through the sortie I called up the control tower to ask if we could 'borrow' the aerodrome for ten minutes. There was little doubt in my mind that the station commander wouldn't object. However, on landing I received a telephone call from an unknown wing commander flying – I wasn't aware that anyone had arrived to fill the appointment – who proceeded to burn my ear off. How dare we carry out aerobatics over the airfield without his permission (which he wouldn't have given anyway)? My apologies and reasons for the practice did nothing to stem the threats of punishments, including court martial, flying down the telephone. We left next morning before I had a chance to meet the man concerned. Nothing ever came of his threats – then. But ten years later a far heavier payment would be subtly extracted.

Although our next display was to be for a relatively small audience, in some ways it was the most interesting of them all – and not without a touch of humour along the way. We were to fly to Schwechat, a small British-operated aerodrome in the Russian sector of Vienna. Two air corridors linked Vienna, a hundred miles or more inside the Russian zone, to the American zone in Germany; no military aircraft from the West had flown along them since the end of the war. When we learned that a couple of months earlier the Russians had twice shot down American fighters that had strayed into their zone, our proposed journey became very interesting.

The route from Wildenrath was to be via the American aerodrome at Neubiberg, just outside Munich, for refuelling; then down the corridor to Schwechat with a change of course near Vienna. Rules for use of the corridor required us to fly at 10,000 feet with 1,000 yards between aircraft. We also had to make radio calls overhead several points along the corridor. Perfect conditions should the Russians wish to make mischief: an undefendable formation with its exact position known every second. Lose our way and step outside the corridor and we would certainly be attacked, and perhaps even when inside it. No wonder the pilot who'd be last in our line of aircraft, nearly two miles back from me, became anxious. The only assurance I could offer was, 'Trust me'.

There was one important instruction missing from the operation order for our flight. We would be carrying long-range tanks, which required either a full load of ammunition or lead ballast to provide the necessary balance. But which? A chat with Johnnie about this oversight produced a typical response: 'I can't advise you on that but I know what I would do.' My answer, 'Yes, and we'll carry it up the spout,' meaning the guns would be ready to fire, was received in silence. A few hours later a signal arrived from command ordering us to carry ballast. The story behind this instruction emerged only later, from a staff officer who'd witnessed a sudden burst of activity in the corridors of power. Concerned about a possible international incident, Johnnie had contacted Group staffs who in turn spoke to Command. Wing Commander Operations was seen to hurry into Group Captain Operations' office. A few minutes later the pair visited SASO. After another short interval what was now a threesome headed off to see the C-in-C. That my thoughts on ammunition had at least sparked some action at senior level was a tale that tickled my twisted sense of humour.

The flight down to Neubiberg on 7 September didn't tax the range of the Vampire but it did tax our abilities. The further we went the lower the cloud and the worse the visibility became. The first the base knew of our arrival was when we crawled into the circuit at 300 feet and requested permission to land. I taxied along behind the 'Follow Me' jeep and on stopping the engine was surprised to find my aircraft surrounded by armed soldiers. A staff car came roaring up as I climbed from the cockpit and out jumped a cigar-chewing colonel who turned out to be the base commander. Without any form of introduction he demanded to know what we were doing on his base and where we'd come from. Had he not received the operation order from my HQ with the flight details? He hadn't. So as briefly as possible, standing there in cold miserable weather, I told him we were on our way to Vienna and why. I explained too that we'd be staging through Neubiberg again on our way back in a few days' time. This seemed to stump him. He rolled the burnt-out stub of his cigar from one side of his mouth to the other for several seconds then revealed that 'the Russians aren't very friendly over there'. I explained that we were fully aware of the situation, whereupon he stuck out a hand, pumped mine a few times and said, 'I wish you the best of luck!' With that and with a screech of tyres he disappeared into the mist.

The entire incident had all the drama of a Hollywood war film, annoying and amusing in equal part. That said, I derived considerable satisfaction from the fact that we'd crept into Neubiberg unaided in rotten weather long after the Americans had cancelled flying. There was no way we could continue our journey that day. But since our request to draw dollars for the trip had been refused, that night we were forced to rely on the generosity of the American transport crew who'd just delivered our ground crew to Schwechat (in a Fairchild Packet if my memory is correct).

Next morning we were on our way to Vienna. Broken cloud at 10,000 feet allowed me to maintain an accurate track down the centre of the corridor. I called Schwechat, as required, about fifty miles out. Up on the air they came immediately to tell me that for the last ten minutes two MiG-15s had been patrolling the aerodrome at 10,000 feet and had just set off in my direction. Well, we were not in any mind, nor our aircraft in any condition to play. The avoiding action was obvious. Knowing the Russian would be monitoring our every word, I thanked Schwechat for the information, emphasising that we too were at 10,000 feet. On went the engine power to maximum cruising and down went the nose of the Vampire into a long dive, all in the knowledge that the three behind me would do exactly the same. A couple of minutes later two MiGs in close formation shot high over the top of us. They hadn't seen us. By the time they'd been alerted and turned round we were all in the circuit at Schwechat. The best the MiGs could do was a high speed low pass as we taxied down the runway.

The weather was bad for the display next day. Cloud cover limited us to rolls and low flying but the small crowd enjoyed themselves and wandered around the aircraft afterwards. Through the British Ambassador in Vienna, Sir Harold Caccia,[178] I learned how we'd come to be there. Earlier, over lunch with Air Chief Marshal Sir John Slessor[179] at the RAF Club, he'd explained that the people in Vienna were complaining that they saw only Russian aircraft and were asking where the RAF was. He suggested that Sir John, as CAS (Chief of the Air Staff), should send some aircraft to Vienna to commemorate Battle of Britain Day and test the Soviet reaction to exercising the right to fly fighter aircraft along the corridor. So there we were, showing the flag and taunting the Russians. We'd become political pawns in an international power game. Truth be told, I wasn't exactly displeased by the role we'd played in this minor test of strength.

That evening we were taken through the Russian zone to a Vienna night club. It was a wet, cold and misty night. Deserted, dimly lit streets with no sign of people or cars and drab black buildings created a grim image of despair. Scenes from Orson Welles' *The Third Man* came to mind and it wouldn't have surprised me if Harry Lime had stepped out from the shadows. The cellar club and bar were as dead as the streets outside and after one quick, tasteless drink our escort took us back to the aerodrome. The return trip to Wildenrath the following day was uneventful and when the Americans arrived with the ground crew we tried to repay them for their kind hospitality with a bottle of whisky each and a crate of beer, at our expense, of course. Once more the prestige of the Royal Air Force was upheld at our personal cost. Sad to say, it was the same almost everywhere we went and often a cause of embarrassment to members of the team.

It wasn't until some weeks later that a copy of Sir Harold Caccia's telegram reporting our visit reached me. Sent to the Foreign Office and copied to the AOC-in-C Germany, the text is below:

On the 9th of September the four Vampire Jet aircraft which had arrived from Germany the previous day, carried out a programme of acrobatic flying over Schwechat aerodrome in commemoration of the 12th Anniversary of the Battle of Britain. In addition to the Acting French High Commissioner and the Deputy United States High Commissioner, members of the Diplomatic Corps and official Austrian guests including the Secretary of State in the Ministry of the Interior, the display was seen by several hundred people from Vienna most of whom had walked nearly two miles to get to the airfield.

2. No Russian representative accepted my invitation to attend. But the Soviet Element did agree to waive all formalities so as to enable United States guests to visit the display without passes. But there has so far been no Soviet reaction: beyond an oral and inaccurate allegation that we had flown outside the corridor on the fly in on September 8th. As was expected, the Communist newspapers, some of which carried a factual report of the display, took the line that this was a provocative military demonstration unwelcome to the Austrian people. There has been no comment in the Russian military newspaper.

3. The whole non-Communist press in Vienna on 10th September carried enthusiastic accounts of the flying despite unfavourable weather and a number of newspapers explained the anniversary and quoted the Prime Minister's words about the debt to the few. My Western colleagues are naturally pleased

that we have stood by our rights for the use of Schwechat airfield and that the Austrians in the Russian Zone have thus been able to see with their own eyes that the Soviet air force is not the only one to be equipped with Jet aircraft.

4. The Vampires returned safely to base without incident on September 10th.

After another display at Wildenrath, during the next four days I flew eight trips over England as a target for a major defence exercise. A week's break preceded yet another major exercise at the beginning of October when Johnnie wheeled along Lord Alexander,[180] then Minister of Defence, to hear my story of the Vienna flight. This quiet, immaculately dressed man in his field marshal's uniform impressed with his dignified attention to what was being said. He had that rare quality of making one feel completely at ease in his presence and it was an honour to shake the hand of this brilliant soldier.

With our final display in October the closed season for aerobatics had arrived and the remainder of the year was taken up with routine training, except for a week's attachment to Florennes in Belgium. As the year came to an end I was asked whether I'd be interested in joining the staff at Sylt next. The possibility horrified me. The thought of giving up my squadron and leaving Wildenrath was more than enough to fret over without throwing Sylt into the mix.

Early in the new year I was back in England for an appointment at Buckingham Palace – the award of an AFC (Air Force Cross). The ceremony was a strange mixture of pomp up front and production behind. The great crocodile queue that wound along passages, around corners and through rooms led finally to a dais where we were to be received. A position close to the tail reflected my relative importance, but standing in front during the hours of queueing was Prosser Hanks.[181] I'd heard of him, of course, but we'd never met. Like Johnnie Walker, his fellow flight commander with No. 1 Squadron in France at the outbreak of the war, he'd previously been a renowned aerobatic pilot. Back of the queue I might have been, but at least I was in distinguished company.

As we shuffled down a long corridor a little man darted from the shadows and with a deft sweep of one hand gaffed the breast of my uniform with a huge forward-facing hook. It was so big that the young Queen could not possibly have missed when the moment came to pin the medal to my chest in what turned out to be a relatively silent procedure. On the way back down a second lengthy corridor another small figure sprang from the shadows. I came to an abrupt halt and in a flash he'd whipped everything from my breast, packaged the medal and handed it over; this was the signal to get moving again. I was left with the impression that these chaps in the corridors must have been pickpockets, so swiftly, silently and skilfully did they perform their tasks.

Back in Germany, with the squadron now at Sylt, I had to find my way there by rail. The journey to Hamburg in an overcrowded carriage brought hostile looks. The RAF uniform was still a hated symbol for the Germans, understandably so given the almost total destruction of Hamburg and the Ruhr just a few years before. This was even more obvious during a slow journey in the stopping train from Hamburg to Sylt. I sat in an uncomfortable old carriage with slatted wooden seats together with four large labourers (miners perhaps?) whose expressions said it all. With my presence a source of anger and irritation, my defence was to sit in dignified silence, ignore them and hope for the best. Thanks to my trip to England I was spared the boredom of Sylt for all but a week. I flew back to Wildenrath at the beginning of March, happy to be with the recent addition to our family: daughter Debbie, born just a few weeks earlier.

The Wildenrath squadrons were now beginning to re-equip with the American Sabre F-86, starting with 3 Squadron. It was a slow process and the few that arrived by the middle of the month were used to set up a Conversion Flight. It would be at least two months before 71 would receive any but I managed to scrounge three trips near the end of March. The Sabre was a jump into a new era of flying and had proved itself against the MiG-15s in Korea, but in my opinion it wasn't suited to the Tactical Air Force role in Europe.

The starting equipment was the size of a small car, cumbersome and difficult to move about by hand. The procedure itself was long and slow by RAF standards, and moderately fast throttle movement sent the engine temperature into the red. It certainly wasn't an aircraft that could be launched into the air at short notice. With warning times of attack coming down to minutes, or even seconds, this was a serious disadvantage. The fuel was gasoline, not kerosene, which increased the risk of fire considerably. And wearing a bulky 'bone dome' cut down visibility to the rear drastically. The Sabre's flying controls also took a little time to master. The control surfaces were hydraulically operated, which meant the control column lacked 'feel'. The ailerons, however, were highly sensitive. It made first take-offs amusing to watch, wings wobbling up and down as pilots fought to keep them level.

The cockpit was full of switches and pop-up fuses, and the flight instruments were peculiarly American. All this unfamiliarity gave the RAF pilot an initial feeling of insecurity, albeit one soon overcome with experience. The Sabre's big boast was that it was supersonic – a claim that contributed nothing to the aircraft's combat effectiveness. This feat could be achieved only in a vertical dive from 40,000 feet on full power and when the control column had become locked solid. On the other hand, flying the Sabre was an experience not to be missed. It was easy to understand why so much of the young blood in the RAF, without war experience, were hooked on these American 'go faster' machines.

Two incidents occurred in April, otherwise a quiet month, that I recall clearly. First, the bane of my life on 72 Squadron in Tunisia arrived at Wildenrath at the beginning of the month. He'd flown Sabres with the Americans, both on exchange in the US and in Korea, and was to run our Sabre Conversion Flight. His attitude towards me was a little different now that we were on equal terms,[182] although it was easy to see he regarded my recent achievements with some disdain. We had little to do with each other, but evidently during the previous ten years he hadn't lost the urge to show he was top dog. Shortly after my departure from Wildenrath he beat up the aerodrome early one morning after a dining-in night. Johnnie had him off the station that afternoon. Word had it that he took a swing at him, whether during the dining-in or after the beat-up wasn't clear. But if the rumour was true it wouldn't have surprised me, given the temperament of the man.

The second event came at the end of the month. My opposite number on 11 Squadron at Wunstorf allowed me to fly one of his recently acquired Venom aircraft. Built by the same company as the Vampire and with a more powerful engine, it was dubbed a 'Vampire with hair on its chest'. No external equipment was needed to start the Venom. It employed a Coffman starter, a cartridge system just like the Mk II Spitfire. Parked at the end of a runway, a Venom could be in the air in fifteen seconds or less – child's play compared with a Sabre. Top speed wasn't as good as the Sabre but better than the Vampire, and unlike its stablemate it could be achieved in level flight rather than by diving. It was less tolerant of rough handling than the Vampire and things could become uncomfortable with the onset of compressibility. But it was a good aircraft, better suited than the Sabre to the type of fighter operations we expected in Europe at the time. Thankfully, neither aircraft was put to the test.

With two quick trips on 12 May 1953, Wildenrath to Gütersloh and back, sadly my flying with 71 Squadron came to an end. It had taken a long time to achieve command of a squadron but it was a gem of an appointment when it finally happened. I couldn't have wished to build and command a better unit, to work with more loyal comrades or to serve with such distinguished and co-operative senior hierarchy. Johnnie, Scotty and all the officers at Wildenrath gave me a grand send-off at my dining-out, and the silver cigarette box presented to me by the officers and airmen is still displayed with pride on my desk. In retrospect, leaving Wildenrath marked the end of my fun time in the RAF, and of my flying career.

My next appointment would be on the staff of HQ Fighter Command, Bentley Priory.

» Chapter 14

THE YEARS OF DISILLUSION

I didn't know it at the time but my posting to Fighter Command HQ would begin a period of disillusionment that was to last the rest of my service life. It would be the source of the odd painful memory thereafter too. So before recording how my subsequent career unfolded, let me try to put these feelings into perspective. The background against which they developed was a simple personal philosophy, a code of conduct based on the belief that striving honestly and selflessly to succeed would bring recognition and appropriate reward. Its origins go back a long way.

My early years were marked by a general disinterest in work, school work in particular. Things changed when I began to develop a competitive urge – possibly from sharing a desk with the brightest boy in the class, the one who earned all the accolades. If he could get to the top, then why not me? It took about a year to knock him off his perch but it turned out to be embarrassing. I'd made my best friend cry, which came as a mild shock – a warning that personal achievements could bring distress to others. But it failed to alert me to the accompanying possibility of bitterness and the damaging consequences that could stem from resentment. Oblivious to such considerations, I remained determined to try harder and do better than others.

It was an approach that certainly paid dividends at college and immediately thereafter in the air force. My simple philosophy did not, however, allow for human interaction. I was about to discover that there were other routes to success, not all of them entirely honourable. I'd had forewarnings of this, of course, in North Africa. But I was still slow to recognise the occasional lack of integrity – possibly because I was reluctant to come to terms with such unexpected failings from fellow officers.

If this was difficult, so was the staff environment – one where logic and practical experience were sometimes given less weight than they deserved, or so it seemed. Add to this the spice of politics and finance, and you have a recipe for subsequent disenchantment. It appeared that in peacetime politics, self-interest and the interests of the party always prevailed over national security.

To be fair, and add balance to these years of labouring in unfamiliar and sometimes unhappy surroundings, there were good times too, and treasured relationships with seniors and juniors alike. But like many, I found it difficult to suppress a cynicism that grew with age, particularly about the system of personal assessment, promotion and appointments. As in the air, luck played a large part in one's survival on the ground.

It's hard to overstate the impact of the sudden jump from the air to the ground. All my previous service had centred on flying – a life full of excitement, enjoyment and freedom. There was a bond then of sincerity, comradeship and respect between pilots sharing a common duty and, particularly in war, a common danger. There was little of this now, and little opportunity to demonstrate tangible results or ability. In the air events moved at pace but on the ground there was a sense of lumbering along on a month-to-month or even year-to-year basis. As for excitement and stimulation, there was none. And the competition that was so much part of my life became a competition of personalities.

Moving from the general to the particular, when Johnnie Johnson back at Wildenrath told me that my posting to Fighter Command was to fill a new appointment in tactical intelligence, misery over leaving 71 Squadron turned to horror. In my experience intelligence posts had been filled by has-beens. The appointment was an insult – it must be a mistake! But it wasn't. So in June 1953, bewildered, annoyed, apprehensive and depressed, I arrived at the headquarters in Stanmore, a north-west London suburb, where I was slated to spend the next two-and-a-half years.

It transpired that new arrangements had been introduced to enable overall control of the UK-based fighter force to be exercised from the Air Defence Operations Centre (ADOC), an underground operations room adjacent to the headquarters. My post was one of five established to organise and run the ADOC. We were also to train other headquarters staff to operate the system on a twenty-four-hour basis in time of emergency. Its purpose was to provide the C-in-C with a picture of the air situation over the whole of the UK and its approaches, thus enabling strategic decisions on the conduct of the battle both in the air and on the ground.

The airspace itself was divided into five sectors, each with its own operations room, fighter aircraft and radar control stations. A sector commander could see the activity only in his own and neighbouring sectors and it was his task to fight the tactical battle in his area of responsibility. In coordinating the activities of the five sectors. the ADOC could reallocate fighters across sectors to reinforce those most threatened by an attack. That said, the fluid nature of the air battle and the speed at which events unfolded would inevitably give rise to control problems that the ADOC would be unable to resolve in timely fashion.

The ADOC staff was headed by Deryck Stapleton,[183] who'd been the station commander at Odiham during much of my time there. Second in command was 'Sam' McHardy,[184] a thrice-decorated New Zealander who had made his mark on Blenheims and later Beaufighters. With no specific task other than to act as Stapleton's stand-in, Sam was far from happy with his lot. Better use could have been made of his operational experience, I felt sure.

A similar situation applied to Dougie Oxby,[185] our signals officer. A little Welshman who captained the command rugby team, Dougie was the top-scoring wartime night-fighter navigator/radar operator and sported four decorations on his chest. Yet all he had to do was make sure our communications worked. What a waste of expertise that could have been fully exploited in the field of crew training. Then there was me trying to make sense of the hostile raid plots during synthetic and live exercises, attempting to decide which were nuclear armed – an impossible task as it turned out. It was also my job to provide a narrative and visual display of air activity for every four-hour period. Finally, the only member of the team employed in a proper service trade was Claire Legge. Known for some reason as 'Sister Anna', she'd started the war as an operations room plotter and knew every detail of the control and reporting system. Many years later she married test pilot Jeffery Quill[186] – back in 1936 he was the second man ever to fly the Spitfire.

It took many months before the various links in the reporting chain that served the ADOC began to function with any degree of reliability. Those of us with an understanding of air fighting and the method by which the air situation was reported didn't have much faith in the ability of the air defence system to cope with the Russian threat at the time. There were far too many manual processes in the reporting chain, giving rise to errors and delays in the picture appearing at the ADOC. No matter what was displayed on the table, it was universally accepted as true – it all looked so convincing.

But confusion could and did occur. For example, filter centres responsible for coordinating plots on a single contact from adjacent radars at different times might identify it as two or more aircraft. And a fighter aircraft could be misidentified as an enemy plot. It took a special skill to sort out such problems. Mistakes could be made, especially under pressure. While the network of telephone cables over which information was exchanged was as secure as possible, it was still vulnerable to disruption, particularly by the electromagnetic pulse produced by nuclear weapons. The magnitude of the devastation this pulse could inflict upon communications and electrically operated services was not fully appreciated until later. Back in the 1950s the most obvious way of disrupting UK air defences was to jam the early warning and fighter control radars; not exactly a simple task but one well within the capability of the Russians. To that end their surveillance aircraft and ships operated up and down the east coast for years monitoring the operation of our air defence radars, often accompanied by RAF fighters sent out to investigate.

The UK's air defence system may have had its faults but it at least complicated the task of an enemy, forcing him to expend money and effort to defeat its mechanisms – or so the argument went. The more complex the defence system, the greater the resource demands on any potential aggressor. To my mind this was a head-in-the-sand outlook. Nothing could camouflage the failings of the UK system if it were put to the ultimate test. With this conviction, with dull and virtually impossible duties to perform, and with no chance of early escape from this soul-destroying predicament, my first six months at Fighter Command were the unhappiest of my service career. Coming immediately after the wonderful years with 71 Squadron, the shock to my morale was that much more severe. Until I finally accepted my fate, it strained relationships with my family too – our misery compounded by having to live in a shoddy little two-up, two-down on the outskirts of St Albans, albeit we managed to escape after about a year there.

Deryck Stapleton was the first to move on after some six months, to be replaced by the most unpleasant man with whom it was ever my misfortune to serve – a Lothario who would unashamedly claim credit for any ADOC successes, even those due to the work of his predecessor. With his qualities and background, JL had no difficulty in climbing the air rank ladder. But then he was a Cranwellian prizewinner – and didn't he let everyone know it.

I did manage one or two interesting escapes from the ADOC during JL's reign. The first was for some six weeks over August and October 1954. JL was on leave and Sam was in charge when somehow it came to our notice that four Shackletons of Coastal Command were to carry out a goodwill flight to Australia, New Zealand and America. After I discussed the delights of such a tour with Sam, to my surprise he raised the matter of getting me on the trip with Dougie Oliver,[187] Group Captain Operations, that same afternoon. Within a day my passage was booked as supernumerary crew on one of the two support Hastings scheduled to accompany the Shackleton. Better still, as supernumerary crew rather than a simple passenger, at airfields along the route I couldn't be replaced by freight, or by those with higher priority. By the time JL returned from leave my trip round the world was signed and sealed.

On arriving at Abingdon in Oxfordshire to join up with the Hastings I discovered that another New Zealander, Mick Ensor, would be on board for a trip home too. I'd never met this much decorated wartime Coastal Command operator but had heard about some of his escapades.[188] He was another who became disillusioned with the RAF and eventually threw in the towel. I ran into him only twice more. In 1964 in the mess at Malta, where we discussed our misgivings about the promotion system, and again some four years later by chance at Euston station; he'd retired three years earlier and was then farming somewhere in Suffolk.

It took the Hastings nine stages and just over fifty-three hours' flying to get from England to New Zealand via the Middle East, India, Ceylon, Singapore, Darwin and Sydney. Most stages ended with overnight stops, a welcome blessing after sitting on a canvas seat in a noisy, unheated aircraft surrounded by boxes of spares and equipment. Thankfully, we two supernumeraries were able to go up front and occasionally sit in comfort and do the flying; it relieved the monotony. Two incidents on the journey out are worthy of mention: the blast of heat, 120°F (49°C), when the doors were opened at Habbaniyah, Iraq, and watching in dismay as the Hastings we'd switched from because of previous unserviceabilities sail past us and disappear into the distance when crossing the Tasman Sea. Our own aircraft had developed an oil leak, which necessitated shutting down an engine. However, we carried on to New Zealand where parents and friends were anxiously waiting to greet us.

We were supposed to spend five days in Auckland before following the Shackletons to Fiji, then home across the Pacific and America. I lost my chance of seeing America when we failed to leave Auckland on time. We supernumeraries had chosen to take the last aircraft to depart. Problems during the run-ups prior to our scheduled midnight take-off led to an engine change that delayed us for sixteen days – time spent with relations and friends. It was three weeks in all before we left Auckland. With no hope of catching up with the Shackletons, we tottered back home along the same outward route. But fate had more problems in store and the Hastings story doesn't end there.

The Australian Air Force base at Darwin was an isolated, lifeless, barren and primitive airfield. After an overnight stop we were keen to leave and got airborne early. As we reached the top of the climb, at about 10,000 feet, I put down my book and peered outside. Against an otherwise clear blue sky, little puffs of white cloud were flashing past the window. I moved forward for a better view, only to find that the white puffs were pouring from a couple of exhaust stubs on the port inner engine. With no signs of any activity in the cockpit I went up front to enquire whether they'd had any engine trouble. They hadn't. But once I persuaded the co-pilot to pop down and take a look he shot off to have it shut down. Then back to Darwin we went with yet another engine change in view. More problems: the dump valves wouldn't work, which meant we couldn't jettison fuel. So to get down to our maximum landing weight we circled the airfield for two-and-a-half hours at low level and high power to burn off the fuel.

Installing a new engine was to keep us at Darwin for five hot, sweaty, boring days and nights. I recall only two incidents from our stay. The barrack blocks were made of wood and fixed high on concrete pillars to prevent attack by termites. A trip to the toilets located underneath at ground level revealed an astonishing site one morning. There, stacked in rows on top of each other, were dozens of frogs, all at eye level perched on the water cistern. For them, it was probably the only water for miles around. The second incident was during our one and only outing, to a hotel on the outskirts of Darwin. As we sat by a swimming pool sipping cool drinks, out strutted a stocky, muscular Australian carrying under one arm a baby of about five months. Without a moment's hesitation he tossed the baby into the middle of the pool. The little mite went down about three feet, struggled to the surface and began to swim. Astonishing!

The rest of the journey was relatively straightforward, though somewhere along the route two army nurses appeared on board, bound for the UK. Keen to impress, the two pilots up front began showing the ladies all the complicated bits of equipment which had to be mastered to keep the Hastings in the air. They even allowed them to sit in the driving seat. The first we in the back knew of this was when we suddenly found ourselves floating about like astronauts in a no-gravity state before being rammed back again onto our backsides. One of the nurses had knocked the flap lever down when getting out of the cockpit seat. Fortunately the lever was lifted before the flaps were bent or torn off.

The trip to New Zealand and back took 119 hours' flying and resulted in my absence from the ADOC for forty-four days. My thanks will always go out to Sam and Dougie Oliver for their support because those happy days with my parents proved to be the last I ever spent with them.

Surprisingly, JL outwardly took my long absence reasonably calmly, remarking only once, rather pointedly, that he wondered what took me so long. I couldn't help but think that he was annoyed at Sam for letting me go. But whether this contributed to the suffering Sam was subjected to later is questionable. Whatever his feelings, he didn't stop me taking a week off for another jolly some eight months later.

With the connivance of the training staff at Fighter Command I managed to scrounge an attachment to the Air Fighting Development Squadron at West Raynham to fly the Hunter aircraft that was just entering RAF service. Few if any at the headquarters at that time had flown a Hunter or knew anything about it. Thus the five-and-a-half hours spent roaring about the Norfolk sky in a supersonic aeroplane did much to bolster my morale and earn a little respect from my contemporaries.

The Hunter was quite a stable aircraft to fly. Its hydraulically operated control surfaces were not as twitchy on the ailerons as the American-built Sabre, and its wide undercarriage made it a delight to land. With the controls in manual, i.e. not hydraulically assisted, it was brutishly heavy to fly, possibly more so than the Sabre, but it went supersonic more easily. Climbs to 50,000 feet and subsequent dives to go supersonic were revealing, though not unexpectedly so. The sky directly overhead was much darker and the horizon lighter than I'd experienced before, and a gentle dive with engine power soon brought up the magic Mach 1 figure. At that speed the control column was immoveable but it gradually returned to life as speed was reduced. There was no buffeting and engine noise was sensed rather than heard. My week at West Raynham was a revitalizing stimulant made all the better by the personal attention provided by a colleague from the Stradishall days. I didn't know it then, but these Hunter trips were to be my last adrenalin-stirring flights – and this despite my later struggles to return to a flying appointment. And I still had a year to serve at the ADOC …

JL was the next of our small staff to leave, during the middle of 1955; in many ways it was a blessing. Earlier in the year I learned that he'd submitted an annual report on Sam which, if it didn't wreck his career certainly put a large black mark on it. An officer from the personnel branch at the headquarters took an unusual risk in passing on some confidential information. JL's annual assessment of Sam had been sufficiently poor for the Air Ministry to suggest it should be treated as 'adverse' and the necessary follow-up procedures taken. This meant that Sam would have to be told formally of his failings and would probably be relieved of his position. My informant seemed to feel that Sam should perhaps be advised who he had as an enemy. This put me in a tricky position. Telling Sam wouldn't rectify matters. It would upset him and possibly provoke a scene with JL, which in turn might involve me and compromise my colleague. Eventually I simply advised Sam that JL was no friend and left things at that. I got the impression that Sam was already aware of the situation. Whatever the truth of the matter, he certainly didn't deserve such criticism.

Poor Sam seemed fated to create the wrong impression, as when all the ADOC staff attended the 1954 Fighter Development Conference at West Raynham. JL stayed there the full three days while the rest of us flew up with Sam in an Anson for a day. In the middle of drinks and a buffet lunch, served in an empty hangar, a white-faced Sister Anna came rushing up to me: 'Quick, get a doctor. Sam's collapsed.' Looking for Sam, I spotted him getting to his feet and rushed over to see how he was. Pale and embarrassed, he began brushing the dust from his uniform and explained to everyone he was fine. It transpired that someone in his circle had been describing a recent medical operation in gory detail, unaware that this bemedaled warrior fainted at the very thought of blood, or the sight of a hypodermic needle. Of course, most of those in the hangar put his fall down to excessive drinking. Thus it took a lot of talking to persuade Sister Anna to join us in the aircraft Sam was flying back that afternoon.

James Leathart,[189] 'the Prof', replaced JL and made for a happier ADOC than did his predecessors. He had a great sense of humour and could see a funny side to everything, even a calamity. The Prof – never did discover how he earned the nickname[190] – was CO of No. 54 Squadron at the beginning of the Battle of Britain. Serving with him then he had two New Zealanders, Al Deere[191] and Colin Gray, who were to survive the war with many a decoration.[192] Earlier, as a flight commander during the fighting in France, the Prof flew a Miles Master trainer across the Channel to pick up 74 Squadron's CO, Squadron Leader 'Droguer' White, who he'd seen carry out a forced-landing at Calais-Marck after being shot down.[193] He was escorted there (albeit not back) by Pilot Officers Al Deere and Johnny Allen[194] in their Spitfires; all three aircraft were lucky to get back to England unscathed, having been set upon by a number of Me 109s (Deere and Allen shot down three and damaged three more). It was a courageous act on the part of the Prof, knowing the risks involved in landing and taking off under the very noses of the Germans. He never spoke of the incident or, indeed, of any other of his experiences.

Sam left in late summer and Dougie shortly after. Sam took over the drone target flight at Llanbedr in Wales, which operated mainly in support of the Cardigan Bay ranges under Aberporth's control. He later moved out to Woomera in Australia. Realising that the RAF held no future for him, he then returned to New Zealand.

I was beginning to feel that the RAF had little room for highly experienced wartime warriors. Dougie, on the other hand, remained hopeful; he still had aspirations and went off to HQ Allied Air Forces Central Europe at Fontainebleau near Paris. For nearly two years I'd shared an office with this clever, cheerful chap who was mainly responsible for making my life at the ADOC tolerable. I was sorry to see him depart. We met again some eleven years later when he was back at Fighter Command HQ, unhappy with his lot. The complete change in him was sad to see. He talked about leaving and going to Canada, which I believe he did shortly after.[195] Expertise in the RAF was by this time shrinking fast and Cranwell reigned supreme. My time to move came when, thanks to the Prof, I found I was to spend 1956 as a student at the RAF Staff College Bracknell, in Berkshire.

Would this be the moment my career turned back in the right direction?

» Chapter 15

THE COURSE AT BRACKNELL

The drive from Watford, where we lived during my last eighteen months at Fighter Command, to the Staff College at Bracknell took a little over an hour one bleak Sunday evening in January 1956. While I was signing the arrivals book an energetic young wing commander came rushing up to ask my name. 'Good,' he said when I told him. 'You're the last. Come and meet the rest in the bar.' The rest turned out to be the other five officers in his syndicate; his name was Neil Cameron.[196]

There were just over a hundred students on the course, divided into syndicates of six, each headed by a member of the Directing Staff. We were shuffled around three times during the year so that each of us shared studies with fifteen other students under three different members of staff. Students were drawn from a wide variety of services and disciplines – from the armed forces of the old Commonwealth countries, the United States Air Force and from the UK Armed Forces and Civil Service. Such breadth of talent made for interesting discussions throughout the year.

With work mostly concentrated on basic grammar and service writing, the first three months were quite boring. But for me, working with Neil made it enjoyable – and at times a little embarrassing. He had a habit of addressing me, fortunately not in front of others, as his 'star pupil'. Even after I changed syndicates he would regularly chat with me, on one occasion asking my opinion on a paper he was hoping to submit to the Royal United Services Institute. I took it as a considerable compliment that he didn't proceed with it. Much to my regret, Neil left the college halfway through the year to command London University Air Squadron, an appointment considered by many to be a dead-end job. However, after a couple of years, and to my pleasant surprise, he moved up, so to speak, to become PSO (personal staff officer) to CAS. We met again during his time at the Air Ministry, after which I lost contact with him for good.

The story may be apocryphal but I heard that, having reached the rank of air commodore, he was advised he had no further career prospects. It was then that an intervention by Defence Secretary Denis Healey apparently occurred. They were known to each other[197] and on hearing Neil was considering leaving the service and taking up the cloth, which he often told me he'd considered, Healey said he would see what he could do. The upshot was that Neil stayed in the RAF and eventually worked his way up to become CAS and then CDS (Chief of the Defence Staff), the UK's highest military post.

There must be a moral to that story. How many officers with the potential to make a major contribution to the excellence of the RAF have been cast aside because they didn't fit comfortably within a managed career system? The evidence of two world wars suggests that it takes time to weed out peacetime commanders misplaced in key appointments. Subjectively, and consistent with my earlier thoughts, I'd argue that the armed forces are better served when commanders are able to select subordinates on the basis of personal knowledge. It was standard practice in the RAF during the Second World War, and shortly thereafter, at all levels of command. Every commander needs around him a team who thinks as he does, has the requisite professional knowledge and upon whom he can rely. There is no question but that comradeship moulded on mutual respect and loyalty is vital for morale and efficiency. A square peg in a round hole is not the fault of that individual, but of the system which put him there.

The average age on our course was older than usual. It was apparently a last attempt to clear the backlog of officers awaiting this important step on the career ladder. The greater age certainly showed in the capacity to consume alcohol, most evident whenever the course went away on visits. The week spent in France and Germany was particularly bad in this respect and rightly earned the worst offenders a reprimand. Not being greatly fond of drinking, the trip gave me a chance to catch up with a few old friends, especially Dougie Oxby in Paris, where we had some pleasant evening meals together.

The course was without a commandant for many months and run by the assistant commandant, a New Zealander by the name of Faville,[198] the officer who'd led the Shackleton world tour. A commandant did eventually arrive, one Denis Barnett,[199] another New Zealander. They seemed to turn up everywhere. He wasn't with us long – whipped away to command RAF forces assigned to the invasion of Egypt when Nasser nationalized the Suez Canal. Denis did, however, come into my life again later, in Cyprus. The resulting international crisis caused a bit of a stir at the college. America was violently opposed to Britain's role in the crisis and US students were withdrawn by their embassy and given a short indoctrination on the attitude they were to adopt towards the British over this Egyptian adventure. It was an unnecessary precaution. When they returned after an absence of several days not one trace of friction arose between us either then or at any time thereafter.

Regrettably, there were a couple of casualties early on in the course. Playing some type of sport was considered to be a tick in a student's character box. 'Doc' Howett, one of four officers from Fighter Command on the course, introduced me to the game of golf, which we played at Wentworth. At our age, rugby was a much crueller test. Like me, 'Tubby' was a member of the college team; he played next to me in the back line and we got to know each other quite well. Outwardly he was a happy chap, always friendly and helpful. The shock to the whole course was, therefore, all the greater when he committed suicide, hanging himself one night in his married quarter. The second loss was a Royal Navy commander, caught by the police one evening in his car in compromising circumstances. Such activity was treated differently in the 1950s, of course.

Only two students on the course eventually made air rank – just. While their elevation to that level came as a surprise, by then it was becoming clear that my ideas on leadership qualities were far from those held by operators of the promotion machinery at the Air Ministry. It was a view borne out by the number of decorated and respected officers on the course who made little progress afterwards – a trend that was becoming par for the RAF course (no pun intended).

The routine of lectures and syndicate work was regularly punctuated by short visits to other service and civilian formations. On one of these outings – a trip to Ventnor on the Isle of Wight to see a demonstration of cliff-scaling by the army – I was pleasantly surprised to meet Billy Whisner, the American from Odiham days. He and Geoff Atherton,[200] an Australian who used to frequent Odiham at the same time, were on the Andover Staff College course. It was good to catch up with the Whisners again and to exchange happy visits at weekends, although we lost contact after 1956. Geoff Atherton, however, continued to pop up in my life every now and then.

The day the course spent at Farnborough has always stood out in my mind too. It was shortly after intensive work there solved the mystery of the Comet airliner crashes. The Comet was the first of the jet airliners. Built by de Havilland, it was a fine-looking aeroplane in its time and had been in operation by BOAC for a year or so when the first major disaster struck: an aircraft was lost in India.[201] Inside a year two more crashed, one near Elba and another near Naples. Most of the Elba aircraft was fished out of the sea[202] – itself a major accomplishment – and taken to Farnborough. Here the accident branch went into hyperactive mode since the Comet stood as an object of pride and a symbol of British engineering ingenuity. Most of the pieces recovered were reassembled on a jig and those that couldn't be positioned on the airframe were placed around the hangar walls.

Outside was a complete Comet fuselage, encased in a tank filled with water. Hydraulic rams had been positioned under the wings to flex them up and down in sequence with changes of water pressure to simulate take-off, climb to altitude, descent and landing. Thus the stresses and strains of a full flight were repeated many times each hour. The whole of our morning at Farnborough was given over to a presentation on the various avenues of thinking thrown up by the Elba wreckage. No sooner did the investigators feel they were on the right track than something would come to light which contradicted their theory. One very tiny clue did, however, begin to make the sequence of events obvious. On the leading edge of the starboard tailplane was the clear imprint of a twelve-sided 'threepenny bit', a coin in circulation at the time. The deduction was that it must have been in the pocket of a passenger hitting the tail with tremendous force. But how had this passenger, and probably others too, come to be out there?

All windows, hatches and doors came under suspicion, as did the breaking up of the fuselage itself. The evidence began to indicate possible failure of a large hatch on top of the fuselage. Had this burst open allowing passengers and bits of cabin furniture to be sucked out? Ideas were firming up on this theory when the water-tank test offered up a conclusion. The fuselage had cracked at a corner of the top hatch and this failure had carried on part-way around the fuselage too. Thus, the sequence of events fell into place. The hatch had broken free, passengers and debris were sucked out, hitting the tail and causing it to break off. The aircraft had then pitched violently nose down, breaking off both wings and the forward part of the fuselage, leaving the wreckage to fall into five main areas in the sea below.

The Comet case became a classic example of accident investigation. No stone had been left unturned in an effort to find the answer to a series of fatal crashes at a critical stage in air transport – the beginning of the jet airliner age. Difficult though it had been to find what lay behind the accidents, the cause came down to a simple design fault. The Comet Mk 1 had square corners to windows and hatches; it's usually these points that become the weakest parts of a material under stress. From then on all Comets were built with rounded corners to fuselage openings.

Besides our away trips we received many visitors to the college which further helped to break the monotony of the syndicate routine. Staffs from the various RAF command headquarters each gave day-long presentations on their responsibilities and activities. Studies with the army and navy each covered a week. During the latter, Lord Louis Mountbatten, personally propped up the bar into the early hours one morning attempting to justify a stronger navy.

The week with the Americans was a laugh from Monday to Friday with a continuous string of jokes. But best remembered was the talk by Chuck Yeager, who in 1947 was the first man to break the sound barrier.[203] He was also a close friend of Billy Whisner and they spent most of their time together the day of his talk at the college. Our other visitors included celebrities from a wide range of disciplines. Even the Archbishop of Canterbury spent a day and a night with us, speaking about the role of the church in modern society and the attitude of the Church of England to war. A group of scientists from the Ministry of Defence, headed by Sir Henry Tizard, lectured too. Previously MoD's chief scientific adviser, Tizard was now scientific adviser to the Defence Research Policy Committee. My question to him seemed to produce a mild reaction – as if asked by an idiot. I'd been swatting up the German V-2 weapon programme in preparation for a short lecture (each student was required to give one to the course) and discovered that the Germans had carried out tests firing rockets from underwater, with some success. Tizard said he knew of these tests but to my question whether we'd followed up on the experiments he simply answered no, rather sarcastically. I sensed unspoken ridicule from many of the course students too. Little did we realise that within a few decades the nuclear deterrent would be carried not by aircraft but by submarines capable of launching missiles underwater.

It seemed that a lethargy in forward thinking and research had already overtaken our scientists and military masters. Indeed, most air force officers at that time felt that the era of ballistic missiles, if it arrived at all, was many decades away, and that bomber aircraft would be around long into the foreseeable future. They were doubtless reflecting the party line. Bomber Command was in the process of re-equipping with three large and expensive V-bombers.[204] The belief that anything that flew had to have a man in it prevailed in such strength and for so long as to seriously impede advances in other defence technologies. It was an attitude, a prejudice that I, and many of my immediate associates, would have to confront in the coming years.

My syndicate director during the second term was a Canadian exchange officer. We weren't exactly compatible. But I got along happily during the last term under the direction of a secretarial branch officer who'd earlier been at Fighter Command with me; the common background helped. During this phase of the course we had to hand in an essay on a military subject of one's own choosing. Mine was titled 'Foundations of Modern Strategy' and examined the interplay of politics, service attitudes and the sciences in military thinking and their consequence for defence. I discovered many years later that it attracted considerable attention amongst the college staff and was a close contender for the Brooke-Popham prize that year. Pity it missed out because such an accolade would have been a handy weapon to counter criticism by an officer I was unfortunate enough to serve under some years later.

It was a pity too that the wartime code-breaking work by Bletchley Park, and the tremendous contribution to victory of the scientific intelligence efforts of Professor R.V. Jones[205] weren't then public knowledge. Both these examples bear out the theme of my essay and illustrate what can be achieved by the pooling of scientific, political and service knowledge, and by the concentration of national purpose and effort. The Manhattan Project – the building of the atomic bomb – was another outstanding example of combined endeavour. Sad to say, and it's a coda in Professor Jones' book, *Most Secret War*,[206] it's a somewhat forlorn hope we might see the lessons of these events pursued further.

As the end of the year approached attention turned to my future employment so I went to see Jimmy Ronald, who I knew from my Wildenrath days. He was now in the postings branch of the Air Ministry and only too willing to accede to my request to return to flying – until his assistant pointed out that it was against policy to have two flying appointments in the same rank. So off I went with the assurance that Jimmy would 'see me right'. When the posting did arrive it was to the operational section of the surface-to-air guided-weapon department at the Air Ministry. The department was under the direction of Chris Hartley,[207] who'd worked for Professor Jones during the war. I learned that he'd asked the college about my suitability for the job and they'd given him the thumbs-up.

The thought of having to spend three years in the 'mad house' didn't appeal, but it was comforting to know that my work would be near to, if not at, the forefront of new technology.

» Chapter 16
THE AIR MINISTRY YEARS

My arrival at the Air Ministry at the beginning of 1957 coincided with 'Splinters' Smallwood[208] taking over the air defence department from Chris Hartley. We were both quite new to the field of air defence and the first month or so was spent visiting the many government research establishments and civilian companies engaged on Bloodhound, the surface-to-air weapon system for which we'd become responsible. These excursions began a working relationship which was to grow into a bond of mutual understanding and respect.

Splinters' recently established department was unique. Complete in its own right, it wasn't part of the operations department, which dealt with the commands, and the guided weapons branch had its own operational requirements staff who were also divorced from the rest of the ministry. The reason for this was that the RAF was entering a completely new and rapidly developing field of defence technology – computers, data handling, radars, explosives, performance envelopes and weapons, all being integrated into a single system. It was important, therefore, that those directly involved on the service side be brought together to function as a unit away from the day-to-day distractions of a command headquarters. And because of the difficulties that would arise when operating fighter aircraft and guided weapons in the same airspace, it was sensible for the fighter branch of the ministry, then dealing with the introduction of the supersonic Lightning, to also be an integral part of the air defence department. This caused some displeasure among the hierarchy at Fighter Command, who considered they should have the lead on air defence, as they had in the past, leaving the Air Ministry to concern itself with political and financial matters and liaison with the Admiralty, War Office and Ministries of Defence and Supply.

That the new department worked wonders during its relatively brief existence is without question. Besides getting Bloodhound deployed and working in record time, it broke new ground in future defence thinking, equipment and in the coordination of technical skills and manual effort. This was because we were eventually able to bypass the Ministry of Supply and establish direct contact with the weapon design authorities, the manufacturers and the scientists within the Air Ministry and the various research establishments. The breadth of knowledge we thus acquired was extensive, simply because the characteristics of Bloodhound meant we had to take into account all possible aspects of the threat: aircraft, ballistic missile and guided-bomb performance, radar-jamming capabilities and countermeasures, nuclear weapons' effects etc. Meanwhile, for light entertainment there were parliamentary questions to be answered and cost-effectiveness studies to be prepared for defence reviews – distractions from what we saw as more important work. Despite our success, the department was later disestablished, possibly reflecting a general RAF prejudice against surface-to-air weapons. But that came after my time.

As one of the slaves in the operations section, there was not one operational or technical aspect of air defence development I did not become involved in during the next three years. Back, though, to the beginning of 1957, when the go-ahead had been given for Bloodhound to be deployed in defence of V-bomber bases and, where possible, the American Thor medium-range ballistic missile sites about to be set up by the RAF. This was a difficult assignment given the number of Bloodhound missiles ordered, about 200, and the demanding criteria for a deployment site, e.g. no obstructions higher than half-a-degree above the horizon, and certainly not in the likely threat direction, and no housing or industrial buildings inside the fall zone of the missile's four solid-fuel booster rockets.

Bloodhound was the first air defence weapon to be designed as a complete system – a means of engaging an enemy aircraft from detection until destruction, from 'blip to bang' in the vernacular. A number of technological firsts enabled the system to function quickly and effectively. The tactical control radar, at the main control centre where aircraft were initially detected and tracked, provided not only the plan position of an aircraft but also its height – determining the latter was previously a slow process involving two radars working separately. Again for the first time, this information could be quickly labelled in the control centre and displayed synthetically on a screen. A good operator could accurately maintain up to fifteen plots at a time. To engage a target, stored data would be sent down a landline to the best placed missile site, which could be up to forty miles away. A missile site had four groups of eight missiles sitting on their launchers with a target illuminating radar and control post associated with each group. Once the illuminating radar and missile locked on to the target, after they compared reflected signals to ensure they were both seeing the same object, the operator in the control post could select one or more missiles to fire. It may seem simple enough now but this was before the introduction of the microchip.

By the middle of 1957 construction of the first Bloodhound sites had begun and attention within the operations section was turning increasingly towards new air defence problems, not least Russian progress with guided weapons. The effort they were putting in to arming their forces with offensive weapons was massive. In October 1957 they startled a world cynical of their scientific progress by putting the first satellite into orbit, Sputnik. While this spurred on American ballistic missile projects and the space programme, bomber diehards in the Air Ministry were focusing attention on what the Russians might be doing to develop a stand-off guided bomb similar to our own Blue Steel.[209] Were they developing such weapons and, if so, how could we defend against it? Down came the question from on high to land on Splinters' desk. His reaction was to set up a working party – the standard Whitehall panacea: experts from research establishments and from within the Air Ministry with me as secretary. It meant drafting the paper on the guided-bomb threat.

The first question which came to mind was why would the Russians want to develop a guided bomb? They had already demonstrated with Sputnik that they were well on the way to a ballistic-missile capability. Moreover, on cost effectiveness grounds alone ballistic missiles had a considerable advantage over a guided-bomb/aircraft combination. Bearing in mind that there was no defence against ballistic missiles other than attacking them at source, the odds clearly lay in favour of the Russians concentrating their efforts on such weapons. The single factor which might change this conclusion was accuracy of delivery. After a good deal of delving it turned out that despite a big difference in their ranges (1,500 miles for a ballistic weapon and 150 for a guided bomb) delivery accuracy was comparable. My first draft paper therefore concluded that a ballistic-missile system had major economic and military advantages over a stand-off bomb; there seemed no reason why the Russians would wish to develop such bombs.

The paper received a hostile reception in the upper echelons of Fighter Command. There was still a struggle going on with the Treasury over financing the Lightning and the command's case would be weakened if there was no threat from stand-off bombs. With a number of working party members sympathetic to the introduction of the new fighter, my paper had to be rewritten on the basis that because the West was developing stand-off bombs the Russians would do likewise. This was a difficult pill to swallow, but at least there was satisfying support from Splinters and the scientific branch in the Air Ministry. My paper also had to conclude that the Lightning had the potential (undefined) to deal with the stand-off guided-bomb threat to the United Kingdom. I did, however, manage to squeeze in that the next generation of surface-to-air guided weapons could provide a good level of defence, depending on the numbers deployed. This paper was yet another case of emotions and personal interests overriding logic. While the Russians never did produce stand-off bombs for operational use, their development and deployment of ballistic missiles became worrisome.

While all this was going on, occasionally I would have to act overnight as Air Ministry duty officer and sleep in the building. The room, with orders on the action to be taken in the event of an emergency, was on the top floor of the building. The gates across the access corridor were locked by a security guard and the door to the room had to be kept locked by the duty officer himself. Contact with the duty civil servant was maintained by telephone; it was his responsibility to handle matters with the press and the public. One was incarcerated in this unfriendly room for nearly fifteen hours, without radio or television, wondering what international crisis might thrust itself down the telephone. The last thing I heard before falling into a deep sleep when on duty one night was the chimes of Big Ben striking midnight. It must have been an hour or two later when there was a thunderous banging on the door. Who the hell could that be, and how the hell had they got through the gate?

It turned out to be the duty teleprinter operator from the signals room. 'Christmas Island is on the line wanting to talk to you. I'm patching them through to the teleprinter across the corridor.' Christmas Island? Was this a joke, a hoax or some kind of security test? I opened the door to see that a message was already coming through. 'Had we any information on an aircraft crash off the coast of Iceland?' Back went my answer: 'No, but will contact Bomber Command operations room and let you know.' A quick telephone call established that a Canberra had crashed into the sea during its approach there. Off went the information to Christmas Island, only to be followed by the next question: 'Had any Canberras landed at Blackbushe?' Bomber Command's confirmation shot off from our teleprinter only to bring another enquiry: 'What was the serial number of the Canberra at Blackbushe?' Again Bomber Command came up trumps. All this back and forth took about three-quarters of an hour, when one single question and answer would have sufficed. However, it all ended amicably with the last question: 'This is Air Marshal Grandy[210] here. Who have I been talking to?' I gave my name and, with some embarrassment, my lowly rank, and since we'd met at Fighter Command I took the liberty of adding, 'Good to be in touch with you again, Sir!'

At the time Grandy was commanding Operation Grapple, the testing of Britain's thermonuclear bomb, so it was easy to deduce that one or both Canberras had classified material for Harwell[211] onboard. What did come as a bit of a surprise that night was how the magic words, Air Ministry duty officer, could spur those in lower formations into action, even if they were of higher rank – and just how quickly a rush of adrenalin could get me thinking clearly on my feet. Those were the days.

And in those days we lived as a family in Lightwater, Surrey. A small motorbike took me four miles to the nearest railway station, from where the stopping train to Waterloo took just under an hour; a ten-minute walk over the Thames finally brought me to the mad house by 0930. The working day was supposed to finish by 1800 but rarely did for me. We were also required to work half days on Saturdays, a practice thankfully abandoned after about a year. My working routine made for a very tiring day and left no time to be a loving part of my family. Even with five-day working it seemed that Friday night's sleep became Monday morning's awakening. When each day brought a bigger pile of files to my desk, the journey to London gave time to wind up for the challenge ahead and the run home a chance to unwind, often half asleep.

The next edict from the upper echelons of aeronautical power to arrive on Splinters' desk, and thence mine as secretary of his working party, was a demand to know 'the type of ground environment required to control fighters and surface-to-air guided weapons'. This task brought me into close contact with the future head of the scientific department at the Air Ministry and with a number of officers at the Royal Radar Establishment (RRE), Malvern, who had close contacts with the defence industry. We'd already kicked this problem around within the department and arrived at a few ideas on what might be required. Even during my days at Fighter Command we'd begun to think of future fighter pilots differently – simply as monitors of automatically controlled interceptions. But now we had the benefit of the best information available, on Lightnings and on present and future surface-to-air weapon performance. RRE personnel, equally well-informed, were the main source of input on future radars, electronic developments and computer capabilities. It took about four months to firm up on a system which, when the paper was published, gripped the air defence protagonists with enthusiasm over its unique, imaginative and progressive ideas, especially the counter-jamming measures.

There was virtually no opposition to the first draft, presented under the code name 'Plan Ahead'. Once the plan was accepted in principle there followed a period of weekly meetings at Malvern to finalize details. This entailed me travelling to the RRE every Monday evening for about six months and returning late the following day. It left even less time to deal with all the other work waiting in the office – a period when the added burden of heading the operations section of the department fell on my shoulders. With only two officers to assist, where previously there had been three, the demanding work would probably have undermined my morale and defeated me had it not been for the knowledge and satisfaction that I was working on the threshold of a new and exciting era in air defence. And doing so alongside some of the best technical brains in Britain, as well as serving under two excellent masters in Splinters Smallwood and 'Zulu' Morris,[212] who backed me in all my work and decisions.

I recall only two incidents from my trips to Malvern, each a lesson in humanity. The first highlighted the benefit of individual specialists grouped together and working as a team. We were examining a counter-jamming method of controlling fighter aircraft using an electronic means of plotting their position with a new version of IFF (Identification Friend or Foe). After the designer of this piece of equipment had given a run-down of its capabilities we, the users, began to ask questions: Could it do this? Could it be made to do that? What if … ? Where this electronic wizard couldn't provide an immediate answer he'd disappear and return later, interrupt any subsequent discussion and proclaim excitedly, 'I've got it. I've got it!' This only led to more questions, so back to the drawing board he went. This scene was enacted at least twice more that evening during our after-supper session. Then, first thing next morning he assured us that he'd cracked the problem. And he had – after working on it all night. We were fortunate to work with such enthusiasts.

The second incident showed how easy it is for highly intelligent people to lose all sense of logical reasoning when a conflict of personalities emerges during discussion. After the head of RRE, a PhD of some repute, had described two radars which the establishment might develop to meet our control needs, he was questioned by the head of the signals department at the Air Ministry, another member of our group. He could be a bit aggressive at times and wanted to know the relative reliability of the gear used for rotating the radar aerial heads. Turning gear unserviceability on existing radars was a sore point at that time with the signals department and the man was determined to press home his point. 'Would the reliability of the two gears be of the same order? Both must have a very high serviceability rate. Failure of either meant failure of the complete control system.' These were questions to which the good doctor could not give specific answers. The more he tried to explain, the more the man from the ministry sensed moral victory and pressed on. As each repeated his point more forcefully, things became more heated and personal until reason no longer prevailed.

This personal conflict had gone on long enough. 'Gentlemen,' I said in a firm voice. All heads turned towards probably the most junior person there. 'Doctor, you said in your presentation that it was planned to use the same turning gear for both types of radar?' He agreed. 'Since the gears should have the same reliability in manufacture any difference in reliability of operation will depend on other factors such as aerial weight, windage and speed of rotation, which at the moment haven't been determined. There's no point of argument.' There was a pregnant pause and a featureless stare from my signals colleague as slowly the message began to sink in. He began to smile, most unusual for him, and said: 'The lad's been listening.' At least the tension had been broken and we were able to get on with the business at hand.

I struck up good friendships with a number of RRE personnel during these regular meetings, which sometimes went on until midnight. Indeed, it was a privilege to work in company with the Malvern staff, many of whom could trace their activities back to the early days of radar, in some cases to experiments with Watson-Watt,[213] the father of British radar. A particularly close friend once remarked that he wondered if all this work we were doing would produce an end result. It turned out that rarely had anything he worked on ever come to fruition, 'except perhaps once', he revealed. He'd been working on an afterglow problem on new PPI (radar) tubes. The spot that marked an aircraft's position didn't glow long enough with sufficient intensity to be useful. The answer was eventually found in a woman's face powder. When sprinkled over the tube it would congregate at an afterglow spot. Clearly, that particular powder carried an electrical charge which caused it to react with the radar display: a temporary solution at a time of emergency. A simple answer to a complex problem seemed such a minor reward for all the years of experimental work carried out by this RRE officer. So much knowledge is acquired by observation, by simple trial and error – and purely by accident.

All this while back at the ministry we were also juggling with possible deployments of successors to the Mk 1 Bloodhound. The missile, and the radars used for homing it to the target, worked on pulse transmissions and had only limited resistance to enemy interference. The Mk 2 model employed a continuous wave transmission which would give it a slightly better range and improved anti-jamming characteristics. On the other hand, the Mk 3 missile was to use a command guidance system – steered in flight by instructions passed to it from the ground – and carry a nuclear warhead; it would also have greater range than its predecessors. Both the Mk 2 and Mk 3 systems required completely different types of radar where development was still in the early test or design stage. With so many unknowns, developing a plan for future deployment and effective control was challenging. But they were exciting times, not least because we were effectively playing with hundreds of millions of tax payers' money – something which helped discourage radical thinking.

Around the beginning of 1959 there was a panic: we needed to survey Singapore and Cyprus for possible deployment sites. Splinters took Singapore and the Cyprus task was assigned to me. The island's emergency had just been resolved and the British had earmarked several sovereign base areas solely for their own military use. The reason for my visit was to ensure there was sufficient suitable space within one of these areas for the deployment of surface-to-air missiles. The signals department at the Air Ministry took advantage of my trip to ask for an assessment of two sites for possible deployment of a new search radar. Only one officer could accompany me and he did a great job in organising the trip in a mad twenty-four-hour rush.

We were pretty tired on reaching Cyprus. Much to our annoyance we were wheeled into a conference room the moment we arrived at HQ Middle East. It seemed that all the staff had been gathered there ready to deal with any and all of our needs, having been alerted only to the urgency of our task. Our requirements were, in fact, very simple: wheels to take us to wherever we wanted to go. The RAF Regiment were detailed for this task and, because one of the places we were to visit was in a remote anti-British area, an armed guard would accompany us. We appreciated the wisdom of this decision when we experienced a surly reception from villagers we passed on our way to the site. However, the half-hour or so we spent there proved a restful and welcome break from the exertions of our journey from London. The view overlooking the blue sea, crashing white on the rocks far below where we were perched, was inspiringly peaceful – a dramatic contrast with the hustle and bustle of London to which we were shortly to return.

Captured as I was by the beauty and isolation of our surroundings, I couldn't resist a compulsion to reflect upon the history of this lovely island, strategically placed at the head of the Mediterranean: a crossroads for generations of civilisations surging around Europe. And now, here we were, the latest representatives of countless races who, over thousands of years, had marched this land – but with weaponry incomprehensible to that of earlier warriors, even those a generation previous. We had little difficulty in making our decisions. Ample area was available, ideally suited for the deployment of Bloodhound. This became obvious from a visual inspection – there was no need for a detailed survey. And siting of the new search radar was equally simple to resolve. Importantly, our report and presentation once back appeared to make everyone in Whitehall happy.

As the year progressed the reputation of the department for progressive thinking and planning grew on the back of new electronic techniques under development by the defence industry and research establishments. A whole new and exciting field of scientific exploration was underway, but the great majority of service personnel were unaware. A reluctance to acknowledge the implications of technical change has prevailed in each of the three services to varying degrees at times.

This much was evident in the strength of RAF opposition to any possible threat to the continued operation of manned aircraft. It was lack of information about technical progress and a natural reluctance to accept change that induced in our comrades a tendency towards hostility regarding the work we were doing on guided weapons. At best we were considered to be not much more than an extension of the old anti-aircraft gun crews. At worst, traitors to the honourable flying traditions of the RAF since, at the time, Fighter Command was about to enter the supersonic era and Bomber Command was equipping with the latest V-bombers. The size and performance of these aircraft made them ideal targets for surface-to-air missiles, which made us uneasy about the emphasis and direction of the RAF's offensive strategy. On the other hand, endless pronouncements from the department that there would always be a role for manned aircraft failed to allay our critics. Nonetheless, our masters at the Air Ministry had begun to wonder and finally asked: 'What measures might be taken to provide a defence against ballistic missiles?'

Again, the task of producing this study fell to me, though most of the thinking this time was done in conjunction with RRE alone. It was feasible to bring down a ballistic missile using, at that time, a nuclear-headed, command-guided Bloodhound. But defending major targets like cities, or providing an effective defence of point targets against saturation missile attack employing decoys and multiple warheads, was neither technically nor financially practicable. The overwhelming advantage lay with the ballistic missile when launched in numbers, and it still does. It takes only one thermonuclear warhead to virtually annihilate a small city. The old adage that the bomber will always get through had at last been fully justified by the ballistic missile.

In the main, 1959 proved a happy year for the department, and for the surface-to-air side especially. The first sites for the operational deployment of Bloodhound were underway; information on the expected performance of the next generations of Bloodhound was to hand; and the pressure of work in the office had dropped almost to routine level. There was now time to look up from the desk and to share interests with my staff and others. As one who shared my office said earlier, he'd never met anyone like me who could cut himself so completely from his surroundings when concentrating. I guess it had become a habit when trying to think through a problem. The work was certainly varied and demanding. It was about this time that I had to update the Air Ministry directive to the C-in-C Fighter Command to include his responsibility for the effective operation of the surface-to-air missiles shortly to be deployed within his command. I was struck by the novelty of a situation where a wing commander gives an order to a C-in-C, despite the edict not going out under my signature.

Then there was the agreement leasing RAF sites to the American forces in the UK to look over. Not much for me on that one, but remembering the difficulties I'd experienced trying to get information on American missile and space programmes prompted me to raise a point. In Splinters' absence I did so with my director. Would it be possible to use the leasing to negotiate the inclusion of RAF personnel in the American space programme? The bewildered look the director gave me reinforced his view that, 'We don't want to get into space, do we?' There was no point in pressing the matter further. But it was a sad reflection on the attitude the RAF of the time adopted to space flight, despite claiming to be a young and visionary service.

Apart from Splinters and myself there had been a complete change of staff in the section since we came. One new arrival, who worked under me for little more than half a year, was later to make Marshal of the Royal Air Force.[214] I never ceased to be surprised by some promotions; they always caused me to wonder whether my own standards were seriously at fault. But there are no memories of why, usually at the end of a week, I found myself in Splinters' office with some minor issue to discuss. Perhaps it was the easing of my workload that made time to help restore a sense of humour those Friday evenings. Conversations that began in a serious vein would rapidly degenerate into a humorous distortion. Our senses of humour were infectiously compatible and before long we would be in speechless hysterics – laughter that once brought the director bursting through the door pleading to be let in on the joke. However, the workload didn't lift for long. An election was coming up the following year and the ministry was under pressure to provide the incoming government with a review of defence plans and expenditure. What started as a slow-paced, routine exercise built up over the next few months until different sizes, shapes and costings of deployments were being called for at the rate of two a week.

Money, not defence, was the driving force behind these exercises. As usual, it wasn't a question of what was necessary and affordable, only of what we were prepared to afford. Clearly, the Ministry of Defence – then separate from the Admiralty, War Office and Air Ministry – was itself on the defensive against the Treasury. My small contribution to the review brought me into contact with the head of the Air Ministry secretariat, a civil servant. I was called to provide a statement on surface-to-air weapons, their deployment and future developments, in the minimum words possible. When I visited his office to hand over my two-and-a-half pages of type he immediately had my sympathy. The whole of the floor was covered with stacks of files, the desk just could not hold any more, and people were passing through as though it was Piccadilly Circus. Pressure of work? My own labours were of midget proportions compared with his. Yet he was so calm, cool and considerate during our discussions. The comings and goings of others didn't distract him for a second. His draft paper, when it arrived on my desk, reduced my own writings to less than a page without losing a single critical point. It was humiliating since it was my firm belief (after several rewrites) that my submission could not be further reduced. Here was a civil servant who certainly had my respect.

Things were still going along smoothly towards the last quarter of the year when the bomb burst. There were to be no further surface-to-air missiles other than those already ordered – about half of what was planned for deployment. Bloodhound was not the only missile affected. Blue Streak – the British ballistic missile then undergoing propulsion-system tests on the Isle of Wight – was also cancelled. Blue Steel, the air-launched missile for Bomber Command, was under close scrutiny too.[215] But by this time, Thor, the American nuclear-armed intermediate-range ballistic missile, was already being deployed in limited numbers in the UK for operation by RAF personnel. [216] In both America and Russia the ballistic missile was beginning to dominate deterrent philosophy, while Britain was plodding along with complete faith in its V-force aircraft – only one of which had neared its expected performance. The bomb which hit us clearly had its origins in the figures thrown up in the defence review and in the never-ending demand by the Treasury to cut defence spending. It was all too easy to conclude that the items to be cut had been decided by service officers and civil servants with little understanding of technical developments and their potential impact on building cost-effective defences. Thankfully, the consequences of these decisions were never tested in a war between the major powers, although they undoubtedly had an inhibiting effect, both scientifically and technically, on British missile and space research.

The announcement terminating further development of certain missiles came at a very unfortunate, indeed uncomfortable time for me. In just a few days I was due to give my regular forty-five-minute lecture to the Air Warfare Course on weapon deployment and future plans. What could I say now to an audience containing many guided-missile sceptics? I couldn't even explain why our plans had fallen from favour. And their cancellation implied that missiles were a proven failure – nothing short of expensive fireworks. For me the lecture was an embarrassing humiliation and contrasted completely with the enthusiastic reception I'd received six months earlier. All credibility in our work had been undermined, a setback that coincided with the time that postings were due, Splinters' as well as mine. It was a sad end to our three years' work at the Air Ministry.

In expectation of my coming move I'd arranged a visit to the Air Secretary's department to discuss my future. The two officers I met were known to me and receptive to my plea to be sent back to flying. My hope was for a Lightning squadron, in my view the only flying appointment worth having then. Splinters had been earmarked as CO of the first operational Bloodhound Wing at Watton in Norfolk. My two friends in the postings branch left shortly after my visit, but true to their word they left instructions for me to be returned to flying. The offer when it came was Javelins. My impression of this aircraft had always been far from favourable. It was a two-seater, a huge and ugly machine. In expressing my disappointment to the postings officer when he telephoned to say what he had in mind, I referred to the Javelin as 'a heap of junk' – a comment brought to Splinters' attention shortly after. During a subsequent exchange of views about my posting he agreed with my assessment of the Javelin and pointed out that for the past three years my work had been concerned with the latest defence technologies. Then, after a moment's hesitation he said: 'Why not come to Watton with me?'

So there it was, the biggest and hardest decision of my Air Ministry tour. To go flying, which I wanted, but in an aircraft which had never appealed to me, or to stay with a friend who was destined for high rank? A few days pondering this tricky dilemma resulted in a decision to stay with Splinters – just. But who can alter the course of fate? Within a couple of weeks of Splinters' fixing our futures the Reaper swung his scythe. A group commander was killed in a flying accident.[217] Chris Hartley, who was in charge of the Bloodhound trials station at North Coates, was promoted to group commander. And Splinters' move was switched to North Coates. This left me flat on my face with no option but to go to Watton without the very reason for my choosing to go there. Nothing could have been worse.

My one and only attempt at controlling my career had ended in disaster. In retrospect it was the start of my downward slide in the air force.

» Chapter 17

THE WING AT WATTON

Watton wasn't a happy station, at least for me. To start with, it was in Signals Command and two types of special reconnaissance aircraft operated from there.[218] The Bloodhound Wing Headquarters and the missile squadron deployed on the station were parented administratively by Watton, although operationally we came under Fighter Command. The other two missile squadrons were located remotely: one on a site parented by a nearby Fighter Command station, the other on (and parented by) a station in Bomber Command. This seemingly muddled arrangement worked reasonably well without much interference from the parenting stations. In Splinters' absence, the new officer appointed to command the wing, together with the operations room staff, weren't due to arrive for several months, so all the problems of set-up fell upon me.

Civilian contractors were still working on the main search radar while others were installing the data-handling equipment in the control building. None of this equipment had yet undergone acceptance trials or been handed over to the RAF. Hence it was improper for me to interfere in any way with the contractors' progress. It was a testing time, trying to work my way harmoniously through RAF problems reliant only on the goodwill of civilian contractors, RRE staff and Ministry of Supply officers, all of whom worked at their own separate pace. There were only two other officers on the wing at the time: the engineering officer, Jim Masters, who had considerable experience with Bloodhound from the firing trials at Woomera, and the signals officer – a reluctant cooperator. It wasn't until many months later that I learned he and his family had been in Kenya at the height of the Mau Mau troubles. Their two-year-old son had been hacked to pieces in the garden by a trusted houseboy. He had every reason to bear a grudge against humanity in general and the air force in particular.

If life was pretty miserable those initial months, there were times subsequently when the outlook became even worse. We weren't particularly popular with the Watton officers, who looked down on us missile operators with the usual contempt, seeing us as interlopers and an administrative burden. Their cooperation was minimal and although my post was *ex officio*, no married quarter was made available for over four months. This meant living in a practically empty mess and travelling a considerable distance to be with my wife and family every second or third weekend. Not a happy situation and a very lonely one. My only mess companion was a Catholic padre, Father O'Brian, who had been at Gütersloh during my time there. Golf was about the only thing we had and enjoyed in common.

The only relief was to bury my head in the work. And there was plenty to do in preparing the RAF's first missile site for operation. There were divisions of responsibility to decide, procedures to write for each individual in the chain of control, orders to prepare detailing the do's and don'ts of working and, above all, the safety measures to be enforced. The last thing I wanted was for a missile full of fuel and explosive to go roaring off accidentally. Despite more than twenty interlocks in the system to prevent a misfire, as a last precaution we always pointed the missiles away from nearby inhabited areas. These were just a few of the issues which had to be resolved without any previous experience to draw on. Fortunately, my prior knowledge of the Bloodhound system, together with Jim Masters' practical experience, enabled us to anticipate problems and get men and machinery working safely in harmony when the time came for the system to go operational. With no help whatsoever we did a good job of breaking entirely new ground for the RAF, for which we received neither thanks nor recognition. Our seniors were ignorant of just how much was involved.

The CO and control personnel arrived in May after completing their six-month training course, but still the contractors hadn't completed their work in the operations room. By this time the data-handling cabinets, which stood about seven feet tall, were spread over an area about thirty yards square. Much of the equipment had to be installed, wired and tested on site, hence the length of time to complete the task. However, Fighter Command had a big exercise coming up and after a bit of fast talking on my part the contractors agreed to let us have access to the control system for a few days. This was an unprecedented and generous gesture by those who would carry the responsibility if we broke anything, and who would face humility if the system failed to function properly because of incomplete testing. The exercise itself was a total success. The system worked perfectly, which caused the contractors' personnel considerable boyish excitement and satisfaction. We, on the other hand, got some much-needed training.

The work at Watton was dull and routine once the wing was up and running. My family had moved into a married quarter at last when, inconveniently, the task of president of the officers' mess committee was lumped on my shoulders for a year. The commandant at Watton, an air commodore, had been angling for some time to pass the chore my way. So besides the routine of running the operations side of the wing, and lecturing the few dignitaries who visited, I had the officers' mess finances and entertainments to deal with in my spare time. I recall the tedium being interrupted only a couple of times. First came the day the wing was open to the press, who spent most of the time probing issues requiring nifty thinking to avoid revealing classified information. Then there was the virtually no notice arrival in my office of Sir John Salmond.[219]

Within the RAF Sir John was held in as much esteem as Lord Trenchard.[220] Officers of his rank never retire and hence he had a flight lieutenant regular officer as his personal assistant. It was a completely informal visit for this living legend of the Royal Flying Corps and early RAF history. The Royal Flying Corps – my boyhood heroes. And here was the man who took command of the RAF after Trenchard left,[221] actually sitting beside me while I described how Bloodhound worked and sketched things out in simple terms and diagrams for him. This tall, slim, erect, white-haired eighty-year-old may have served in a totally different era but he understood exactly what he was being told; he was even able to substitute the correct terms for the simple ones I used to help him understand the missile's control and guidance system. He was most courteous in his quiet acceptance of my underestimation of his knowledge of modern techniques. It was impossible not to be impressed by everything about this man: his bearing, stature and mild manner, quite apart from his outstanding service record. Sir John certainly had my full respect.

As the years at Watton dragged on there was always a worry that an important time in my life was being wasted – a deeply rooted feeling of imprisonment in a service backwater. A sort of punishment, perhaps, for having had the temerity to sit at the centre of air defence strategy when at the Air Ministry? And, yes, for having the impudence to add an order to the Commander-in-Chief Fighter Command's directive. As my two-and-a-half years of purgatory dragged to a close, 'Black' Smith,[222] another New Zealander, brought some light to the end of my tunnel. He'd attended the same college as me but some five years earlier. Our paths didn't cross during the war and we first met when serving together at Fighter Command. Black did well during the Battle of Britain but was best known for his later efforts leading low level precision bombing raids, notably on the prison at Amiens.[223] Now at HQ Signals Command, he often visited Watton and would drop in to see me whenever he did so. On one occasion he walked into my office in a highly agitated state. A pheasant had just smashed the windscreen of his new car, fortunately without injuring him. The news he brought me on the evening of the 1962 summer ball was more propitious. On the previous day he'd been a member of a board convened to agree wing commanders' future appointments. I was to be sent on an exchange posting to Colorado Springs in America. Brilliant! America at last, some twenty-one years after gazing at it across the falls at Niagara.

During the following weeks, while waiting for the news to become official, Barbara and I spent much time working out what needed to be done before and after arriving in America. We'd even decided on the type of car we'd buy. But fate still had some dirty tricks to play. Our hopes were dashed when the posting finally came through: Plans, HQ Middle East, Cyprus. It was becoming impossible to escape to a world away from a planning desk. Well, at least it was an escape. Or was it?

I felt I'd better go out to Cyprus on a quick visit and check the place out; it would give us an idea of what to expect and what arrangements to make for the family. A word with the wing commander flying at Watton next. With a little urging on my part, he decided it was time to do a route check, out to Aden via Malta and Cyprus, bases regularly used by Watton aircraft. He'd drop me off at Cyprus and pick me up when returning a few days later.

We flew out in a Canberra in perfect weather. My arrival on the beautiful island of Cyprus became a nightmare on meeting the man who would be my immediate superior. What had I been doing? Why had it taken so long for me to get there? When I explained that this was only a brief exploratory visit and that my actual arrival date was a month or so away, he became highly agitated and said that he would not allow me to leave. His attitude astounded me, but I made my points firmly. There were still matters at Watton to be attended to and my allegiance was still to Fighter Command. While he began to cool down, he was still angry enough to grab the telephone and start an argument with the postings officer at headquarters: why the delay in my arrival and why wasn't it possible to keep me there? It was a disturbing exhibition that didn't auger well for the future.

Back at Watton during a visit by David Scott-Malden, who was then our group commander, he asked who I'd be working for. He pulled a long face when told, which only made me press him further: 'What's wrong?' He paused, leant closer and said, 'He's an old woman.' Just my luck.

» Chapter 18

CYPRUS

All four of us in the family arrived in Cyprus in the middle of summer 1962. We handed over the cat at Waterloo station to be sent on later and bumbled our way out in an old RAF transport aircraft. The cat travelled out later in a BOAC Comet. When it was thrust on me as a kitten, I was assured by my wife that it wouldn't become an expensive liability!

We were met at Nicosia airport by the secretary of the planning department who'd already organised accommodation for us in a Limassol hotel. He then whipped me out next day to find a house in the town, with the housing officer there to do the financial negotiations. Within an hour we had a nice apartment in a good, quiet area. A married quarter wouldn't become available at the headquarters for some time. This meant catching the RAF bus at the bottom of the road at 0630 hours, to begin work at 0700, and effectively cut us off from evening social events there. A car was therefore a paramount priority, although the one I ordered took several weeks to arrive on the island.

As to my responsibilities – plans – what there were of them were mainly to meet contingencies which might arise in our area of interest: the Middle East theatre. Since this stretched from Malta to Tehran and embraced all the Mediterranean countries in between as well as Arabia, the possible military and political contingencies were enormous. How was one expected to draw up sensible plans when most of the forces needed would have to come from the UK, with the approval of the government? It's one thing to plan when the forces required are available and under command, quite another when there are only hopeful thoughts to work with. No wonder the plans were in a mess. However, my master, he of the hostile reception on my exploratory visit, clearly expected me to create order from chaos in a matter of weeks.

It soon became evident that this officer (a group captain hereafter referred to as CC) really *was* an old woman. He seemed to go out of his way to find fault and criticize my work. It was a blessing when I swapped roles with a colleague in the operations department. I've no idea which of the two group captains involved initiated the move, my guess would be CC, but it pleased me. Then fate struck again when CC himself was moved from plans to operations shortly after. There was to be no escape.

At this point (though unknown to me until six years later) I should mention that CC was the same officer who shouted down the telephone, threatening me with court martial for doing aerobatics over the airfield at Sylt back in 1952. Had he a long and vengeful memory? A Wykehamist MA and a pure academic, he was all theory and little practice. He'd picked up an OBE during his travels but few campaign ribbons and it's doubtful he ever heard a shot fired in anger. Yet he once had the gall scoldingly to express horror at my 'low number of flying hours' and instruct me to, 'get out and do some flying'. This insulting remark truly tested my patience. But restraint held and stopped me from dumping my four logbooks on his desk and informing him that at least every use had been made of *my* flying.

I knew no one in the headquarters apart from Bill Crawford-Compton, but he had no responsibilities on the operations side. My initial impression was that the quality of staff work fell short of the high professional standards in the Air Ministry. However, matters seemed to improve with the turnover of staff. Either that or I was adapting to the new environment. After all, the stint in Cyprus was for three years.

The main reason for the RAF being in Cyprus, apart from adding to the British military presence in the area, was the Canberra bomber force, this both in the context of global strategy and as a contribution to CENTO, the Central Treaty Organisation.[224] There were three squadrons of Canberras based at Akrotiri, each at half strength. Most of the operations staff were concerned with the support of these aircraft. Everything else landed on my desk: radar and associated control-room exercises, Hastings, helicopters and fighter aircraft (at times there were three different types to deal with). I had two squadron leaders to help me, one with a Hastings background and the other fighter experienced. With UK fighter and transport aircraft bidding for exercise time in our airspace, plus our own requirements, coordinating the yearly exercise schedule was demanding enough without the associated need to keep a watching brief on these events when in progress. There was always something new happening to keep our noses to the grindstone, though none of our efforts satisfied CC. Did he have some kind of complex? There was certainly no love lost between us, as a particular incident suggests.

A Hunter aircraft from the UK, on attachment to El Adem in Libya, crashed at Benina near Benghazi. Word had it that the aircraft had caught fire and started to break up in the air. The summer ball was a few days away, so guess who was landed with the job of president of the Board of Inquiry into the accident? I got away to a bad start by ringing up the postings officer and asking why he hadn't had the courtesy to consult me first. This move was referred back immediately to CC, who had me on the carpet for daring to question his decision.

So off I went to El Adem to meet up with the other members of the court, and then on to Benina. It was a Libyan-controlled airfield used by oil company aircraft flying personnel and equipment to wells in the desert. We were met there by Geoff Atherton and Micky Martin, now an air commodore. These two Australians had come out in a great hurry from the UK in response to stories of the Hunter breaking up in mid-air; they were worried that the aircraft might have a serious defect. This was my first meeting with Micky despite him being at Odiham prior to escorting the Vampires across the Atlantic. My memory of him shooting off the end of the runway there in his Mosquito was diplomatically not mentioned. After impressing on me the need for urgency in letting them know what happened, they left for home.

There were three other members on the court: a Hunter pilot, an engineer and a civilian from the Accident Investigation Branch. The latter was a Pole who didn't take long in gathering up sufficient important bits to confirm that all control surfaces and trims had been in their normal settings and that the engine was under power at the time of impact. Under his instructions, most of the aircraft remains had been removed from the crash site before we arrived, but something struck me about it on inspection. To me, the marks on the hard ground indicated that the aircraft had been almost inverted and had hit the ground at about thirty degrees from the horizontal. I needed a second opinion, so I asked the Pole to re-examine the impact marks and advise his findings on the attitude of the aircraft at the time of the crash. He reappeared some hours later and confirmed my opinion exactly.

Taking evidence from witnesses was a bit of a problem. Almost all were Arabs and their evidence was required to be taken on oath. A copy of the Koran was eventually found, to be wrapped to prevent it being touched and to be handled only with the right hand. An interpreter was produced and sworn in. As expected, there was conflict between statements taken, but a common trend began to appear. The pilot of the Hunter had beaten up the airfield at low level and been doing aerobatics when he hit the ground upside down. Earlier, we'd quickly established that the aircraft hadn't broken up in the air and I'd immediately signalled Micky Martin accordingly. Then halfway through the taking of evidence a signal arrived recalling me to Cyprus to report on progress, a very puzzling request. An aircraft arrived to pick me up and a Canberra was waiting at El Adem. What was the rush and why the bother? All was revealed on reaching the headquarters. Bill Crawford-Compton, who was now the SASO, had done my wife and I a kindness by bringing me back for the summer ball. CC didn't say a word; his sour face said it all.

Back at Benina we caught up with the one witness we could trust: an ex-RAF officer who'd been waiting to take off for the oil wells when the Hunter crashed. He'd seen the pilot's whole performance. It was a pity we'd spent so much of our time with less reliable Arab witnesses, but the conclusions were clear. Unauthorised aerobatics over a civilian airfield had ended in a crash while inverted during a slow roll.

The report on our inquiry gave great scope for CC's vindictiveness. Not a thing was right, its composition and length as well as the findings. The sequel, contradicting his opinions, was played out a few weeks later when I again bumped into Micky Martin. He immediately congratulated me on an excellent report and went on to say that his air officer commanding had been 'tickled pink by it'. My plaintive response was to express the wish that he'd tell that to my group captain.

Around this time Johnnie Johnson was serving as AOC RAF Middle East. En route to his headquarters in Aden he stopped off at Cyprus in a V-bomber. Bill Crawford-Compton laid on a dinner at his house and Johnnie brought along some of the beef he was carrying in the Victor's temperature-controlled bomb bay. It was a great evening, full of laughs and good spirit, just like the old days at Wildenrath. Johnnie had to depart Akrotiri at first light and on leaving the party vowed to wake us all in the morning. Sure enough, at 0500 hours the sound of approaching engines made me sit up to look out of the window. There, looming ever larger, was an aircraft at window height. The Victor flashed over the house, all four engines at full power, making a terrific noise. Everything in the house was shaking. Not a soul in the married quarters was left asleep and no one, apart from Bill and myself, saw the funny side of the prank. Certainly not CC, who lived two houses away and was soon on the telephone to the operations room in one of his hopping mad fits. Of course, nothing happened when he found out who it was. Later, when he grumbled about it to me in his office, it gave me much pleasure to explain that those of us at the party had been forewarned and greatly enjoyed the joke. Even the C-in-C dryly remarked to Bill, 'I suppose that was Johnnie'.

The C-in-C was none other than Sir Denis Barnett, from Bracknell, who'd taken over shortly after my arrival. A quiet, reserved fellow, he was to surprise me one morning on the way to work. As my little motor scooter slowly chugged up the steep hill to the headquarters his big black staff car would often sweep past with flags flying. But on this occasion Sir Denis's grinning face, just visible below an RAF cap covered in scrambled egg, suddenly appeared in the rear window – together with a vigorous two-finger salute. I nearly fell off the scooter with laughter.

Lady Barnett was the complete opposite of her husband: a press-on type, always leading the charge. An evening rehearsal in the officers' mess for a formal dinner in honour of the Princess Royal bears this out. A disagreement arose between Lady Barnett and the president of the mess committee on a point of procedure, so she telephoned Sir Denis at their home, Air House, for advice. There was no answer. She then got through to the picket post at the entrance, a little distance from the house. It so happened that the airman who answered the telephone had arrived in Cyprus only a few days earlier and it was his first time on guard duty. Lady B instructed him to go to Air House, wake Sir Denis and have him telephone her at the mess. Wake the C-in-C? The poor chap must have been overawed by this sudden and heavy responsibility. 'Yes Ma'am. But can you tell me where Air House is?' Back blasted Lady B, 'You're guarding the place, you bloody fool!'

The time had come for CC to be on his way. About a week earlier, at a party in my house, I'd spotted him sitting quietly by himself, handling the silver cigarette box presented to me when I left 71 Squadron. He was deep in thought as he studied the inscription.[225] What was going through his mind? Was it the aerobatic incident? Did he remember the squadron's reputation, which at Sylt stood second to none? Or was he conjuring up another reprimand – for accepting a gift contrary to Queen's Regulations? My impression of that incident, and his expression, burnt itself deep into my memory. I've wondered about it ever since. Why had I accepted this man's criticisms and insults without riposte? In the first place, it was difficult not to feel some sympathy because of the flaws in his own character. In the second, nothing I could do would have eased the situation. Any response to his behaviour – satisfying though it would have been – or appeal to higher authority, would probably have made matters worse. And as I discovered six years later, it would have made no difference to my career. In the third place, there was always the hope that more senior officers saw me in a different light. And finally, there was the knowledge that he would soon be on his way, out of my orbit.

'Paddy' Finch,[226] who replaced CC, was a jovial, easy-going Irishman who'd unfortunately been prejudiced against me by CC. Early on, to his embarrassment, I learned he thought that I couldn't write – one of CC's regular criticisms. But later he was shaken when a senior officer began eulogizing my Staff College essay. Paddy's response? 'I don't believe it!' It was noticeable, however, that he approved without alteration all the paperwork I placed in front of him. He spent most of the time sitting in his office puffing on his pipe. Such orders as he gave were always verbal. Frantic calls would occasionally arrive in my office from Akrotiri or Nicosia complaining about them. Paddy knew nothing of the times his instructions were countermanded, leaving me to carry the can if found out. Whenever he went on leave, requiring me to take over, it was no hardship to clear the backlog of thirty or more top secret files locked away in his cabinet. Others were aware of this habit because Bill Crawford-Compton was once heard telling him sharply to 'clear that lot of files' in his cabinet. What was the problem? None was difficult to answer and some could be cleared in a day. But that was Paddy. He probably considered them unimportant, which of course some were.

I've occasionally mused about the nature of courage in these recollections. One of my squadron leaders, Tom Stafford, who looked after the Hastings squadron and other transport aircraft operations, once offered an interesting perspective on what it takes to earn a decoration for bravery. Leaving my office after one of our regular discussions he suddenly turned and said that he could have won a Victoria Cross. My enquiring silence led to further elaboration of this startling claim.

Transport Command was running a trial using a Hastings with two full crews and a doctor on board. Its purpose was to test the physical effect on the crews of keeping the aircraft in the air following a fast refuel and switch of crew after each landing along the route to India. They were on the final leg home after leaving El Adem with Tom and his crew resting. About an hour into the flight a propeller (or a blade) flew off one of the inboard engines, cutting into the fuselage and seriously injuring the navigator. It also cut the elevator controls, leaving only the trim to control the aircraft's climb and descent – a desperate situation. With no parachutes, it would require great skill and enormous luck to land an aircraft successfully in these conditions, and at night too.

Tom said he went forward to see if he could be of any help but the pilot seemed to have things in hand so he left him to carry on. The navigator was in a bad way and being attended by the doctor. What to do? They were in radio contact with Transport Command who could offer no advice or assistance. The options were to ditch in the sea, to try putting down on a long beach somewhere, or attempt a landing at an aerodrome. The advantages lay in favour of the aerodrome and the nearest was Benina. After floating around for some hours they commenced their approach. Tom said that it was during this period he had so much adrenalin surging through his body that he could have carried out any act of bravery without thought of safety; a Victoria Cross would have been there for the taking. The approach was going well until a wing struck an unlit pillbox near the end of the runway and was torn off. The aircraft flipped over and slid down the runway on its back. Tom said it seemed like an age as he hung in the straps upside-down in the dark, although it was only a matter of seconds before he and his companions released themselves and forced their way out onto the tarmac. Fortunately, the aircraft didn't catch fire. But the pilot, co-pilot, navigator and, Tom believed, the doctor all died. A sad story, told not in a boastful way, and one with a moral that was undeniably true.

By the end of 1963, growing friction between the Greek and Turkish communities on the island led to the threat of a Turkish invasion. Our Christmas lunch had just reached the pudding stage when the telephone rang: all staff were now on an emergency footing. Forty-eight hours were to pass before I got back home to the pudding. On top of the usual office work, the headquarters staff were established on twelve-hour watches in the operations room. Sir Denis went to Nicosia to hold Makarios's[227] hand, representing the British government, while Bill Crawford-Compton took charge of the headquarters. Sporadic fighting continued between the Greeks and Turks, with the small contingent of British Army on the island attempting to keep the warring parties apart until, eventually, the United Nations (UN) stepped in. For me, this meant the arrival of Whirlwind helicopters to work with the UN forces. Separately, and a little later, Lightnings and a token Bloodhound element arrived, all adding to my workload.

The need for Lightnings arose in response to the Greek air force flying fighters on reconnaissance flights into Cyprus air space. The prospect of Lightnings arriving sent the technical staff there and the station commander (who'd commanded a Lightning unit in the UK) into fits of protest. While the latter thought it 'impossible to maintain the aircraft in the comparatively primitive operating conditions at Akrotiri,' he had no experience of Tactical Air Force operations, or of the resourcefulness of ground crews working under field conditions. My counter-argument was based on Air Ministry knowledge. One argument for introducing the Lightning was that it would have the capability quickly to reinforce overseas bases. Now was the time to put that claim to the test and for squadrons to learn from the experience of overseas reinforcement and operations. Cyprus was a gentle beginning, and it involved in-flight refuelling. So the Lightnings came and had no difficulties in maintaining serviceability or in operating. Indeed, squadrons vied for the privilege of getting to Cyprus. A few interceptions by Lightnings and the intruders from Greece soon stopped. On one occasion a Greek pilot wasn't aware of a Lightning's presence until he turned and saw it in close formation a few feet away. He reportedly turned for Greece in a great hurry.

Tension on the island was slow to reduce. One was liable to be challenged by armed vigilantes on the road at any time when outside British sovereign base areas. Such was the case one evening when driving to Limassol for a meal. Johnnie Johnson, Bill and Chloe Crawford-Crompton and my wife were in the car when we came to a stop behind a truck with a number of armed civilians surrounding it. Since no one was taking any notice of us, I attempted to move gently round the obstruction, whereupon an individual brandishing an automatic rifle jumped in front of the car, bringing me to a halt. He approached waving the gun at me as I lowered the window. 'You tried to run me down,' he shouted. 'Rubbish,' I replied. He kept on shouting the same accusation but there was no point in replying, so I simply stared at him with disdain. It took him about a minute to realise he wasn't making any impression on us so he decided to wave us on. It was a few months before life for us settled down under the presence of the UN forces, who were expected to be on the island for a short period only. They're still there, adding to the Greek economy.

Life in the office had become more tolerable and there was much on the island to enjoy after work, which during the summer months finished at 1300 hours. There was yacht racing most afternoons, always exhilarating in the consistently fresh winds which made capsizing a regular occurrence. Horses at the riding stables were in constant demand, especially by my two children who spent all their spare time swimming their favourites in the sea bareback. My wife's mount and mine, when together, had a habit of bolting quite uncontrollably. Luckily they would stop when reaching a cliff or ditch, often leaving us on our backsides, staring up at them. Dinner dances at the officers' club were very popular and private parties at someone's married quarter featured at least twice a week. And department beach barbecues, using Turkish cooks from Limassol, were well worth the time and effort spent setting up all the equipment needed for a wonderful evening. In short, off duty we lived a lotus-eating life in a wonderful climate. There was certainly more to life than work.

Our Cyprus location provided ready access to a number of tourist centres rich in Middle Eastern history. On one occasion my wife and I set off for a holiday in Egypt, despite the arrival of a signal from London just a day before, warning against such visits. The arrangements had been made weeks earlier, so we decided to risk the trip. Our arrival at Cairo airport could not have been more welcoming. We were accommodated in one of the best hotels in the bustling city, had an Arab guide to ourselves and every minute of our time was arranged for us.

Our guide had been employed by the British Army during the war, spoke excellent English and had an extensive knowledge of Egyptian history. He was a real asset. There was a trip to Giza with a ride on camels up to the pyramids and the great sphinx; visits to the step pyramid of Djoser at Saqqara, to the burial chamber of a wealthy merchant and to a huge underground excavation of burial chambers for sacred bulls – all under the supervision of our personal guide, with lengthy explanations at each stop. It was the same at the sites of worship in Cairo and at the museum. Here we virtually had the place to ourselves. We were even able to peep behind large canvas drapes and spot a number of mummified bodies lying about on the floor. The most spectacular sight, however, was that of Tutankhamun's mask. A climb to the top floor of the museum culminated in a moment never to be forgotten. There in an alcove stood the glass box holding the mask of gold, glowing brilliantly in the sun. It was breathtaking. The perfection of the workmanship was astonishing. Not a mark could be seen on the mask's finely polished surface. We spent some five minutes or more entirely alone circling this magnificent work of art and symbol of an ancient dynasty.

A move from Cairo to Luxor provided two days full of interest: one at the impressive ruins at Karnak, the other at the Valley of the Kings. Tutankhamun's tomb there was a striking contrast with that of Ramesses. Its entrance and chamber were small and in an excellent state of decoration and content, whereas Ramesses's was huge, all but bare and displayed little of its former splendour. Then on our return to Luxor we viewed the Temple of Hatshepsut and the Colossi of Memnon. Back in Cairo we had an afternoon sailing in our own felucca and an evening meal in the tented Sahara City, watching a floor show by whirling Dervishes. Finally, we spent an entertaining night of son et lumière at Giza with the pyramids and sphinx as lit backdrops to a script of an imagined life in 2500 BC. To me there is a mystic fascination about Egypt. Once back in Cyprus we reflected on an enjoyable week's experiences – at a total cost of about sixty pounds.

I managed two other interesting trips while in Cyprus, the first to a CENTO conference in Tehran. One of our Hastings on a routine run dropped me off, to be met and ushered to a lavish hotel where all the other service nationals were accommodated. There we were briefed on the arrangements the Iranian air force had laid on for us. The Shah was still on the throne with an air force that was American trained and equipped. The programme was mainly social, with only two of the five days set aside for afternoon conferences. Travelling around the city by air force car was hair-raising. Being flown in the big C-130 transport was just as frightening, but the places we visited were well worth the scares. The open-air buffet lunch at a radar site near Tabriz was delightful. It was my first introduction to caviar – it's never tasted the same since – and the barbecued sturgeon steaks were quite wonderful. If this was an example of what it meant to be a representative of the British government, I'd quickly transfer to the diplomatic service!

It was Isfahan next day. The dominating feature over this city was the massive, glazed tile dome of the great mosque,[228] glistening a brilliant dark green in the sunshine. The centuries rolled away as we stood on the wooden balcony provided for potentates and gazed down on the large oval expanse reserved for ceremonial. Then we watched young girls learning the art of carpet making at a school. They sat on wooden planks four tiers high with three or four to a tier, each working independently to a pattern. How the patterns matched perfectly when they came together was a mystery to us. Apparently it took three years to make one carpet, then worth thousands of pounds. The girls were under training even longer, for five years.

Persepolis, near Shiraz and about 400 miles south of Tehran, was on the programme next day, together with a lunch and lecture at the air force base where we landed. Both places were located in a desolate, semi-desert area devoid of growth except for a bit of scrub here and there. It seemed unusual that such a relatively barren site should have been chosen for the building of Persepolis, the ceremonial capital of an empire dating back before 500 BC.[229] The city's splendour and wealth were legendary, as was evident from the remains still standing after the destruction wrought by Alexander the Great and by the ravages of over 2,000 years. Known for its many pillars,[230] what remained standing of these were giants of polished marble, a few with the great gleaming black torso and head of a bull, weighing nearly a ton, still on top. It was an unbelievable sensation, sitting quietly alone amid the evidence of an ancient civilization and watching the miniature figures of my companions appear and disappear as they moved between these massive monuments.

Back at the airfield we were lectured on the operational role of the base by the Iranian pilot in charge of flying. He spoke with an American accent more pronounced than any American I'd ever encountered. They were flying some of the latest American fighter aircraft, of course.[231] The afternoon conferences were dull affairs after the marvels of the previous three days, although the high-speed drives to and from the meetings proved characteristically exciting. Thankful to have survived, I was relieved to enjoy an uneventful airline flight back to Cyprus, via Beirut.

With the Cyprus conflict effectively resolved, relations with the Turkish Air Force were back on track. This resulted in a weekend liaison visit to the HQ at Izmir, a social trip with an archaeological interest once again. Bill Crawford-Compton headed the Cyprus delegation of some half a dozen officers and their wives, and we travelled in Sir Denis's Hastings aircraft. It was lovely weather as we approached the Turkish coast. My wife was sitting in the co-pilot's seat with me standing behind, telling her to gently move the double-handed control column and see how the aircraft responded. She quite enjoyed the quarter-hour experiment and the view of Turkey especially. The evening's official dinner, in formal dress with ladies present, was a colourful if dull occasion. It began and ended with a rather ordinary meal and there was no after-dinner hospitality.

But not so the next day, when the few British and American officers attached to the headquarters took charge of us. They arranged a sandwich lunch, a bus and guide, and escorted us to Ephesus for the day. The guide was an American warrant officer who'd made a study of ancient Greece and had wangled his appointment to the area. He certainly knew his history, which he recited in great detail. At the height of its importance, about 500 BC, Ephesus was second only to Alexandria as a major trading post in the Mediterranean. In those days the sea came right up to the city. Today it can barely be seen in the distance thanks to the gradual silting up of the harbour. But this took nothing away from the pleasure of our leisurely outing.

There was one other formal visit, to the NATO HQ at Naples, but not with my wife. It hardly justifies a mention except for the highlight of the trip, which was to be a tour of Pompeii, organised by the Italians. A bus was provided for the journey and we all climbed aboard with great expectations. But when we got to Pompeii the place was closed, and had been for several days.

The dominating feature of all my trips from Cyprus was the evidence of vandalism and desecration, in particular of historic structures, things of beauty painstakingly assembled over hundreds of years. These scenes of destruction appalled me. I wondered what type of person, what mentality, could commit such barbarous devastation? Then the past came back to mind. We'd tossed bombs at the constructions of earlier generations of Europeans during the war, and we'd done it without a conscience or thought. That's possibly too much of a generalisation, but it becomes easy to blanket the mind from the realities of actions taken in the name of moral righteousness.

As the end of my tour in Cyprus drew near, so the urge and readiness to move on grew, despite the making of new friendships and a reluctance to leave our lotus life existence. By 1964 Sir Thomas Prickett[232] had replaced Sir Denis and had become a member of my yachting syndicate. We sailed a lot together in the fastest boat in the club and whenever he had the helm it became Bill Crawford-Crompton's fanatical aim to beat his C-in-C. As Sir Thomas's crew and mentor, I was equally determined to stop Bill from winning. They were always needle-sharp matches, but never without amusement. Another valued friend was John Manning[233] who took over when Bill moved up and across to the operations side of the headquarters. John just loved my wife's apple pies, something he never failed to mention whenever we met in later times.

Almost all service personnel on the island, regardless of rank, owned cars purchased from new. The RAF, therefore, ran a list of those hoping to have cars flown back to the UK whenever an empty aircraft became available. Quite a number of cars were shifted this way each year, with the customs arrangements at both ends of the flight well organised. I'd reached about fourth from the top when the day came for me to leave. Typical of my luck to miss out. However, Bill and Chloe Crawford-Compton threw a delightful formal party a couple of evenings before our departure. It was typical of the many enjoyable and hilarious times we'd spent with them and others on the island. A cloudless heaven, a warm and gentle breeze and a sea shimmering bright from the light of a large orange moon was the backdrop to a memorable occasion of friendship, hospitality and festivity.

It was a rather silent and thoughtful drive to Famagusta with my wife to catch the drive-on, drive-off Greek ship we'd booked for the start of the journey home. Our children had been sent back to England about a year earlier because of the relatively low standard of education provided by the service schools. The ship was typical of the Greek Mediterranean passenger fleet – modern and attractive from the outside, congested, dirty and slovenly worked on the inside. We did at least have a cabin on deck, giving access to fresh air, but it would accommodate only one of us standing at a time. A large number of travellers were squashed on the deck aft without cover for the whole of the trip. Food was greasy and often inedible, while the car was regularly dowsed with sea water through a porthole on the car deck. The only moments of relief during our journey were at the ports of call: Piraeus, Corfu, Dubrovnik and Venice.

Piraeus gave us the chance to get in to Athens and to walk the Acropolis, there to reflect yet again on the ruthless destruction of the engineering ingenuities of ancient man. That night the ship passed along the Corinth Canal, a late-nineteenth century construction that represented an impressive accomplishment at the time. At Corfu the ship anchored and lowered a boat which ferried us ashore for a bus ride around this lovely little jewel set in a deep blue sea. Then on to Dubrovnik. From where the ship berthed we had only a gloomy view of the medieval wall that surrounds this fortress city. We didn't go ashore. Venice and its approaches were more pleasant. Our ship passed close to the Doge's Palace, providing a good view of the Bridge of Sighs and parts of St Mark's Square. The sights increased our determination to return and see Venice at close quarters. But there was no time to do so then if we were to make our cross-Channel booking after a long drive across Europe. We stopped near the Swiss border, and at an hotel in France which put me off staying there ever again. Next day the cliffs of Dover hove into sight.

Back in England we spent a few days in nearby Folkestone with my wife's parents, awaiting the next phase of my life in the Royal Air Force.

» Chapter 19

A NAVY INTERLUDE

Returning from an overseas appointment was always something of a problem for me – and for my wife. Many of our belongings were in store while more boxes, including most of our clothes, were following along somewhere behind. But the main problem was temporary accommodation. The only relations we had in England were Barbara's elderly parents, who lived in a flat where a few nights' stay was about the best they could manage. The only solution to our immediate need was to apply for a vacant married quarter. A visit to the Air Ministry office dealing with such requests was, therefore, a priority. All the quarters near London and along the south coast, which were my first choices, were occupied. The nearest available was at Honington, a Bomber Command base near Bury St Edmunds in Suffolk. There we moved to await my next appointment, which turned out to be the Senior Officers' War Course at the Royal Naval College Greenwich in two months' time.

Sixty days with nothing to do apart from some recommended reading. At least we could recover our belongings from store since, allowing for the length of the course, we knew we'd be at Honington for at least eight months. The free time did, however, allow me to buy and install a radio and a much-needed heater in the car, to visit a few friends and to buy myself a full set of golf clubs. Barbara arranged riding for herself at a stables near Bury St Edmunds, which later helped her fill the lonely days during my spell at Greenwich.

It was during this time that Bill Crawford-Compton's name hit the newspapers. He was cited as the senior officer who'd flown his car, family and belongings back from Cyprus at public expense. Bill did well to keep his head below the parapet while the flak from the press burst overhead. Certainly he'd moved the family and belongings in the C-in-C's aircraft, which had been lent to him for that purpose, but a movements officer at Akrotiri had blown the whistle on him for jumping the queue with his car and heavy kit. Regrettably, a number of movements officers earned themselves and their branch a bad name for seemingly taking delight in inconveniencing senior officers in this way.

After the longest period of limbo in my air force career, I finally joined the course at Greenwich in September 1965. There were twenty-three of us: ten navy, five RAF, five civil servants and three army. At the time, the RAF didn't recognise the status of the course. A pass was not, therefore, included in the Air Force List as a career qualification like the Joint Services Staff College (JSSC). I felt the war course should have rated higher than the JSSC since the latter catered for foreign students; it therefore operated at a level of security below secret. The war course had no such limitations and could deal with subjects at top secret classification. It seemed to me that the RAF saw it as a holding slot for officers waiting for a suitable vacancy and for others they weren't sure what to do with. It took another ten years before the course was recognised as a career qualification.

The students spanned a wide range of experience in military and associated disciplines. There was a doctor from the Chemical Defence Experimental Establishment (CDEE) at Porton Down which, during the Cold War, was under constant critical attack by the anti-defence brigade.[234] A quiet, reserved individual, never to the fore during discussion or course functions, he became a valuable source of information and explanation during our visit to the establishment halfway through the course. Another notable was a civil servant from the Foreign Office, a Scot. He mixed well with the rest of us and was clearly an intelligent man, but he never spoke of his work or background. This added to his air of mystery and importance.[235]

Then there were two navy officers with interesting backgrounds. Captain Douglas Poynter[236] had been lucky enough to survive taking part in the Great Escape from Stalag Luft III in March 1944.[237] He'd been captured more than three years earlier, in September 1940, after taking part in an attack on shipping in the Trondheim area. The raid was launched from HMS *Furious*, stationed off the Norwegian coast, and comprised six Skuas and twelve Swordfish. Poor weather meant they were unable to locate their targets and only twelve aircraft returned safely. A Skua and five Swordfish, including

Poynter's, got lost and were forced to carry out emergency landings: three in Norway, two in Sweden and one ditching. Regrettably, diplomacy suppressed my curiosity and stopped me pressing him to tell more of this extraordinary tale, despite the friendship struck up between us.

The second navy man, Captain Tony Kidd,[238] was witness to the winning of a Victoria Cross. A submariner, he was the engineer on the *Torbay* when his skipper, Lieutenant AOC-in-C,[239] took her into the shallow waters of Corfu harbour in 'a daring and successful raid';[240] there he attacked several ships before escaping. For this action Tony received the Distinguished Service Order, AOC-in-C the Victoria Cross. AOC-in-C hit the headlines years later after his death when it became publicly known that he was responsible for the gunning of survivors in a lifeboat following another of his sinkings. Tony never spoke about either of these events. While it reached my ears from others on the course that he had been at Corfu, nothing was said, or perhaps then generally known, about the machine-gunning.[241] Pity he never discussed the Corfu incident. He had plenty of opportunity during the weekend runs when he ferried me to and from Honington. I'd have been fascinated to hear his account.

We even had a knighted student on the course. This fact puzzled me when the list of students arrived but there was further enlightenment once the course assembled. It turned out that Sir Peter Anson's knighthood was hereditary. The Ansons had a long history of association with the military, high office in the Royal Navy in particular. It dated back to an admiral in the 1700s who returned to England with proceeds from the sale of a captured Spanish treasure ship worth nearly half a million pounds![242] While there wasn't an Anson at Trafalgar, over the years an impressive number of naval vessels have carried the family name.[243]

Only one of the three army officers had an unusual background, Colonel Kenneth Timbrell.[244] He'd just returned from Saudi Arabia. There he'd been military adviser to King Faisal, although this didn't come to our notice until well into the course. Timbrell was a loner and kept very much to himself. No one seemed to know much about him. But one evening a group of us popped down to a nearby pub and there, sitting by himself in a corner, was Timbrell. After we joined him, primed with a few drinks he warmed to the conversation. In a way he was a bit of a Lawrence of Arabia, well versed in Arab customs and with direct access to the king.

The story I remember from that evening was of how he was woken in the middle of the night and surrounded by armed guards. His first thought was that he was about to be murdered, but all they wanted was for him to dress and go with them to Faisal. The king was with all his top advisers and they questioned Timbrell on what actions he would take to bring off a *coup d'état* in Riyadh. As he said, it was a fast ball to field in the middle of the night when still half asleep. He listed what he thought would be the right moves, including seizing control of the radio station, the police headquarters, military barracks and residences of the royal family. This seemed to satisfy his inquisitors and he was returned to his rooms. Apparently Faisal had heard rumours of a coup and wanted advice on where to deploy his forces in order to forestall any attempt to take over the country. It was the only time we managed to loosen Timbrell's tongue. His knowledge of Arabia must still have been of value, since now and then he would disappear for the day to the Foreign Office or even the War Office. It's surprising what sometimes lies hidden behind an unpretentious facade.

There was a lesser assembly of personalities in the air force contingent. Three only were aircrew, one being the officer who went to Colorado Springs instead of me. There was no doubt that he had a good time, though what he had to say set me wondering whether perhaps it was all fun and little work – more of a diplomatic exchange on the Americans' part? But it would certainly have been exciting to see their country and perhaps have had the opportunity to fly a number of their aircraft.

The course members who 'lived in' were accommodated in a house just outside the side gate leading to the Naval College. These extensive buildings, designed by Sir Christopher Wren, served first as a royal hospital before being taken over by the navy almost 200 years later in 1873. The spacious and solid structure, kept in excellent repair, is now on show to the public, with the Painted Hall as the main attraction.

The hall is impressive, with its two-level marble floor and polished surrounds leading to a ceiling adorned with baroque paintings by Thornhill.[245] It was here, on the upper level, that we took all our meals, the lower floor being used by students on the staff course and others. We dined in the pomp and elegant style of the privileged – the hall was at times used for the banqueting of visiting royalty and government dignitaries. Being accustomed to dining rooms in service messes, it felt almost unnatural eating ordinary meals in such ornate surroundings, the great echoing space of the Painted Hall. As war course officers we also had our own private room, or 'cuddy' in navy parlance, for relaxation. There we could help ourselves to drinks, catch up with the newspapers and magazines or just snooze.

The course was spread over six months with studies and lectures punctuated at regular intervals by visits to service, industrial and commercial establishments. Studies didn't greatly tax our time or intelligence and were mostly done in syndicates. Only the final study, 'The threat to the United Kingdom and forces necessary to combat it,' was a challenge. It took the best part of a morning to persuade the syndicate's thinking away from a Russian military threat to an economic one (British industry was suffering from union disruption at the time). I felt that without an economically secure and financially sound home base it would be impossible to build or operate effective armed forces. Thus convinced, the syndicate was eventually able to hammer out an appropriate defence philosophy.

Lectures by visiting speakers were more interesting and relaxing and covered a wide range of disciplines. There were shadow defence ministers, scientists from the Ministry of Defence and universities, nuclear physicists, including Sir John Cockcroft,[246] economists from the government and the City and so on. There was even a representative from Australia House lecturing on that government's military and domestic policies. I well remember his statement that the distance from one side of Australia to the other was greater than from London to Cairo.

It was the outside visits that provided the real fun. We travelled far and wide, from Portsmouth to Barrow-in-Furness, from Plymouth to the Humber, and to Ireland. A look at the tank museum at Bovington was the highlight of the army week. It was followed by a ride in the latest tank (was it a Centurion?) on the range at Lulworth, where I determined the range of a target vehicle using tracer from the half-inch machine gun; we then blasted it with the first shot from the main armament. But for me the most memorable visit was to Londonderry to observe a NATO maritime exercise.

Submarines had always fascinated me. I'd read every book on them that came within reach with the same enthusiasm as those on flying. I felt that submariners and aircrew had much in common and were motivated by similar traits – a love of excitement, the risk of adventure, surviving and succeeding against the odds and an ability to suppress fear. I'd always wanted to meet members of the underwater race and to get a first-hand experience of submarines.

At Londonderry we had a choice of aircraft, destroyers or a submarine. It was only by exchanging preferences with a navy officer that I realised my ambition. The boat was American, given to NATO and manned by a Dutch crew. She'd been built quite late during the Second World War for long-range operations in the Pacific and was therefore large and roomy. Course members had a free run of the boat, though most of our time was spent alongside the captain at the periscope. To my surprise, we were never detected throughout the day by the three or four destroyers taking part in the exercise, or by the Shackleton aircraft dropping sonar buoys.

Looking through the periscope on high power at the action going on around us gave the impression that it was all happening a few hundred yards away when the distance was more like miles. After carrying out one attack the captain told each of us to take a quick look at the target. Those few seconds are forever imprinted on my memory. The destroyer was head-on, travelling fast in a tight turn and leaning outwards at a steep angle. The sight of great sheets of white water being thrown up either side of the bows, almost as high as the ship's superstructure, was awesome. Through the periscope we looked frighteningly close to a collision.

A quiet spell alone in the engine room was quite enlightening. There, over the almost silent whirr of the electric motors, it was possible to hear and mentally plot the passage of the destroyers on the surface. Occasionally, and for short periods, I could hear the impact of sonar pulses quietly hitting the hull as the searchers groped for us. And I could sense the slightest movement up or down of the submarine by the change in pitch of the floor. Standing there alone with my thoughts, responding to the sounds and movement, my imagination conjured up the stories of submarine warfare I'd read about. Only the sound of propellers overhead and the explosion of depth charges were missing. From fantasy to reality, my association with the undersea navy ended at Barrow-in-Furness, where I was able to go onboard Britain's second nuclear submarine, HMS *Renown*, when she was on the stocks and in the building stage.

A visit to the Houses of Parliament with Tom Harvey was an eye-opener. Tom was an air force man and had a cousin who was a prominent member of the Conservative Party. We were welcomed and entertained with morning tea in the Members' Tea Room. A look in at proceedings in the Commons and the Lords was a shock and a disappointment. Only four or five members were sitting. some asleep, in each House, while a lonely figure was on his feet speaking about some obscure topic with an enthusiasm that matched the interest of his audience. What a way to run a country!

As for entertainment at the college, the Christmas party was a lavish affair. Of all the service functions I'd ever attended, the Greenwich spread was the most luxurious. The quantity and variety of food, and the glittering display of silverware, represented a display of opulence that bettered any Hollywood Roman orgy. There seemed to be more food on offer at the end of the party than at the beginning. As usual, my wife was in constant demand as a dancing partner, mostly by senior officers trying to rekindle that last spark of youth that remains only in the mind. Then, finally, near the end of the course, one of the navy officers organised a farewell evening at an old-time music hall show under the railway arches near Charing Cross. It was just like the real thing – period dress, songs, make-up, moustaches and compering. Only the timescale differed from the original. The attention we as a course received from the stage, and from the audience, all added to the fun of an enjoyable evening.

At this point in my tale I should add that a small nuclear reactor had been installed at the college for the training of personnel manning the new submarines coming into the navy. The local Greenwich paper proudly claimed at the time that the district was the first in Britain to enter the new scientific field of reactors. Jumping ahead seventeen years, after I'd left the air force and was working for Hampshire County Council, I returned to the college for a course on nuclear reactors. The headlines then emblazoned across the local paper were to the effect that Greenwich was 'nuclear free' and proud of it. The newspaper, left-wing councillors too, began to look silly when the attention of the public was drawn to those earlier, forgotten headlines – and to the fact that the college reactor was still working. In reality, there's nuclear radiation everywhere. What hospital could function properly without radioactive isotopes for medical purposes (e.g. sterilization) and machines for radiotherapy?

To continue with events at Greenwich, during my second visit to the college in 1983 there was a coincidence which took me back to my childhood in New Zealand. Back in the early 1930s murders were a very rare occurrence. When they happened they were headline news and the main topic of conversation for weeks. There was a particularly gruesome killing involving two families working adjacent farms about fifty miles south of Auckland. Farmer Bailey shot farmer Lakey and his wife, cut them up, boiled down their remains and fed them to his pigs. After a few days neighbours noticed Lakey's cows hadn't been milked and, failing to find him, they notified the police. Bailey soon became a strong suspect and disappeared; he was believed to be in hiding in Auckland. The alert went out followed by a hue and cry: a murderer was on the loose in the city. Overhearing related conversations was a frightening experience for an eight-year-old. I've never forgotten what it was like going to bed in fear of waking to find a murderer hiding in the room.

But what has this to do with Greenwich? Seated there at breakfast one morning, the other occupant of the table and I were joined by the professor in charge of nuclear studies. Evidently the other two had known each other many years earlier and began to investigate the course of their lives since. During this conversation the professor was asked if he ever returned to the Scilly Isles, at which point my ears fine-tuned to the conversation. A friend of mine in New Zealand and his family had come from there. Had the professor known them? I held my curiosity in abeyance while the conversation continued. It turned out that as a young lad of seventeen he'd been due to go to New Zealand to work on a farm with his uncle, but it didn't happen because his uncle was murdered. The penny finally dropped. The professor's name was Lakey, He looked at me astonished when the words, 'the Lakey-Bailey murder case' slipped from my lips. He hadn't been aware of my citizenship.

Back now to the war course and to the spring of 1966. Our studies were coming to a close and we'd soon learn of our next appointments. It was a similar feeling to the end of school, awaiting exam results. There was a sense of resignation: 'Well, we've had our fun, now for the real-life consequences.' Some of the navy officers were promoted on posting, but they were the only ones. We air force officers were the last to be notified of our new jobs, none of which was cause for excitement. As for me, there would be a wait of several weeks before taking command of the missile station at North Coates. Back to Bloodhound again. My expertise had chained me to a part of the air force seen, incorrectly and unjustly, to be of little importance – as, indeed, were the people serving in it. The one redeeming feature about North Coates was that the only boss there would be me.

It was about this time that Johnnie Johnson retired and to my surprise an invitation arrived to attend his farewell dinner, laid on by 'Bing' Cross,[247] Commander-in-Chief Bomber Command. The evening was at Hendon, a gathering of the elite of Fighter Command wartime pilots. It was probably the last time most of the well-known RAF fighter pilots were assembled together. But typical of Johnnie, his lower-ranked friends were included. In his world loyalty worked down as well as up. It's my belief that he wasn't impressed by the support he was receiving from on high and that this was the main reason for him taking early retirement. Also, by then his mentor, Harry Broadhurst, had left the RAF – as had most, if not all, the other wartime senior officers who knew him intimately. Things were certainly changing. There appeared to be less emphasis now on skill and reputation, more on structuring a peacetime Royal Air Force. It was a situation that so many, like Johnnie, had to struggle against.

Among my own close friends bidding Johnnie farewell were Brian Kingcome, not seen since Biggin days, and Paddy Barthropp, both of whom were out of the air force; Bill Crawford-Compton and Alan Deere each shortly to retire; and Splinters Smallwood, on the verge of becoming an air marshal. Alongside the record of these people my own achievements paled. On the other hand, I hesitate to include Bader's name in the list of those present. Not because he wasn't a friend of mine, and not because I hadn't admired him for flying with tin legs, but because I thought him an arrogant and opinionated egotist. Had Johnnie known my views he would have dropped me as a friend. He held Bader in high esteem, although it was obvious his sentiments weren't reciprocated. Interestingly, something of the real Bader began to emerge for public consumption many years after his death.

Before leaving Greenwich I called the commandant at Manby and a bit of pleading got me attached there for a short flying course to fill the time before reporting to North Coates. It was a good move since Manby was very near North Coates and it opened the door to more flying in the future. The amount of flying and personal attention I received came as a pleasant surprise – a welcome break after many years at a desk, the more so since my presence at Manby was completely unofficial. Flying was under strict financial scrutiny and money for 'joy riding' was no longer available. The time at Manby was like my early training days. I was in the air at least twice a day and often at night. My experience of night flying over England was very limited, done previously in the total darkness of wartime, without a feature in sight. In contrast, a night flight in 1966 over the Midlands was a panoply of twinkling lights as far as the eye could see. Unfortunately, my three weeks of fun flying ended abruptly when my father-in-law died suddenly. He was a kind and wise adviser and his departure cast a shadow of gloom over the family.

And so the time arrived for me to move on to North Coates, although unbeknown to me then, two other appointments had been under consideration. The first was as personal assistant to Alan Deere, who was in charge of a sector in Fighter Command,[248] with a small staff based near Norwich in Norfolk. However, his post was disestablished and with it went my prospective appointment. The second was to the Air Fighting Development Squadron at Binbrook in Lincolnshire, run by another New Zealander, Bill Tacon.[249] It was Bill who told me that this posting was changed on the instructions of the SASO at Fighter Command who put in his own protégé, later killed in a flying accident. Since Binbrook and North Coates were reasonably close, it was no surprise to meet Bill on a number of occasions. What did come as a surprise, however, was his open dislike of the aforesaid SASO who, he considered, had no time for New Zealanders.

If true, the second of these events suggests that the outwardly democratic appointments process may have been less so in practice.[250] But such is life.

» Chapter 20

NORTH COATES

North Coates was a small airfield in an isolated part of Lincolnshire, on the east coast near the mouth of the Humber, ten miles south-east of Grimsby. If one travelled due north from the airfield, first stop would be the North Pole. A winter at North Coates could therefore be hell. During the war it was a Coastal Command airfield operating Beaufighter aircraft on anti-shipping strikes over the North Sea. And it was from here that Sam McHardy, of my time at Fighter Command HQ, flew when he commanded 143 Squadron.

A colleague from Cyprus provided a further link. He'd flown a torpedo bomber[251] mission from the airfield on which his Beaufighter, and three others with him, were all shot down. It was pure luck that he was the only one to survive. His story, which came to light forty years after we first met, was probably typical of numerous other tales of human endurance locked forever in personal memories, far from public knowledge. His aircraft was hit by flak, starting a fire in the starboard engine and wing which destroyed the aircraft's dinghy. He had no option but to ditch and was fortunate that the aircraft didn't flip onto its back, as the Beaufighter was prone to do.

He and his navigator were thrown clear; he in a dazed state, his navigator unconscious. His second stroke of luck was that he'd changed his normal parachute to one with a dinghy pack, as worn by fighter pilots. But he remembered this only when the pack lanyard began to drag on his Mae West. This type of dinghy was quite small, only large enough to support one man in a sitting position. After inflating the dinghy he paddled over to the navigator, still unconscious, and managed to heave him over the narrow end of the dinghy and hang onto him. This he did for the rest of that day, all night (when he could hear the engines of rescue boats but had no means of attracting their attention) and part of the next day. By this time he was so cold and exhausted he couldn't hold his crewman any longer and let him go. He felt sure that the navigator was dead anyway. After another night and day he drifted ashore in Denmark but was unable to move up the beach because of an injury to his leg. This was his third stroke of luck. The beach turned out to be mined.

He was spotted next morning by Germans who cleared a path and rescued him. Following a period in hospital he finished up in Stalag Luft III, where the Great Escape tunnel was discovered just before it was his turn to enter – a fourth piece of good fortune. With a lower number, he might well have become one of the fifty escapees who were shot.

North Coates had a chequered post-war history, including periods under care and maintenance, and had fallen into disrepair when in 1955 it was chosen as the site for the RAF's Bloodhound Mk 2 trials. Its selection was mainly for safety reasons, being both in an isolated area and facing directly out to sea (as well as towards the direction of a probable air attack). It was a one-off, though, and didn't fit the pattern of deployment eventually adopted for Bloodhound. On its revival as a station in 1957 it was commanded by Prof Leathart, of my Fighter Command days; by Chris Hartley, who left the Air Ministry as I arrived there; and then by Splinters Smallwood, following the disastrous attempt to coordinate our moves from the ministry. After Splinters, and completion of the trials, the station was downgraded and commanded by lesser mortals.

When I arrived in 1967 there was to be no gentle handing over of the reins and gradual easing into the seat of power. The AOC's annual inspection was due within three weeks but no preparations had been made. The importance and urgency of the event had me searching out every nook and cranny on the station, getting to know those in charge and tasking them with righting any wrongs. Checking everything out with them again and again was only marginally more popular than my parades and marching drills. However, all went well on the day and the station got a good report from the inspecting officer, who happened to be my wife's apple pie-loving friend from Cyprus, John Manning. Was it my efforts or the pies which influenced the report?

John was an enormous help to me and to North Coates. He would readily open the command's public purse to provide much-needed improvements to the station – demands which were always kept within reason. I was able to show willing by building a small church at little cost under the guidance of my works department officer and using volunteer labour. The C of E padre, who was a civilian and the village vicar, provided all the internal fittings from church sources. He even had the Bishop of Lincoln open and bless the church, though the bishop's day was not without mishap; he dropped his plate of food all over the mess carpet. Besides the padre, the station was also served by the local doctor, who attended the medical centre twice a week or when called. Indeed, the station had excellent relations with the local community. We organised fetes, raised funds for the village and were twinned with the nearby town of Cleethorpes for ceremonial purposes. There was rarely a mess function without some local dignitary being present, often with a brace of pheasants for me. Fortunately, in those days we had help: a full-time batman to take care of such gifts, manage our seven-bedroom married quarter and serve at the obligatory dinners expected of an officer in my position – events which my wife always hosted stunningly. I was a lucky man.

The office duties at North Coates were far from exciting. If ever work was routine, then it certainly was for me there. The only virtue of the work habit, if there is one, and of being your own master is that pleasures such as holidays become matters of personal choice. For the first time in my service life it was possible to disappear on travels, usually to the continent, for reasonably long periods with my family. Even so, at no time was I able to take the full quota of my annual leave entitlement. As station commander, I was on duty twenty-four-hours-a-day every day when not on leave.

Initially, I was offered a flight once a month at Manby. But eventually this avenue of diversion from the office was closed off on financial grounds; my sorties were non-productive and offered no value apparently. There was, though, one interesting break: a trip to an oil rig in the North Sea. It was arranged with the rig's BP manager. He controlled operations from a hut in a field near the station, from where helicopters ferried crews and supplies to and from the rig. Oilfields in the North Sea were then in the early stages of exploitation but it came as a surprise to see the massive size of these platform structures, albeit the concentration of rigs in that particular field was quite small compared with some others.

North Coates was small too. An insignificant unit, or so most of the air force thought, tucked out of sight in a remote part of England. But we did have a few notables on strength. There was the airman who for several years carried off first prize in the inter-services cooking competitions – a great asset when it came to mess functions, needless to say. One of the guard dogs was also a service champion and we had an engineering officer with an unusual claim to fame: involvement in the 1968 London to Sydney marathon. The winning car was a works Hillman Hunter which had been stripped out and strengthened for the purpose. It looked like an ordinary car from the outside but inside it was just a mass of criss-cross tubes.

The isolated position of the station, its proximity to the North Sea and the weather combined to cause some anxious moments at times. The land on which the missiles were sited, together with all the living and administrative accommodation, was below high-water level and protected from the sea by an earth wall. As a safety measure, the station was included in the East Coast Flood Warning Scheme set up after the serious flooding in 1953. A combination of strong north winds and a tidal surge up the Channel could lead to unusually high tides in the lower part of the North Sea, which is what happened then.[252] This phenomenon was partly the reason for the construction of the Thames Barrier protecting London. But why the worst flood alerts always came at night was a puzzle. I pondered this while sitting freezing in the early morning hours watching the tide creep ever higher up the sea wall. Fortunately, in my time the highest tide reached just under a foot below the lowest part of the wall, saving me from giving the order to the surrounding company of duty officers and police to evacuate the station.

One February there was a severe fall of snow which cut the station off for over a week. All went well until a wife ran out of vital medication. My solution was to call in the physical training sergeant, whose hobby was running survival courses in Scotland, and instruct him to get his skis and go cross-country to the nearest pharmacy, some ten miles away. He was there and back in a few hours despite the poor visibility and onset of darkness. It was incidents such as these that relieved the monotony of life at North Coates, albeit rarely.

There were also moments of personal pleasure, as when Sir Frederick Rosier, Commander-in-Chief Fighter Command, dropped by. He'd been in charge of the squadrons at Selsey over the D-Day period. For some reason he seemed to enjoy my company. Often on his trips elsewhere he would arrive in his personal aircraft for a chat and a 'cuppa'. It was never shop talk, rather some recent event he'd experienced or a new procedure which was contrary to the common sense practice of earlier flying days.

Sir Fred had that rare gift of making his juniors feel important, although he once nearly caused me much embarrassment. It was during a dinner dance for station commanders at Fighter Command where my wife and I were being hosted by a colleague from the Wildenrath days. I suddenly felt the impact of a changed air force when entering a room where a lot of young officers, most of them senior to me, were with their partners on the dance floor. They were all strangers, a startling realisation that prompted me to enquire of my host, 'Who are all these people? I know more people hanging on the wall here than on the dance floor.' My host went straight to Sir Fred and repeated my comment. He obviously thought it a huge joke and when all were present at the dining table he turned and waved in my direction announcing, 'Do you know what this fellow said?' The look of embarrassed astonishment on my face stopped him from continuing, which was a great relief. That said, my remarks were a true reflection of my inner feelings. The air force was no longer the one I'd known and respected. This change was rammed home to me more strongly by two subsequent events.

The first came in 1968 with the demise of Fighter Command. The shrinking air force, brought about primarily by the massive and ever-increasing cost of aircraft and a withering defence budget, pressured the fighting arms of the service, both Fighter and Bomber Commands, to combine into a new organisation, Strike Command. The cost savings in personnel could only have been minimal, but the blow to morale of wartime personnel, and to the prestige of the nation, with the passing of two historic commands – commands that had made a major contribution to the winning of the Second World War, and at great sacrifice – was soul destroying.

It was left to dear old Sir Fred to preside over a lunch attended by a huge gathering of past and present fighter notables to mark the death throes of the command. The closing address was given by Sir Sholto Douglas, the man who'd come to Biggin Hill in 1942 to ask what we wanted in our Spitfires. He was now very old, crippled and in a wheelchair. His voice echoed feeble and wavering over the speaker system, like that of a ghost whispering of days of glory long past. 'Why had this terrible decision been taken to give up the name

Fighter Command and blot from memory a glorious part of British history?' It was a sad and mournful cry, almost from the grave, for salvation. It had Sister Anna, who was sitting a little distance away from me on the opposite side of the table, dabbing away at the tears pouring down her face all the while.

As to the table plan, my wife had been agonizing over being seated alongside Douglas Bader. She need not have worried. He'd moved himself to a table of more importance. There was, of course, the usual press call for photos and it was surprising that the gathering of Battle of Britain pilots comprised only Johnnie Johnson, Peter Townsend[253], Alan Deere, Bob Stanford Tuck[254], Douglas Bader and, of course, Sir Fred. Five of these were now civilians.

Then in 1969 came a gathering of station commanders at the new Strike Command HQ. There was the usual movement to the bar after dinner, where I was catching up with another old comrade from Wildenrath days, now an air vice-marshal, when two young group captain products of the post-war air force came bouncing up to us and butted in. They hesitated for a moment, wondering perhaps if they'd been discourteous, then forced on with their intrusion. Seeing they outranked me – that was the clear impression I gained – they pressed on and asked my companion to arbitrate on some facile disagreement. Being pushed aside was an insult difficult to bear and I departed the fray. But it drove home what had been happening to me, and to the air force. I was no longer important or needed. In fact I was in the way and being brushed aside on the career ladder. Let's face it; my time was up.

The situation was such that unless promoted, my service career would end at age forty-seven. It was time for the air force to spell out my future and to this end John Manning arranged a visit to the Air Secretary's department for me. The interview was with an air commodore who gave me the impression that his service days were numbered too. He made it clear that promotion was out of the question and that all my years of ambition and striving would soon terminate. He did add with some sympathy that when I was in Cyprus a report had been submitted which, in his words, 'was so unlike you that it had to be set aside'. Taken aback by his remark, regrettably I missed the opportunity to explore his statement further. If it was so unlike me, then what credibility had been given to it when my promotion was under consideration?[255] And who had submitted the report? My bet was the 'old woman', CC. So there it was. I'd been shot down at last.

Not only shot down but wounded – financially. Although I was granted a few extra weeks' service to round up the years accountable for my pension, more than two years' war service before the age of twenty-one counted for nothing in this respect. Moreover, the substantial service pay and pension increases then in prospect – they would have added roughly a third to my pension – were not implemented until six months after I retired in August 1969. Given the bitterness I felt over my discharge, this was a difficult pill to swallow. While many others fared much worse, finding myself effectively on the employment scrapheap without civilian qualifications and at a certain age was demoralizing, particularly for an ambitious and conscientious soul. Sadly, it happened far too often to those who served at a time of national need; they left quietly but with burning hurt. Why was this? Parsimony on the government's part, or perhaps the need to shape a new air force? Whatever the reasons, many good men of irreplaceable experience and skill left the RAF with a grievance – great servants of their country yet discarded.

It may be stretching a point, but there's a parallel here with Winston Churchill's rejection by the electorate in 1945. Small comfort that it took the great man considerably longer to secure worthwhile employment thereafter. It was still a year before I found a job as an officer in local government. But that's another story, one best left untold.

» Chapter 21
REFLECTIONS

On reflection, I should be honest and admit that I enjoyed my war. I should admit, too, that I wasn't prepared for the armistice and felt disappointed and lost when the war ended. I'd joined the air force with a spirit of adventure and a head full of ambition. Aeroplanes and flying were my inspiration. Twenty-eight years later I left feeling lost. Worse still, I was disillusioned, bitter and felt betrayed – a failure.

The humiliation of standing in a queue with the unemployed, collecting the dole each week, was unbearable. My spirit was broken and on occasions I wept in despair. Even after all these years I still feel a bitterness when I recall the silent suffering to which my family and I were subjected following my rejection by the Royal Air Force. That many others had been similarly treated, more harshly in some cases, was no compensation. The suffering was all the more painful knowing that less able, less experienced colleagues still serving were scaling the promotion ladder – and would continue to do so until age fifty-five, when far better pension rewards awaited. My only consoling thought, if it could be construed as such, was that I'd achieved more and done better than most of those who, like me, had rejoined the air force during its post-war expansion. I've often wondered, somewhat uncharitably, whether the service's need for us then meant that we were never intended to have normal career prospects. Who knows?

Looking back, I can see now an RAF focussed on the post-war regeneration of its officer cadre. It seemed no longer a fighting service. There remained an element of elitism but it appeared focussed on the college at Cranwell and its product. But for those, like me, who'd given their all, there seemed to be a deficit in loyalty – the ingredient which holds a proud, efficient and effective fighting formation together. Loyalty to the RAF per se was demanded and given unreservedly but my experience suggests that it wasn't fully reciprocated. The upper echelons of the service seemed to concentrate their energies on impersonal aspects such as politics, finance, materiel, plans and operations. They seemed less concerned with loyalty to the people who were the backbone of the service. I well remember Johnnie Johnson telling me that when he made up his mind to retire he thought it courteous to first tell the Chief of the Air Staff. Approaching him during an interval at a meeting, he was effectively rebuffed. Johnnie was fuming with anger. Years of service, of loyalty, dismissed with just a nod. There was no comment; he'd been heard and dismissed.

After retirement I turned my back on the Royal Air Force and never participated in any of its functions or affairs. But I was always honoured to be with erstwhile comrades in arms and to call them my friends. Glancing now at old photographs, I'm shocked by the number who didn't survive. Was their sacrifice worthwhile? Too often, perhaps, I'm tempted to think not. But most of all I think how very fortunate I was to get through it all, deeply thankful that my name isn't among those listed on an RAF wartime memorial somewhere.

EPILOGUE

It seems somehow fitting that as he neared the end of his life, Owen Hardy should receive further recognition for his RAF exploits. In 2016 he became a *Chevalier* of the *Légion d'Honneur*. In a private ceremony at his Portsmouth home, he was presented with the highest French order of merit, in recognition of his services to that country during the Second World War.

The following year came another memorable experience. To celebrate his ninety-fifth birthday he once again climbed into the cockpit of a Spitfire, albeit his flight on 31 July 2017 was in a two-seater – unheard of in his day, of course. 'Every flight in a Spit is a thrill. But after seventy years, the one I had on my birthday was just a bit more exhilarating,' he said. 'It was just like going back and being in the office again really, everything was so familiar.'

On his flight with the Boultbee Flight Academy[256] from Goodwood, flying alongside Owen in another aircraft was a fellow New Zealander, Auckland-born Flight Lieutenant Emmet Cox, at the time a pilot with the Red Arrows. The fact that 72 Squadron was celebrating its centenary at the time added further poignancy to a very special occasion.

This would be the last entry in the logbook of Owen Hardy's long and remarkable life; he lived just long enough to see in the new year.

Black Robertson

SPITFIRE CLAIMS — 72 SQUADRON

DATE	AIRCRAFT	LOCATION
4 May 1942	Me 109 — half share, confirmed	Le Havre
5 June 1942	Fw 190 — damaged	Abbeville
19 November 1942	Me 109 — confirmed[257]	Bône
3 December 1942[258]	Fw 190 — third share, damaged	Tebourba–Djedeida
22 December 1942	Ju 88 — damaged	Medjez-el-Bab, Pont du Fahs
5 January 1943	Fw 190 — confirmed	Mateur
6 January 1943	Fw 190 — third share	Mateur
26 March 1943	Me 109 — confirmed	Djebel Tebaga
10 April 1943	Me 109 — damaged	Pont du Fahs, Enfidaville
16 April 1943	Me 109 — probable	NW Beja
19 April 1943	Me 109 — damaged	Tunis
3 May 1943	Me 109 — damaged	SW Mateur
7 May 1943	Me 109 — destroyed on ground	Tunis

Summary

	DESTROYED	PROBABLY DESTROYED	DAMAGED	DESTROYED ON GROUND
Totals	3 and 3 shared	1	5	1

ABBREVIATIONS

ADC	Aide-de-Camp
ADOC	Air Defence Operations Centre
AE	Air Efficiency Award
AFC	Air Force Cross
AOC	Air Officer Commanding
AOC-in-C	Air Officer Commanding-in-Chief
ATA	Air Transport Auxiliary
AWOL	Absent Without Leave
Bf	Bayerische Flugzeugwerke
BOAC	British Overseas Airways Corporation
BP	British Petroleum
C of E	Church of England
CAS	Chief of the Air Staff
CB	Companion of the Order of the Bath
CBE	Commander of the Order of the British Empire
CD	Canadian Forces' Decoration
CDEE	Chemical Defence Experimental Establishment
CDS	Chief of the Defence Staff
CENTO	Central Treaty Organisation
C-in-C	Commander-in-Chief
CMG	Companion of the Order of Saint Michael and Saint George
CO	Commanding Officer
CSI	Companion of the Order of the Star of India
cwt	Hundredweight
DFC	Distinguished Flying Cross
DSC	Distinguished Service Cross
DSO	Distinguished Service Order
Fg Off	Flying Officer
Flt Lt	Flight Lieutenant

FRS	Fellow of the Royal Society
Fw	Focke-Wulf
GBE	Knight Grand Cross of the Order of the British Empire
GCA	Ground-Controlled Approach
GCB	Knight Grand Cross of the Order of the Bath
GCIE	Knight Grand Commander of the Order of the Indian Empire
GCMG	Knight Grand Cross of the Order of Saint Michael and Saint George
GCSI	Knight Grand Commander of the Order of the Star of India
GCVO	Knight Grand Cross of the Royal Victorian Order
GOC	General Officer Commanding
HF	High Frequency
HM	His/Her Majesty
HMS	His/Her Majesty's Ship
HMT	Hired Military Transport
HonFRSE	Honorary Fellow of the Royal Society of Edinburgh
HQ	Headquarters
IFF	Identification Friend or Foe
JSSC	Joint Services Staff College
Ju	Junkers
KBE	Knight Commander of the Order of the British Empire
KCB	Knight Commander of the Order of the Bath
KG	Knight Companion of the Order of the Garter
KIA	Killed in Action
lb	Pound
LMF	Lack of Moral Fibre
MBE	Member of the Order of the British Empire
MC	Military Cross
Me	Messerschmidt
MIA	Missing in Action
mm	Millimetre
MU	Maintenance Unit
MV	Motor Vessel

NATO	North Atlantic Treaty Organisation
NCO	Non-Commissioned Officer
NZDF	New Zealand Defence Staff
OBE	Order of the British Empire
OC	Officer Commanding
Ofw	Oberfeldwebel
OM	Member of the Order of Merit
ORB	Operations Record Book
OTU	Operational Training Unit
PC	Privy Counsellor
PC (Can)	Privy Council (Canada)
PhD	Doctor of Philosophy
Plt Off	Pilot Officer
PPI	Plan Position Indicator
PT	Physical Training
R/T	Radio Telephone
RAAF	Royal Australian Air Force
RAF	Royal Air Force
RCAF	Royal Canadian Air Force
RFC	Royal Flying Corps
RMMV	Royal Mail Motor Vessel
RMS	Royal Mail Ship
RNZAF	Royal New Zealand Air Force
RRE	Royal Radar Establishment
SACEUR	Supreme Allied Commander Europe
SASO	Senior Air Staff Officer
SFTS	Service Flying Training School
TB	Tuberculosis
TSS	Turbine Steam Ship
UN	United Nations
US	United States
VC	Victoria Cross
WAAF	Women's Auxiliary Air Force

ENDNOTES

CHAPTER 1

1   Later Flight Lieutenant R.J.H. Robertson DFC.

2   Christopher Shores and Clive Williams, *Aces High* (Grub Street, London, 1994).

3   Air Marshal 'Black' Robertson, *Fighters in the Blood* (Pen & Sword Books Ltd, London – Philadelphia, 2020) and *A Spitfire Named Connie* (Pen & Sword Books Ltd, London – Philadelphia, 2022).

CHAPTER 2

4   Also known as 'Queen of the Tasman', the 13,482-ton *Awatea* was launched in 1936. In December 1939 she was requisitioned by the Royal Navy as a troopship. She was damaged and eventually sunk supporting the Operation Torch landings in November 1942.

5   The Auckland War Memorial Museum, one of New Zealand's most important museums and war memorials.

6   Dick Branch was Auckland middleweight boxing champion for two years pre-war and lightweight champion post-war, in 1944 and 1946. A navigator during the Second World War, he died in a car accident in 1946, aged 27.

7   The speaking tube between front and back cockpits.

8   An early simulator, produced by Link Aviation Devices, used mainly for instrument flying practice.

9   Completed in 1928, this twenty-two-storey building stands 121 metres (397 feet) high.

CHAPTER 3

10   The RMMV *Capetown Castle* was converted to a troopship under the government's Liner Requisition Scheme.

11   Resembling a rigid inflatable, men could either sit around the rim or cling to rope loops strung around its sides. The largest model could accommodate up to fifty men, half inside the raft, the others in the water holding onto the ropes.

12   Later Group Captain A.G. Malan DSO*, DFC*, he was credited with twenty-seven and seven shared destroyed.

13   Later Flying Officer Francis Malan, he was known to his RAF colleagues as George.

14   Later Wing Commander W.P. Hopkin DFC.

15   Wing Commander R.H. Holland DFC was killed in a mid-air collision between two Vampires on 17 November 1954.

16   Later Squadron Leader D.N. Forde DFC.

17 Lieutenant M.P.C Choron was the first French fighter pilot to take part in the Battle of Britain.

18 Wing Commander M.L. Robinson DSO, DFC.

19 They were flying together over the Channel on a sweep, 10 April 1942.

20 Later Wing Commander P.P.C. Barthropp DFC, AFC.

21 Two days after joining 122 Squadron, on 17 May 1942, Barthropp was shot down and captured. In March 1944 he was one of only 26 to survive the Great Escape from Stalag Luft III. Of 76 escapees, 73 were recaptured, 50 of whom were summarily executed.

22 Later Group Captain C.B.F. Kingcome DSO, DFC*.

CHAPTER 4

23 On 4 April 1942 Flight Sergeant Watson was KIA (killed in action) while Flight Lieutenant Gillespie (RCAF) and Sergeant Hake (RAAF) were shot down. They became Stalag Luft III POWs; Hake took part in the Great Escape, was recaptured and murdered by the Gestapo.

24 Later Squadron Leader H.T. Armstrong DFC*, his first DFC was awarded in May 1942 and followed his fifth claim.

25 George Gilroy owed his nickname to pre-war sheep farming. In March 1943 he added a DSO to his DFC in North Africa and earned a second DFC as a group captain the following year.

26 Air Marshal Sir William Sholto Douglas KCB, MC, DFC, later Marshal of the Royal Air Force the Lord Douglas of Kirtleside GCB, MC, DFC. His visit was on 7 June 1942, in company with Minister of Aircraft Production, the Rt. Hon. Colonel J.J. Llewellin MP.

27 A member of the Women's Auxiliary Air Force.

28 The Air Council (or Air Force Council) was the RAF's governing body until the Air Ministry merged with the other service ministries to form the Ministry of Defence in 1964. It was succeeded by the Air Force Board.

29 Later Air Commodore J.E. Rankin DSO*, DFC*.

30 Nos. 124 and 403 Squadrons, the latter based at Gravesend, Biggin Hill's satellite airfield.

31 A vertical roll.

32 Group Captain P.R. Barwell DFC.

33 Now popularly referred to as the Bf 109. For consistency with the original narrative, the Me nomenclature has been retained throughout.

34 Later Group Captain R.W. Oxspring DFC**, AFC.

35 Both were from 129 Squadron; the leader was on his second operational sortie, the number two on his first.

36 The occasion was a Fighter Pilots' Symposium at Hendon on 20 August 1994; see also the Introduction and Chapter 10.

37   Wing Commander E.G. Barwell DFC* ended the war with nine confirmed victories. Flying a Mosquito he also shot down a V-1 flying bomb.

38   Later Air Marshal Sir Richard Atcherley KBE, CB, AFC*.

39   Angels was the code for thousands of feet; thus a scramble to angels fifteen meant climb to 15,000 feet.

40   Operation Jubilee on 19 August 1942, a classic example of how not to conduct an amphibious landing, was abandoned as a fiasco. Within ten hours more than half the troops involved (over 6,000 and predominantly Canadian) were either killed, wounded or became POWs.

41   Aircraft were painted with white stripes similar to those used for the D-Day operation.

42   Later Admiral of the Fleet the Right Honourable the Earl Mountbatten of Burma KG, GCB, OM, GCSI, GCIE, GCVO, DSO, ADC, PC, FRS.

43   Pilot Officer R.E. Smith.

44   According to the 133 Squadron ORB, Pilot Officer R.N. Beaty suffered a 'petrol shortage [and] crash landed in a small field near Kingsbridge, Devon'.

45   Slang for captivity.

46   By Ofw Heinz Gomann over the Channel on 5 February 1943.

47   On 4 May 1941 Hardy was credited with sharing an Me 109 with Armstrong. There's a note in his logbook that explains his misgivings: 'I am pretty sure that I shot this 109 down; not with Flt Lt Armstrong.' Between 27 April and 26 July on 72 Squadron Armstrong claimed three Me 109s destroyed, a half share in another, a Fw 190 destroyed and another damaged.

48   Kingcome ended the war with eight confirmed and three shared destroyed, one shared unconfirmed destroyed, five probables and thirteen damaged.

49   It's possible that this might have been Wing Commander Brendan 'Paddy' Finucane DSO, DFC**, KIA 15 July 1942, just after taking over the Hornchurch Wing. Credited with twenty-six confirmed and six shared destroyed, eight and one shared probables and eight damaged, his final sixteen claims all came at Kenley as OC 602 Squadron. While news of the unknown individual's demise broke after Kingcome left 72 Squadron, which tends to give the lie to any Finucane link, he was back at Biggin Hill on 22 July. It was possibly then that he made his reported remarks. We will never know.

50   Flight Sergeant J.G. McCutchan was KIA on 25 April 1942. It was his second sortie of the day and the squadron's third fatality in forty-eight hours.

51   Two weeks later, on 9 May 1942.

52   The 72 Squadron ORB, May 1942, records that Red 3 'was seen by Red 2 to go into the sea'.

53   Pilot Officer R.C. Kitchen.

54   A pilot officer at the time, later Wing Commander J.R. Ratten DFC.

55   Wing Commander E.N. Woods DFC was posted missing in December 1943.

56   Under the ill-fated Operation Jupiter, later abandoned, Wing Commander H.N.G Ramsbottom-Isherwood DFC, AFC was slated to command No. 153 Wing.

57   Arctic convoy PQ 17, which sailed from Iceland on 17 June 1942, was a disaster. Only eleven of thirty-five merchantmen arrived at Archangel. It was not until September that another convoy set off for North Russia.

58   At the time Oxspring had earned a DFC and Bar. His father, Major Robert Oxspring, was awarded an MC and Bar.

CHAPTER 5

59   MV (Motor Vessel) *Staffordshire*, built in 1929 for passengers and cargo, was designated HMT (Hired Military Transport) when requisitioned as a troopship in 1940.

60   These landings were part of Operation Torch. Three amphibious task forces planned to seize simultaneously the key ports and airfields in Morocco and Algeria, targeting Casablanca, Oran and Algiers.

61   The other pilot was Pilot Officer Robbie Robertson.

62   The Tunis valley referred to here and elsewhere is the Majardah (or Medjerda) River valley. Once the granary of ancient Rome, it remains Tunisia's richest grain-producing region.

63   CO of No. 324 Wing, which included 72 Squadron. Later Air Marshal Sir Ronald Lees KCB, CBE, DFC*.

64   K-rations were daily combat food rations, individually boxed meals: breakfast, lunch and dinner.

65   *Jagdgeschwader 53*, a Luftwaffe fighter wing better known as the '*Pik As' Geschwader*, was one of the oldest German fighter units of the Second World War; its origins go back to 1937.

66   'Paddy' Griffin.

67   The opening two lines of *Honey.*

68   On 3 December, only four days after he arrived in North Africa, Malan was shot down by an Fw 190. After crash-landing he returned to Souk-el-Arba almost immediately, miraculously unscathed.

69   72 Squadron moved to Souk-el-Khemis, codenamed Paddington. The RAF operated from a number of temporary airfields in the vicinity, all built by US Army engineers; the others were Euston, King's Cross, Marylebone, Victoria and Waterloo.

70   Later Flight Lieutenant R.D. Scrase DFC.

71   For the elevator and rudder respectively.

72   Farish (also known as 'Greggs') was serving with 111 Squadron at Lago, near Salerno, in February 1944 when he 'appropriated' a Spitfire and flew it to Nettuno, a beleaguered temporary airfield next to the Anzio beachhead, to repair an aircraft. 'Bamby' Taylor, from 111 Squadron, had been forced down by engine failure and was trapped there. Court martialled for his efforts, Farish was found guilty and awarded a severe reprimand

and six months' loss of seniority (later remitted by the Air Council as 'too severe'). His only previous flying experience was dual in a captured SAIMAN 200, an Italian Tiger Moth lookalike.

73 Flight Lieutenant T.B. Hughes held the almost certainly unique RAF distinction of baling out from an Me 109 – a captured aircraft.

74 The 'Dangerous' individual who'd aroused Hardy's suspicions when his fellow New Zealander, Dave Waters, was killed.

75 All ranks above group captain, each with 'Air' in the title.

CHAPTER 6

76 Serving as an RAF pilot officer.

77 The award was announced officially on 20 May 1943. The citation read: 'This officer has completed seventy sorties, including a number in the campaign in North Africa, where he has rendered excellent service. In air combat he has destroyed three enemy aircraft, while in low-level machine-gun attacks on enemy transport he has achieved success. Flying Officer Hardy is a keen and skilful section leader.'

78 Flying Officer D.E. Hogan DFC served with 111 Squadron.

79 Later Flight Lieutenant J.M. Cleland was the only New Zealander to fly with an American unit, the 363rd Fighter Squadron, during the war.

80 Group Captain D.O. Finlay DFC, AFC, who retired in 1959, was severely injured and paralysed in a motor accident in 1966.

81 Later Air Commodore P.M. Brothers CBE, DSO, DFC*.

82 Later Group Captain C.F Gray DSO, DFC**.

83 Later Squadron Leader J.N. Mackenzie DFC.

84 George 'Screwball' Beurling claimed twenty-seven 'kills' during the Malta campaign, more than any other RAF pilot. He ended his career as Squadron Leader G.F. Beurling DSO, DFC, DFM*.

85 A Canadian flying with the RFC, Bishop's decorations included the VC, DSO*, DFC and MC. In later years there was controversy over his claimed seventy-two airborne victories.

86 Beurling transferred to the RCAF from the RAF in September 1944.

87 Flight Lieutenant G.E. Jameson DSO, DFC. After both his older and younger brothers were killed and his father died, his mother requested his return to New Zealand; he left in August 1944 to run the family farm.

88 Later Group Captain P.R. Walker DSO, DFC, he performed with 1 Squadron at the 1937 Hendon Air Pageant. Flying Hurricanes, by May 1940 he was already credited with some eight victories.

89 Given that Walker retired as a group captain, this is arguably a somewhat harsh judgement.

90 A note in Hardy's logbook, in July 1943, reveals he felt 'forgotten and condemned to imprisonment'.

91 This accident looks to be that on 23 August 1943 which Pilot Officer H.M. Goldsmit survived. It was put down to pilot error on the part of Pilot Officer J.J.A. Noizet, like Goldsmit a Belgian.

92 Later Squadron Leader A.C. Bartley DFC**.

93 Entertainments National Service Association. It provided entertainment for British Armed Forces personnel during the Second World War.

94 New Zealander Air Commodore K.L 'Grid' Caldwell CBE, MC, DFC* served with the RFC and later with the RNZAF.

CHAPTER 7

95 Squadron Leader J.B. Niven DFC.

96 Later Air Chief Marshal Sir Frederick Rosier GCB, CBE, DSO.

97 At the time a well-known cleaning product.

98 Portsmouth received two V-1 attacks. No-one was injured in the first, on 25 June 1944, but the second, on the night of 15 July 1944, resulted in fifteen fatalities and eighty-two injuries.

99 According to Antony Beevor (*D-Day, the Battle for Normandy,* Viking, London, 2009, p.266) 457 Lancasters and Halifaxes attacked the northern fringes of Caen on the evening of 7 July with delayed-action bombs.

100 Air Chief Marshal Sir Arthur Harris, later Marshal of the Royal Air Force the Lord Harris of Stowford GCB, OBE, AFC.

101 Later Wing Commander R.H. Harries DSO*, DFC**.

102 Anti-aircraft guns were responsible for shooting down over 1,800 V-1s. Similar numbers were downed by fighter aircraft and some 200 were destroyed by barrage balloons.

103 At the time Hardy would have been eligible to wear campaign medals including the Africa Star and Aircrew Europe medal.

104 The DFC.

105 One possibility is Group Captain J. (John) Cunningham DSO** DFC*, the RAF's most successful night-fighter pilot at the time; then serving at HQ 11 Group, he received the second Bar to his DSO in March 1944 and later a CBE. Another is Squadron Leader 'Branse' Burbridge, later Wing Commander B.A. Burbridge DSO*, DFC*, who went on to become the RAF's highest-scoring night-fighter pilot. Then serving at West Malling, his first DFC came in May 1944.

106 Flight Lieutenant A.B. Stead, later awarded the DFC.

107 Incendiary ammunition, more effective than standard armour-piercing .303 bullets.

CHAPTER 8

108 Shot down on 15 July 1943, Flying Officer T.S.F. Kearins reached England more than three months later, on 25 October. The story of his escape is a compressed version of that

recounted by his son, Stephen, on Radio New Zealand, 22 October 2010, and reported in the *Manawatu Standard*, 4 December 2010. He hid first in the Lambus forest and was then sheltered for more than two months by the Forgez family in Le Quesnoy-en-Artois, some four miles away.

109 Flight Lieutenant J.N. King was known by his middle name, Norby, and sometimes 'Reverend' (he later went into the church). His aircraft was hit by returning fire from a concentration of German infantry.

110 Like 485 Squadron, 349 (Belgian) Squadron was part of 135 Wing.

111 The date was a coincidence. Operation Bodenplatte was planned for 16 December 1944 but delayed due to bad weather. Launched finally on 1 January 1945, it was an attempt to cripple Allied air forces in the Low Countries. It's aim was to gain air superiority during the stagnant stage of the Battle of the Bulge, allowing the German army and Waffen-SS forces to resume their advance.

112 In a remarkable parallel with Hardy's own strafing incident, on 6 January 1945 near Breda, Stead was strafing a train which blew up. With his aircraft badly damaged he was forced into an immediate crash-landing and was killed. (His posthumous DFC was gazetted shortly afterwards, on 27 February 1945.) Stead's number two, twenty-year-old Pilot Officer Francis C. Matthews, suffered a similar fate.

113 Flying Officer Edward Te Keu Bennett.

114 Later General Sir Miles Dempsey GBE, KCB, DSO, MC.

115 Powered lifeboats made to be dropped into water by fixed-wing aircraft to aid air-sea rescue operations.

116 Squadron Leader K.J. Macdonald took over from Squadron Leader J.G. Pattison DFC in February 1945; he was awarded the DFC in May 1945, the same month that Pattison was awarded the DSO.

117 Just over a month later, on 14 September 1945, Flight Lieutenant Hardy was awarded his second DFC. The citation read: 'This officer has now completed his second tour of operational duty. Since the award of the Distinguished Flying Cross after the first tour he has destroyed one enemy aircraft, probably destroyed another and damaged two. During his second tour he has destroyed fifteen mechanical transports, one locomotive and ammunition train. He has also damaged one ship, several barges and other transports. This officer has never been deterred by enemy opposition from completing his allotted tasks. Flight Lieutenant Hardy has always displayed courage, determination and a fine fighting spirit.'

CHAPTER 9

118 Home of the New Zealand High Commission in London.

119 The delay was due to the move of the RAF's Central Gunnery School from Catfoss to Leconfield in October 1945.

120 The RMMV (Royal Mail Motor Vessel) *Stirling Castle* was requisitioned as a troopship during the war and released in 1946.

121 Later Group Captain Sir Douglas Bader CBE, DSO*, DFC*.

122 Squadron Leader H.N. Sweetman DFC flew extensively with 486 (New Zealand) Squadron and later commanded 3 Squadron.

CHAPTER 10

123 Launched in 1928, shortly after the outbreak of war the RMS *Rangitiki* was converted into a troopship.

124 Part of the Port of London, a major deep-water port handling bulk cargo.

125 Totalling 770, this was the largest number of people ever to leave New Zealand in a liner in peacetime.

126 Later Sir Ernest Marsden CMG, CBE, MC, FRS.

127 Ernest Rutherford, the Lord Rutherford of Nelson OM, FRS, HonFRSE.

128 One of these looks to have been Robert Mathieson, a 1922 All Black.

129 The November 1968 cover showed Habgood's 'Coastguard Cottages at Duntulm, Skye'.

130 The mutiny on HMS *Bounty* took place on 28 April 1789.

131 Later Group Captain L.H. Bartlett DSO.

132 Squadron Leader F.J. Howells DFC*.

133 The event of 20 August 1994 mentioned in the Introduction and Chapter 4.

134 The effects, such as abrupt changes in control characteristics, that result from changes in the airflow around an aircraft when the velocity at some point reaches the local speed of sound and the air ceases to behave as an incompressible fluid.

135 Intentional spinning was prohibited in single-seat Vampires. The spin itself was erratic. While recovery was possible, unless control inputs were precise the aircraft could flick into another spin in the opposite direction.

136 In the event, the RAF completed the first crossing, one leg ahead of the Americans, on 14 July 1948.

137 Built by the Americans in 1941, and originally named Bluie West One, it was renamed after the end of the war.

138 Otherwise known as New York International and later renamed as John F. Kennedy airport.

139 Later Air Marshal Sir Harold Martin KCB DSO* DFC** AFC.

140 Whisner was an ace in both the Second World War and Korea, one of the few Americans to accomplish this, and the only one to earn three DSCs in the former conflict. As Major William T. Whisner he won the Bendix Trophy in 1953 flying an F-86.

141 An American comic actress and singer who also performed on Broadway. She toured extensively during the Second World War entertaining American troops.

142 An ace before it began, during the Battle of Britain Lacey was third behind Eric Lock's twenty-one confirmed 'kills'. Flight Lieutenant E.S. Lock DSO, DFC* was posted MIA on 3 August 1941.

143 He arrived at Odiham in 1947 as a flight lieutenant and eventually retired in 1967 as Squadron Leader J.H. Lacey DFM*.

144 Kingaby went on to command 72 Squadron and retired in 1958 as Wing Commander D.E. Kingaby DSO, AFC, DFM**. See also Chapter 10.

145 At the time Gatwick operated as a civil airport for charter airlines and cargo flights. In 1950 it was designated London's second airport; after closure and renovation it was officially opened in 1958.

146 From 29 July to 14 August 1948.

147 Later Group Captain R.N.H. Courtney CB, DFC*, AFC; he commanded 72 Squadron from February 1947 to February 1949.

148 Later Air Vice-Marshal J.E Johnson CB, CBE, DSO**, DFC*.

149 He retired in February 1950 as Group Captain P.H. Hugo DSO, DFC**.

150 Later Group Captain H.P. Pleasance OBE, DFC*.

151 AOC No. 11 Group, Air Vice-Marshal S.F. Vincent CB, DFC, AFC.

152 Otherwise known as the Morlaix disaster; see Chapter 4 above.

CHAPTER 11

153 Later Wing Commander R.M. Mackenzie DSO, DFC, AFC.

154 He was finally credited with seventeen confirmed and five shared enemy aircraft, three probables and two shared, sixteen damaged and two shared; all but three (one a floatplane on water) were fighters.

155 Squadron Leader J.R. Stoop.

156 Later Sir Adrian Stoop MC, between 1901 and 1939 he played 182 times for Harlequins and won fifteen England caps. Harlequins' president from 1920 to 1949, the club's ground, The Stoop, is named in his memory.

157 Stoop died at a club meeting at the Croft circuit on 19 May 1968. Driving a Porsche 911S, he suffered a coronary thrombosis; his car mounted the banking at the exit to Barcroft, rolled and crashed through fencing.

CHAPTER 12

158 The airfield served the RAF's Command Headquarters, then the British Air Forces of Occupation; a few months later, in September 1951, it reverted to its previous name, Second Tactical Air Force.

159 An air commodore at the time, later Air Chief Marshal Sir Harry Broadhurst GCB, KBE, DSO*, DFC*, AFC.

160 An air commodore at the time, later Air Chief Marshal the Earl of Bandon GBE, CB, CVO, DSO.

161 Later Group Captain T.F. Dalton-Morgan DSO, OBE, DFC*.

162 Later Air Commodore J.H. Chaplin DSO, DFC, AFC.

163 An interesting observation on a man who studied Theology and English at Cambridge and concluded his RAF career as Air Advisor to the UK High Commissioner in India. For twenty years after retirement he worked for the Foreign & Commonwealth Office.

164 On 29 September 1942 No. 71 (Eagle) Squadron became the 334th Fighter Squadron, part of the 4th Fighter Group, US Eighth Air Force.

165 Then a wing commander, later Air Vice-Marshal W.V. Crawford-Compton CB, CBE, DSO*, DFC*.

166 The Norwegian explorer, writer and Academy Award winner who led the 1947 *Kon-Tiki* expedition, a journey by balsa wood raft across the Pacific from South America to the Polynesian islands.

167 General Eisenhower arrived in Paris to take up his appointment as SACEUR on 1 January 1951.

CHAPTER 13

168 Later Air Vice-Marshal F.D.S. Scott-Malden DSO, DFC*.

169 Scott-Malden was only twenty-four when granted the acting rank of group captain – younger than Leonard Cheshire, who at twenty-five was earlier feted as the youngest group captain in the RAF.

170 The leader was Major H.K. 'Harry' Evans and the brothers, twins, were Lieutenants C.A. 'Bill' and C.C 'Buck' Pattillo. The fourth pilot was Lieutenant L.D. Lawrence 'Dag' Damewood. Later in July 1952 the team composition changed as responsibility moved from 36th Fighter Bomber Wing, Fürstenfeldbruck, to the 86th Fighter Bomber Wing, Neubiberg.

171 A practice that has continued over the years amongst US demonstration teams.

172 The second Noratlas prototype.

173 In the 1930s Maryse Bastié set a number of international flying records for women, including a solo flight across the Atlantic. She served in the French Air Force as a captain, logged more than 3,000 hours' flying time, and was a commander of the *Légion d'Honneur*. By coincidence, in 1926 her husband Louis, a First World War pilot, had also been killed in an aircraft crash.

174 A second lieutenant aged eighteen at the time, Air Marshal Sir Robert Foster KCB, CBE, DFC was seconded to the Royal Flying Corps as a flying officer in 1916.

175 David W. Morgan joined Vickers Supermarine after service in both the RAF and the Fleet Air Arm; he was later awarded an MBE.

176 The Swift entered RAF service in 1954 but proved less than a success. Fewer than 200 of the original order for 497 were built. By 1955 it was clear that the RAF preferred its Hawker Hunter rival.

177 A test pilot at the time, in 1953 flying a Hawker Hunter Squadron Leader N.F. Duke DSO, OBE, DFC**, AFC set a world speed record of 727.63 mph.

178 Later Lord Caccia of Abernant in the County of Brecknock GCMG, GCVO.

179 Later Marshal of the Royal Air Force Sir John Slessor GCB, DSO, MC.

180 Field Marshal the Earl Alexander of Tunis KG, GCB, OM, GCMG, CSI, DSO, MC, CD, PC (Can), PC.

181 Group Captain P.P. Hanks DSO, DFC, AFC was there to collect his own AFC.

182 Both were squadron leaders.

CHAPTER 14

183 Later Air Vice-Marshal D.C. Stapleton CB, CBE, DFC, AFC.

184 Wing Commander E.H McHardy DSO, DFC*.

185 Wing Commander D.A. Oxby DSO, DFC, DFM*.

186 J.K. Quill OBE, AFC learned to fly with the RAF, took part briefly in the Battle of Britain as a test pilot on secondment and later served with the Fleet Air Arm as a lieutenant commander.

187 Group Captain J.O.W. Oliver CB, DSO, DFC.

188 The flying career of Wing Commander M.A. Ensor DSO*, DFC*, AFC, encompassed much more than U-boat hunting. After the war he flew 200 missions on the Berlin Airlift and served with the US Navy during the Korean War.

189 Later Air Commodore J.A. Leathart CB, DSO.

190 He'd previously studied electrical engineering at Liverpool University.

191 Later Air Commodore A.C. Deere DSO, OBE, DFC*.

192 Ironically, Gray's twin brother, Kenneth, a bomber pilot and one of the first New Zealanders to be awarded a DFC, didn't survive; he was killed in a flying accident on 1 May 1940.

193 Squadron leader F.L. White was KIA seven weeks later, on 8 July 1940.

194 Pilot Officer J.L. Allen DFC was KIA two months later, on 24 July 1940.

195 Oxby retired from the RAF in 1969 and emigrated to Canada where he worked as a civil servant for the Ontario Ministry of Health in Ottawa until 1984.

CHAPTER 15

196 Later Marshal of the Royal Air Force the Lord Cameron of Balhousie KT, GCB, CBE, DSO, DFC.

197 During Healey's time as Defence Secretary, 1964-70, Cameron served with him in the Air Ministry; he was promoted to air vice-marshal in 1968.

198 Air Vice-Marshal R. Faville CBE.

199 Later Air Chief Marshal Sir Denis Barnett GCB, CBE, DFC.

200 Later Wing Commander G.C. Atherton OBE, DFC*.

201 The aircraft broke up in mid-air shortly after take-off from what was then Calcutta on 2 May 1953.

202 By September 1954 the Royal Navy had recovered 70% by weight of the main structure, 80% of the engine section and 50% of the aircraft's systems and equipment.

203 Later a brigadier general, as a twenty-four-year-old air force captain, Yeager reached Mach 1.05 in level flight, piloting the Bell X-1, *Glamorous Glennis,* over California on 14 October 1947.

204 The Avro Vulcan, Handley Page Victor and Vickers Valiant.

205 Jones was instrumental in identifying and countering the *Knickebein* radio navigation system used by German bombers as well as developing 'chaff', which confused radars by creating false targets.

206 *Most Secret War: British Scientific Intelligence 1939–1945* (Hamish Hamilton, London, 1978.).

207 Later Air Marshal Sir Christopher Hartley KCB, CBE, DFC, AFC, AE.

CHAPTER 16

208 Later Air Chief Marshal Sir Denis Smallwood GCB, KCB, DSO, DFC.

209 The Avro Blue Steel was an air-launched, rocket-propelled, nuclear-armed stand-off missile, built for the V-bomber force.

210 Then an air vice-marshal, later Marshal of the Royal Air Force Sir John Grandy GCB, GCVO, KBE, DSO.

211 Then the Atomic Energy Research Establishment.

212 Later Air Marshal Sir Douglas Morris KCB, CBE, DSO, DFC.

213 Sir Robert Watson-Watt KCB, FRS.

214 It seems likely that this was the young David Craig, later the Lord Craig of Radley GCB, OBE.

215 It entered service in 1963 and remained Britain's primary nuclear deterrent until the advent of the Royal Navy's Polaris system.

216 Sixty missiles were based on twenty Bomber Command stations.

217 Air Commodore (acting Air Vice-Marshal) J.R.A. Embling CBE, DSO, AOC No. 12 Group, was killed in a Meteor accident at Leconfield on 15 July 1959.

CHAPTER 17

218 A separate 'secure unit', No. 51 Squadron operated the Comet C2R and Canberra from Watton in the signals intelligence role; American U-2s were also occasional visitors.

219 Marshal of the Royal Air Force Sir John Salmond GCB, CMG, CVO, DSO*.

220 Marshal of the Royal Air Force the Lord Trenchard of Wolfeton GCB, OM, GCVO, DSO, regarded as the 'Father of the RAF'.

221 Salmond took over from Trenchard as CAS on 1 January 1930.

222 Group Captain I.S. Smith CBE, DFC*.

223 Operation Jericho breached the walls of the prison, enabling members of the French Resistance to escape, many of whom were under sentence of death by the Gestapo.

CHAPTER 18

224 A mutual security organisation dating from 1955 to 1979. It comprised Iran, Pakistan, Turkey and the UK, with the US as an associate member.

225 It read: 'Presented To Squadron Leader O.L. Hardy D.F.C., A.F.C. By The Members Of 71 "Eagle" Squadron 1950-1953.'

226 Group Captain J. Finch CBE, DFC, AFC.

227 Archbishop Makarios, at the time president of Cyprus. On 26 December 1963 his government formally accepted that forces stationed in Cyprus should be placed under a British command. Later the same day Air Chief Marshal Barnett (Commander-in-Chief RAF Near East Air Force and Commander British Forces Cyprus) and Major General Young (Commander Land Forces), flew to Nicosia from RAF Episkopi.

228 The Jāmeh Mosque of Isfahān, also known as the Atiq Mosque.

229 Persia's Achaemenid Empire, c. 550–330 BC.

230 An inscription from 311 AD refers to the site as *Sad-stūn*, meaning 'Hundred Pillars'.

231 The F-84 and F-86, to be followed later, in 1965, by the F-5.

232 Air Chief Marshal Sir Thomas Prickett KCB, DSO, DFC.

233 Air Commodore F.J. Manning CB, CBE.

CHAPTER 19

234 There were persistent allegations of unethical human experimentation at Porton Down. In 1953 a young airman died after taking part in sarin nerve agent toxicity tests. In August 1962 a scientist died from an accidental infection of the plague bacterium. The same month an autoclave exploded, shattering two windows. These incidents generated considerable media coverage.

235 Likely to have been a member of MI6, the Secret Intelligence Service.

236 Captain D.A. Poynter CVO, MBE.

237 Poynter was one of only twenty-three to survive recapture.

238 Captain H.A. Kidd DSO, DSC.

239 Later Rear Admiral Sir Anthony AOC-in-C VC, KBE, CB, DSO*.

240 An extract from AOC-in-C' VC citation: 'For valour in command of H.M. Submarine *Torbay* in a daring and successful raid on shipping in a defended enemy harbour, planned with full knowledge of the great hazards to be expected during seventeen hours in waters closely patrolled by the enemy. On arriving in the harbour, he had to charge his batteries lying on the surface in full moonlight, under the guns of the enemy. As he could not see his target, he waited several hours and attacked in full daylight in a glassy calm. When he had fired his torpedoes he was heavily counter-attacked and had to withdraw through a long channel with anti-submarine craft all round and continuous air patrols overhead.'

241 AOC-in-C died in 1985. Nothing was in the public domain until four years later when Ludovic Kennedy published his autobiography where he describes 'a submarine atrocity' on the night of 9 July 1941 that led to an accusation of war crimes.

242 Admiral of the Fleet George Anson, 1st Baron Anson PC, FRS (1697–1762).

243 There had been eight at the time. The first HMS *Anson* was commissioned in 1747 while a ninth was launched in 2021, an Astute-class submarine.

244 Colonel K.F. Timbrell CBE, MC.

245 It took nineteen years to complete 'Britain's Sistine Chapel'; the work earned James Thornhill a knighthood.

246 Master of Churchill College, Cambridge at the time, Cockcroft had previously been director of the Atomic Energy Research Establishment at Harwell.

247 Air Chief Marshal Sir Kenneth Cross KCB, CBE, DSO, DFC.

248 12 (East Anglia) Sector.

249 Air Commodore E.W. Tacon CBE, DSO, LVO, DFC*, AFC*.

250 Having previously argued the virtues of commanders filling posts with those they know and respect, Hardy is in danger here of being hoist with his own petard.

CHAPTER 20

251 These Beaufighters were known as the 'Torbeau' variant.

252 The overnight surge of 31 January/1 February 1953 was the worst natural disaster Britain experienced during the 20th century. An estimated 307 people died on land (224 more at sea) while some 40,000 were made homeless.

253 Group Captain P.W. Townsend CVO, DSO, DFC*.

254 Wing Commander R.R. Stanford Tuck DSO, DFC**, AFC.

255 It wasn't unusual for an officer to have a report 'set aside' when it was inconsistent with previous recorded performance. If it was seen as markedly out of character it would normally be given little credence. A conflict of personalities was the usual reason.

EPILOGUE

256 Since renamed as Spitfires.com, The Spitfire Academy.

APPENDIX

257 Flying with the editor's father, Robbie Robertson, who provided the confirmation.

258 Shared with the editor's father and George Malan (shot down the same day but returned uninjured).

INDEX

Where military ranks are shown, these are the highest reached by the individuals concerned.
n = *endnote reference*